3

FATHER, SOLDIER, SON

FATHER, SOLDIER, SON

*Memoir of a Platoon Leader
in Vietnam*

NATHANIEL TRIPP

STEERFORTH PRESS

South Royalton, Vermont

For information about permission to reproduce selections
from this book, write to: Steerforth Press L.C., P.O. Box 70,
South Royalton, Vermont 05068.

Library of Congress Cataloging-in-Publication Data
Tripp, Nathaniel, 1944–
Father, soldier, son : memoir of a platoon leader in Vietnam /
Nathaniel Tripp. — 1st ed.
p. cm.
ISBN 1-883642-14-0 (alk. paper)
1. Vietnamese Conflict, 1961-1975—Personal narratives, American.
2. Tripp, Nathaniel, 1944- . I. Title.
DS559.5.T74   1997
959.704'3'092—dc21   96-46845
CIP

Manufactured in the United States of America

SECOND PRINTING

To my sons: Eli, Sam, and Ben

ACKNOWLEDGMENTS

This book wouldn't have been possible without the men of Mike Division. It was their courage, their love for each other that got us all through. They will always be beside me. So will Defiant Six, James Rew. He set the standards of leadership and humanity. Then there are the soldiers I met later, on the streets or in correspondence, the men who never forgot what the war was; Chip Troiano, Alan Potkin, Chuck Searcy. We the living do what we can, remembering the army of the dead. Thanks also to my cousin Mike Carlebach and editor Tom Powers for their support and encouragement. And finally, amidst all these men, I wish to thank my wife Reeve for this book in which women are otherwise so conspicuously absent. Her gentle ways made it all possible.

THE DREAM

IN THE DREAM I am at home on my farm in Vermont where I have lived since 1973. It is summertime, with blue skies, shimmering green trees, and sunshine pouring over me like warm honey. There are the rolling hayfields, the big old barn, the house I've fixed up and filled with family. All seems well with the world; I am at peace and my children are playing in the shade of the big maple tree. I am mowing the lawn, or weeding the garden, doing middle-aged weekend things. This is always the way the dream begins.

Then there is a noise, so low and distant at first it seems more felt than heard. It is a beating, a throbbing, a drumming like the mating call of the partridge in May. But it is not the partridge, and I straighten up as I hear it. I turn left and right, trying to determine the sound's direction. It grows louder, resounding off the hills, distinctly coming from the southwest now, and I can hear the turbines, too, and separate that sound from the slapping rotors. I know they are coming for me, and there is not much time. I walk away from what I was doing and head toward a nearby knoll in the hayfields. My arms and legs get very heavy, I am so tired, suddenly so very tired, but I must go. I look back at my children playing, knowing that I may never see them again, yet there is no time to explain. Now the air is throbbing with that familiar sad song, a song I have not heard for so long. The helicopters are still hidden behind the tree line, but I know they are close now, maneuvering into a long line, preparing to descend.

I reach the knoll just as the green tadpole shapes of the slicks emerge over the trees. There are five of them, and I feel myself crying as they swing around. A smoke grenade, which I have been saving for nearly thirty years, appears in my hands. I pull the pin and throw it out in front of me, and tears sting my face as the yellow smoke billows upward. Unholy archangels, why have you come for me? Even though I am so very tired, I place my back to the wind, spread my legs slightly, and raise my arms above my head in a gesture that looks like solemn supplication. All these movements come back to me as the old circuits in my brain, so long unused, instantly rewire themselves. The line of slicks swings to my command, though my arms ache. They are downwind, bobbing gently up and down, headed straight for me. I am mindful of the power lines. I am filled with awe and sorrow. I can see the door gunners leaning out over their machine guns. I can see the sun glinting on Plexiglas. The sound wells up even louder as the machines loom closer, losing airspeed, sinking lower.

I am amused, for a moment, speculating upon what the neighbors must think. And I am pleased, for a moment, with the spectacular show I'm putting on for my family. But these are fleeting thoughts. As the ships settle toward me it is mainly the sadness that keeps surging inside me, the sadness and the fatigue. Now I am engulfed by the thick, kerosene-scented wind. It is the hot breath of death. The grit blown up by the rotors stings my eyes, mixes with the tears. The incredible noise beats on my brain as the lead ship comes in, nose up, and kisses the earth with its skids. I walk toward it. The flight crew looks surreal, like spacemen, mechanical grasshoppers in their flight helmets, flak jackets and dark glasses. The infantrymen are sprawled behind them in the open compartment, sleeves rolled up over bare, tan arms, fighting gear draped on their bodies. As I approach a few of them sit up and take notice, but most continue to show the indifference of men facing combat.

The rotors thwack the air over my head. The scent of kerosene is dizzying, with that constant turbine scream that drowns out everything else. Every cell in my body is in tune. I recognize my men. One of them reaches out for my arm to help me up. It is good to feel his strength. So much time has passed, filled with the relative serenity of things we had once prayed for. But now there isn't even time to say "Good-bye." The war still goes on. I must give up everything and go back. The scream gets louder and I feel the deck sway and lift beneath me. The hayfield falls away. I watch everything I worked so hard on and loved so much slowly disappear behind the skids.

In this dream my unconscious does a good job of reasoning. I know that I will be promoted to captain, and will be given a company to command instead of a platoon. It will, therefore, be somewhat safer than the last time, but still I could get killed. I also reason, as I settle in amid the web gear and feel the grenades and ammo pouches and canteens in their familiar places, that I am wiser now and less apt to take chances; better equipped to survive than the last time. But still the sadness is overpowering. I am no longer twenty-four with little to lose. Fatherhood has changed me. And I am so sad to see that the war still goes on. All that time, while I was safe at home, that war which had left poison in my veins was still going on and nobody bothered to take notice. The protesters had gone home; the television turned to other things. But for a few there can be no end, and I am tired and saddened that once again I have been chosen for this utterly awful and meaningless task. There is the sorrow that I must give up so much, my youth the first time, and now my family. There is the grief for all the people who have suffered and died while I unknowingly mowed my lawn. But I keep these thoughts to myself as I settle in among my men and feel the cool beat of the wind on my skin. We are together again, and even though I hate the war I do not hesitate for a moment.

Why doesn't a part of my subconscious rebel? Why can't I ever walk away? How is it that I can find comfort again in my compass and maps and the cool hiss of the radio, giving up all else? Or is it that the dream is real, that a part of me will always be following Highway Thirteen, which runs north from Saigon to the Cambodian border, which runs like a river through my life. I draw from it while I go canoeing. As the shore slips past, with brooding forest, beach and rock outcrop, I am also exploring the dreamscape of sandbags and concertina wire near Bien Hoa, where the road begins and trucks snort soot into the air and the black asphalt then leads to Di An and beyond, where it turns to red laterite and Herron was killed somewhere off to the right side, past the bulldozed margins of red mud and tree stumps, past rice paddies and children begging for cigarettes to the hills near Lai Khe. Then comes the open plain, then more hills and less of the sandbags and concertina wire. We cloverleaf to the left, form a column of two on the right, passing the place where Douglas and Wearmouth were killed, the highway a red stained artery dividing war zones C and D, sprinkled with the vertebrae of the lieutenant from Delta company, the land rising and falling more and planted to rubber trees, rubber trees forming patterns along-side the road which grows darker and narrower till it reaches An Loc, with the cobblestoned town square and a fountain where South Viet-namese soldiers drank beer and told stories and listened to transistor radios, and you could turn right toward Quan Loi, or keep going straight past Firebase Alpha, where Goodman and the guy whose name nobody knew got killed, and then continue farther up the road, which twists and dips and rises like a road in Vermont, the sandbags and concertina wire gone entirely, deep into the dreamscape of mist-filled valleys and little villages on stilts where the Viet Cong knew me and beckoned to me from thickets of bamboo, to the town of Loc Ninh, with its cobblestoned town square and fountain where North Viet-namese soldiers drank beer and told stories and listened to transistor radios, and where General Ware got killed, and still farther beyond, the road turning to purple clay and the shimmering green forest closing in overhead, to where the border with Cambodia is just a red and white striped pole across the road and two men stand smoking cigarettes, their bicycles leaning against the guard shack and a girl in a black and white *au dai* sells yellow chrysanthemums and the sunlight pours down like warm honey on the land beyond, where my children play in the shade of a big maple tree.

❖ I ❖

I WILL ALWAYS REMEMBER the evenings at An Loc as very still and beautiful. The air was clear and sweet smelling, and the last rays of sunlight seemed to reach the darkest places inside of us. From our muddy knoll outside the north gate of the village we looked out upon a rolling landscape of hills which could have been Vermont except for the rice paddies in the valleys and the melodic voices of Vietnamese villagers drifting like smoke in the air. It was a time when the war seemed to hold its breath. It was a time of horseplay, or of reading, or of writing a letter home.

After the bad times we'd been through down south, this outpost was like heaven. Hot meals were flown in to us by helicopter twice a day from brigade headquarters in nearby Quan Loi and dished out of big green thermos containers. We were awash in C ration sundry packs; cartons of cigarettes, chewing gum, candy bars and toothpaste. Our daytime duty was to sweep Highway Thirteen south from An Loc each morning looking for mines. There were never any mines, and our sweeps were accompanied by vendors with pushcarts selling Coke and French bread. Best of all, we didn't have to pull ambush duty at night.

For most of us, the war was nearly over. We were getting "short." I was expecting my own orders any day; I had almost fulfilled the alloted six months as a platoon leader and was looking forward to the MACV advisor assignment I had requested. Most of the old-timers who had been with me all along were going home soon. Every day brought this closer.

We were not much older than my own children are now, and we still had a child-like innocence, even after all we had seen. It was an innocence which for most of us would not finally end until we returned to the "real world." For the time, our language was the jargon of radio protocol. Our names were our coded call signs. Niner Two, our artillery officer, had a guitar and sometimes we would sing while the sun went down; innocent mid-sixties stuff. I did a rendition of "Tell Old Bill" by the Kingston Trio myself, *Tell old Bill, when he gets home, to leave those Viet Cong alone.* Once, the advisors in An Loc even took part. Two of them took the L-19 observation plane up into the darkening sky and flew above us in lazy circles with a recording of "This Land is Your Land" by Pete Seeger blaring from the aircraft's Psyops loudspeakers. The little plane hummed and danced beneath cloud puffs. The last of the day's sunshine grazed the hilltops and the valleys filled deeper with shadow.

The artillerymen who shared our perimeter used the last of the light to check their aiming stakes and swab the long 105 howitzer tubes with oily rags. They would be up all night firing H&I's, or "harassment and interdiction." Several times an hour they would send salvos of shells crashing into a random selection of trail intersections, suspected base camps, and resupply routes to the north. This was designed to keep the Viet Cong from getting much rest, if nothing else. But for us, the sporadic eruption of howitzers just a few meters away was merely the tympanic accompaniment for our dreams.

We had a couple of dilapidated tanks assigned to us, which in retrospect remind me of the tractors I own now, and the mornings began shrouded in mist, just as they do in Vermont in the late summer. My men would have a hot breakfast of scrambled eggs and fried potatoes, but I preferred two cups of black coffee and a package of M&Ms from a sundry pack. Then the tanks would start, spewing exhaust smoke into the damp air, and I'd climb aboard the lead tank. I'd sit astride the main gun while my men found places around me, and I'd alternate sips of coffee with mouthfuls of M&Ms as we started out. The hot coffee swirling around them made the M&Ms cook off in my mouth, bursting sweetness while we rode through the drowsy town toward the south gate. The tank tracks clattered on the cobblestones and the exhausts resounded off stucco walls in this village half a world away from the villages we had left behind.

An Loc, the illusion, An Loc, the impressionist's canvas screen, a veneer of dappled light and shadow concealing the war within. Our tanks, with their thick armor and heavy guns, would grind to a ponderous halt in front of the south gate, which was made of thin bars with cast iron flowers on them. An old man dressed in black, who had stood guard alone at the gate through the night with a rifle older and taller than he was, would then ceremoniously unlock the gate and swing it open. He'd graciously bow to us, very aware of the irony of our respective security measures, and we'd flip him a pack of cigarettes. Often, there would be a couple of civilian vehicles waiting for us at the gate as well, the three-wheeled *lambrettas* or a motorbike or two. As soon as the gate was open they would rush past us and head down the highway intent upon their missions of commerce; they knew a lot more about mines than we did. Day after day, they knew there were none.

We'd dismount and send the tanks back. The lovely raven-haired Co Dep would maneuver her pushcart into our ranks, and we'd begin our leisurely stroll south on the hard red clay of "Thunder Road." It was August of 1968, and there were tanks and armored personnel carriers in the streets of Chicago. We were still unaware of the irony of this, still unaware that to many at home it seemed their city gates had been stormed by brigands. For us, for a while, Thunder Road south of An Loc was mysteriously silent. The devastating mines, the rocket attacks, the ambushes which had given the road its name had evaporated like the morning mist. Sunshine spilled down in shifting patterns as the fog lifted, shimmering on the leaves of the rubber trees which lined the road. After an hour or so I'd buy a Coke and some bread from barefoot Co Dep and try to look in her eyes, but she would always look away too quickly, reaching into her purse for change and speaking English carefully, with a slight French accent.

We went south about six kilometers, just past the Montagnard village, to where we would meet another unit sweeping north. Then we would hire taxis to take us back to An Loc again, instead of walking back the way we were supposed to. That allowed some time for a beer or two at one of An Loc's sidewalk cafés where we could relax and watch the full flow of midday traffic surge past: *lambrettas* loaded with vegetables, beautiful girls on bicycles, old women carrying ammo cans full of water on *chogie* sticks. After five months of sweeps and eagle flights and night ambushes, it was the first time any of us had really seen the country, or seen it without a sense of imminent danger. I felt my own strength, felt my platoon as my arms and my legs. And Highway Thirteen was becoming a river I was just beginning to explore. It beckoned with swirling eddies and deep holes.

Sometimes I would leave my men at the cafés and wander over to the advisor's compound. I was drawn by that bizarre world of decaying colonial infrastructure, Kennedy-era idealism, and CIA operatives. That part of An Loc could have been the Casablanca of movie fame, filled with intrigue, and I had begun to learn my way through the rabbit warren of red tile roofs and mossy walls, scrounging medical supplies for the Montagnards, whom we were trying to befriend. Then I became acquainted with the province's intelligence officer. Under the slowly churning ceiling fans, over the slightly yellowed linen tablecloths, just beyond earshot of the lingering waitresses, he shared his reports with me and I saw the distant hills in a new light. An Loc was an illusion, but still, we clung to the illusion, because it was so beautiful.

An Loc, the capital of Binh Long province, was an island of nineteenth-century colonialism riding high above a sea of chaos. It had been built during that era by the French, carved out of what was once a wilderness populated only by primitive tribesmen. Now it was the center of the vast Michelin rubber empire, built on the high ground like the walled fortress towns of medieval Europe. Thin though the wall was, just brick and stucco with four gates guarded by four old men at night, it seemed a totally effective barrier against the constant battering reality of war. In fact, the communist revolution had started here in the 1920s, amid the squalor and near slavery of the rubber workers, with attempts to organize labor unions. And forty years later, great tides of Viet Cong and even greater tides of North Vietnamese regulars were sweeping past us every night, going back and forth between their Cambodian sanctuaries and the fighting to the south on well-trodden paths that ran parallel to Thunder Road. Yet a truce of sorts really did exist, allowing the French to keep harvesting their rubber trees, and allowing the Vietnamese soldiers to remain dapper and evanescent while the North Vietnamese and Viet Cong staged battles to the south and rehearsed for the inevitable assault on Saigon. The ARVN battalion stationed at An Loc stubbornly maintained its responsibility for security in this part of the province. Every day they patrolled the outlying countryside, finding nothing. Every night they furnished the advisors with a map liberally sprinkled with red circles showing where their ambushes were. Such diligence was a deception. The local Viet Cong were kept better informed than we were.

The illusions were elaborate and well constructed, like the cobblestone streets. In all my time in Vietnam, sliding down hillsides, digging fighting holes, rooting through Viet Cong tunnels, I never saw a native stone. Not even a pebble. Just red clay, mostly, or sometimes grey clay or sand, so these stones must have been quarried a great distance away and brought here at considerable expense in order to complete this canvas of serenity. And the streets were lined with pastel-painted stucco buildings with long, brightly painted shutters and elegant balconies to further invoke memories of France. There was even a statue and a fountain in the center of town; the traffic ran in circles around the fountain and shade trees drooped above the sidewalks. "White Mice," which was what we called the immaculately uniformed national police, rushed back and forth trying to direct the traffic, waving their white-gloved hands like orchestra conductors. The traffic ignored them. Commerce took precedence over everything else, with a palpable vitality which was fun to watch from a sidewalk table with a bottle of *Ba Mui Ba,* the local beer. The voices and the traffic noise seemed to rise above the town like a song. Everything had to be accomplished by day, for at night, after the gates were swung closed, the world turned inside out. This was the matrix in which we found ourselves, and it seemed to invite insanity.

Military ritual and discipline were continually enforced from above; in the afternoon we might take a short patrol out into the countryside to the north, but more likely we'd work on improving our own fortifications, building ever more elegant bunkers out of sandbags, engineer stakes, and the wood ammunition boxes the artillerymen discarded. Our firebase, called "Camp Alpha," had been a revolting mess when we first arrived. The red clay knoll was strewn with garbage and infested with rats. The fighting holes were collapsing and filled with putrid water. It was hard to imagine an infantry outfit so demoralized and undisciplined that they could live like that. Within our first week there we had rebuilt the base, hiring local kids to help fill the sandbags. Then we went on to design elaborate sleeping quarters, command centers and clubhouses, all with the mandatory three feet of earth on the roof.

Always, no matter what we were doing, there were the fantastic clouds overhead, coming in off the sea in a slow parade. These must have been the same clouds my father saw while he lay at anchor in the harbor at Saipan, suffering his "nervous breakdown," an event which was offered to me as an explanation of his absence, an event which characterized him, an event of such humiliation that I never was able to find out much about it although I kept trying, searching for myself in him, looking for the weak points in both of us and building defenses as a military man does. My inquiries were taken as attacks. His loneliness and mine went forever unshared, as is so often the fate of men.

I knew that his breakdown had taken place at the same time of year that I was in An Loc, with the great Pacific monsoons forming, eclipsing everything below with the play of heat and light and water. Then, I was just ten months old. Then, the sun would beat down day after day upon the glassy stillness of the harbor as he sat in his repair ship, surrounded by the wreckage of war and spirits of the dead, while at An Loc, the sun beat down upon the jungled hills and endless rows of rubber trees, but we were both waiting under the dome of sky: he to go home from a war he had never quite reached, and I was waiting for the war to resume. The wheeling of the day overhead was the same. Clear midmorning skies would gradually give way as the day wore on, first to little puffs of white, then later to great ballooning, mushrooming shapes, billowing ever upward, sometimes just like the bomb clouds that had ended his war. By midafternoon there would be hundreds of clouds, even thousands, stretching to the horizon and beyond, taking on fantastic shapes, lifting the waters of the Pacific skyward.

Entertainment, for men waiting, is generally simple and close at hand. At our knoll at An Loc, for example, there was a very short dirt runway beside our perimeter which ended right at the north gate to the village. The runway was just long enough for the twin-engine Caribou resupply airplane that came in once or twice a day, in fact it had at times proved not quite long enough. The wreckage of two Caribous lay at the foot of a steep slope which marked the other end of the runway. Whenever we heard a Caribou coming we would stop filling sandbags and watch the air force play "Let's see if we can get the White Mice to run." Three or four White Mice took over guard duties at the gate during the day, and the air force pilots enjoyed landing a little hot and heading right toward them, reversing their props and jamming on the brakes at the last possible moment. Such were the highlights of long afternoons.

Then, late in the day, when the shadows grew long, a couple of advisors would come out to the runway and check the tie-downs of the L-19, which was the only airplane that stayed there. The last of the villagers would wander up the road and pass through the gate, and the White Mice would go away. Sounds would carry very far in the still air, and the ripening sun played on the huge towers of benevolent cloud drifting in from the South China Sea. I felt as though I were seeing the sunshine for the first time in many months. Surely, there must have been days of sunshine before we came to this place, surely there must have been sunsets ribbed with red and gold, but I couldn't remember them. I only remembered the gray-green wetness. I was not like my father. In the struggle to distance myself from him, and at the same time get closer, I had achieved a great victory on the distancing side. He would never forgive me for my strength. I would never forgive his weakness.

Camp Alpha was where units were sent to recuperate, although of course we were still at war, and in fact our firebase was perched on the edge of a strategic precipice. From where we stood, outside the north gate of An Loc, all the land northward was in Viet Cong hands. Of course this gave the rolling hills we looked out upon a deeper sense of mystery; it was a forbidden place as well as a beautiful one. There were no permanent firebases beyond ours. Highway Thirteen continued its course across French Indochina, but it crossed a different landscape. Above An Loc the flanks of Thunder Road had not been bulldozed back into a tangle of mud and tree stumps. Instead, the trees still enclosed the road with their spreading limbs overhead, all the way to the Cambodian border and beyond, keeping out the sunlight and shutting secrets in. Sometimes in Vermont, when the sky is clear and the sun is setting, I still see that road and those hills as though I am seeing the light for the first time. The place where a hayfield meets a deep wood becomes the edge of the rubber plantation, and on our neighbor's dairy farm I even see the place on Bad Vibes Hill where the helicopter went down.

Looking out across those hills to the north, there was the urge to simply walk away, answering to no one, perform the ultimate recon and follow the river to its source. As a platoon, we could probably have woven our way through the fabric of Vietnam pretty well, as long as the cigarettes and candy bars held out. This would have been the sane thing to do. Nobody gave a fuck for the war, we were great at performing recon, and we had doubtless made friends with lots of Viet Cong already.

Not only were there kids filling sandbags, wandering around our base all day, but there were also *mamasans* cooking dinners to order and passing them to us through the concertina wire, and a host of other vendors. Best of all, though, were the "short-time" girls who came around at night; Butch and Nancy and the others with Americanized names and hair cut short. The lucky men assigned to listening posts just outside the wire got to share the warmth of their poncho liners with them for a few dollars. Often, while I scanned our defensive perimeter with a starlight scope, I would be startled by the image of a pale white ass bobbing up and down against a hazy background of brush and tree line. Our seduction was complete; there were no more enemy, no more rules. There were just the pastel shades of An Loc, the brightness and shadows of Highway Thirteen, and the almost sickly smell of hibiscus, raw latex, and diesel fuel.

When An Loc had finally been overrun by the North Vietnamese tanks, and bombed by the B-52s, and I had moved to Vermont and was barefoot planting sweet corn and feeling the sunshine and had just seen the photographs of An Loc in the news in which nothing was recognizable but pieces of tank and those stupid cobblestones amid the red clay craters and my own children had not yet been born, there was no way to talk about those things. I was planting corn and planting the seeds of my children in my first wife and keeping An Loc a secret. But now and then I would stop and lean on my hoe and look out across the valley at the next hillside. There was the column of smoke rising like an exclamation point from the side of Bad Vibes Hill, interrupting my reverie on a particularly fine evening. Bravo Six, our company commander, breathlessly explained to me that a helicopter with four men on board had just gone down there, only four kilometers from our position, right where the rancid rubber plantation met an impenetrable bamboo thicket, and I had to get my platoon there fast.

I knew the place was infested with VC; I knew this partly through the intelligence reports I'd scrounged but mainly I knew because of the sixth sense I had developed, that most of us had developed, which had become as real as taste and touch. It was something which could qualify us as crazy, but it was terribly important, as important as the smoke grenades and claymore mines we carried with us, a tool for survival. It was as though we had absorbed some of the Montagnards' animist religion through our skins, and rejected the Western logic which had landed us in this place. Call it ESP. Those who had it, and by now I was one of them, were always on the edge of a precipice, playing with fire in our brains.

Bad Vibes Hill had earned its name precisely because nothing real ever happened there. It was an illusion, a sucking black hole. One time, while out on a rare afternoon's mandatory reconnoiter, there was a feeling as if maybe we all really were crazy. We were at the foot of the hill, on the southeast side, just about a click below where the helicopter went down. We kept going through little square fields enclosed by bamboo hedges, each one just like the one before, so that it began to seem like we were stuck going in a circle even though we were trying to go in a straight line. We all became confused and disoriented. I couldn't get over the impression that I had been there before, even done and said the same things before, like in another lifetime. We looked at each other in wordless communication, eyes rolling. Of course this meant we were all going to die, and talking about it would only make things worse. Within the bamboo, they were watching us through the narrow slits of spider holes. We finally had to stop and sit down for a while, we were so scared. Then we went back to the firebase and reported seeing nothing.

What could we report besides our own hysteria? My platoon was functioning like a family, very close and under siege, more or less autonomous and quite neurotic. We were also the best and knew it, the envy of other outfits, speaking our own language. We saw the most action, yet suffered the fewest casualties. That was one reason we kept getting the recon assignments. There were hierarchies of male bonding, of legends and lore that must have seemed impenetrable to the newcomers who were gradually trickling in and bringing us back up to strength. We really had become tribal and mystical like the Montagnards we admired, feeling our way through a jungle filled with many spirits. If this was insanity, at least I wasn't alone in it. It was how we had learned to survive, teetering on the edge, sensing what is unknowable.

Another time we were in the rubber on top of Bad Vibes Hill and Bravo Six sent us to check out a thicket on the northwest side, near an infamous VC hamlet. The VC liked bamboo because it is nearly impenetrable and the roots form a dense mat which is the perfect cover for a tunnel system. Like the other time, we knew that the VC were in the bamboo, and with each step we took that sense became more vivid, and we kept looking at each other as well as straight ahead.

Then a voice materialized on my radio and began calling me by name. "Mike Six," it kept saying with a heavy Vietnamese accent, "Mike Six, you come here. Come this way."

At first we thought it was a joke so I stopped our movement and gathered the platoon together. We sat in our usual tribal circle with all four of our radios, but the voice kept going. It wasn't a joke. They had a fifth radio and not only did they know my name, they also knew the right frequency. Perhaps they had been filling our sandbags or draining our semen the day before. Now they were watching us, beckoning for us to cross over into another dimension. Or, as I preferred to think, they were warning us not to break the unwritten truce we had forged. I wasn't about to test any of these theories, and ended up doing something I had never done before. We hunched lower in the thick underbrush of the rubber plantation and concocted phony radio reports on a notepad, which we passed around. Then we took turns sending the phony reports over the radio just as though we were doing a thorough cloverleaf search of the bamboo. Actually, we were doing pretty much the same thing the ARVNs were doing. The VC fell silent, either puzzled or pleased. We, of course, reported finding nothing in the bamboo and returned to the base.

Maybe we were just crazy. Maybe we had been in the field too long, and now we had been outside An Loc for too long, and ambivalence and craziness had begun to grow on us like moss or clouds. Maybe I had lost my own sense of identity as an officer and grown too close to my men, and certainly we had lost track of our mission long ago. At any rate, if we had indeed formed our own separate treaty, it was doubly annoying that the truce should be broken by four guys from the rear of another outfit who flew too close to a VC marksman on Bad Vibes Hill. I ran back to our sector yelling "Saddle up, Mike Division," and my men looked at me as if I was being mean and spiteful. Cursing and complaining, grunting and clanking, they began to throw on their web gear and check their weapons. There wasn't much time; the VC would be expecting us. Already that side of the hill was in shadow; the smoke plume rose a hundred feet or so in perfectly still air before it entered the yellow sunshine. I briefed the squad leaders and coordinated some preplanned fires with Oscar Five, the mortar platoon leader, and Niner Two, who was the artillery liaison officer.

The plan was to race up the highway with some M-48 tanks, take a side road up the hill toward the VC hamlet, then cut off and bash through the rubber so fast that the VC wouldn't have time to assemble an effective ambush. The potential flaw in that plan was those tanks.

They belonged to an armor outfit that had been stationed at An Loc for so long they had gone completely to seed. For month after month the crews just ate and slept and went to the latrine and hung their laundry on the gun tubes to dry. I never once saw an officer in their presence, and got the impression they were here because nobody else wanted them. After a lot of clanging and banging and puffs of blue smoke, only two of the tanks could be persuaded to start on this evening, which was OK because most of the crews had managed suddenly to disappear. The malaise which was entirely to overcome our army in the years to follow was already firmly rooted among those tank crews, who'd been a subject of ridicule up to this moment. The man driving the lead tank, a man too new to the game to hide successfully in the bushes upon hearing my orders, began to plead with me as we mounted up. He said he had never driven a tank before in his life. He was an ammunition loader. I screamed at him that he had better learn to drive in a hurry, and he went back down through the driver's hatch like a retreating clam. Then, with a dozen of us riding each tank, clinging to the turret handrails and avoiding the hot engine grates, we were off, lurching across the runway and onto the highway, headed north.

There was still a lot to do en route, and I stayed on the radio while sitting in the turret hatch of the lead tank. A helicopter fire team from Quan Loi had come on station. I could see them circling the smoke plume like angry hornets. I went to their push on my radio and checked in. They had enough fuel for forty-five minutes, which was about as much daylight as we had left. The voices of the pilots, trembling with the vibrations of their ships, sounded grim. They said they couldn't see anything below them through the thick canopy of the jungle, just a smoking hole burned through the leaves, and they didn't want to go down any lower for a closer look. They put one of their radios on my push, and left another on brigade frequency so they could relay back to Quan Loi. Niner Two broke in to tell me he'd gotten a battery of 155s from Quan Loi to shoot for us, adding their massive firepower to the 105s back at Alpha. Oscar Five was cranking azimuth and deflection data to his three 81mm mortar crews, following our progress with the gun tubes so we could count on a quick and accurate response. And brigade radioed down that they had put a team of F-4 Phantom jets on stand-by out of Bien Hoa with a twenty-minute response time.

I had quite an arsenal at my fingertips, and I hoped that the Viet Cong still had their radio tuned in and were listening closely. I also hoped the downed helicopter hadn't inadvertently flown over one of those NVA regiments which kept showing up in the intelligence reports. As we roared through the lengthening shadows, churning clouds of red dust into the air, peasants emerged from their thatch huts on the outskirts of town to see what the commotion was about. Squads of ARVNs on their way to their overnight hiding places gawked and waved. Then we were alone on the road, going deeper into the land I loved and feared. In my mind's eye, each hill ahead had the military symbol for an enemy unit hovering over it, as on the intelligence maps; the Phu Loi Battalion, the Fifth NVA Regiment. I used my mental radio to tell them that we meant no harm by steaming into their midst at thirty miles an hour in a cloud of red dust. And nightfall was coming on with the inexorability of death itself.

The highway was fully steeped in shadow by the time we hit the fork a few kilometers north. We left the main road and climbed up the side of the valley, back in the sunshine again. The view out to the west was splendid: mile after mile of rubber plantations, rice paddies, dark jungle and misty streams rolling toward the horizon. I longed to come back on a bicycle some day instead of a tank, maybe with a girlfriend. The place where we turned off the road and entered the rubber would be good for a picnic, right at the crest of Bad Vibes Hill, with the sunshine flaring up for one last moment before plunging down below the distant hills. All the colors seemed so incredibly bright, iridescent blues and greens, with the stark rows of rubber trees on the left side of the road glowing orange for a few seconds. I knew, at that moment, with a clarity that had taken me long to reach, that I had done my work, and that I had found my way as a leader, as a father of men just a few years younger than I was, and I hated it. There were black butterflies of death fluttering between the tree trunks again.

As soon as we entered the plantation the darkness was a shock, like plunging into icewater. Even at midday, the canopy kept the place in twilight. Now it was almost impossible to see at all until our eyes adjusted. And since this part of the plantation had been abandoned, deemed too infested with things invisible even to bother harvesting the rubber, a dense undergrowth ten or twelve feet tall had sprung up, making visibility much worse. The driver of my tank began to cry on the intercom. He said he couldn't see and he wanted to stop. He had reached the breaking point and was getting hysterical on me. But I knew the feeling, had experienced it myself once, and just kept talking to him calmly in order to keep him going. We couldn't stop. Now and then we would smash head-on into a rubber tree, and my men on the tank would yell and curse, drawing more sobs from the driver. I told the driver to ignore them, that he was doing a great job. And gradually, his driving improved, the sobs subsided, and we smashed into rubber trees less often.

As we drew closer to the crash site I got the whiff of burning meat which was memorable for the irony that, during that split second between levels of recognition, it smelled great. The helicopter had hit in the bamboo right on the edge of the rubber. We dismounted and I set up a security perimeter around the site. Then I went in with my CP (command post) group; just me, my radio man, and our medic. The helicopter had burned a big hole in the bamboo, so it was easy to get in. Nothing recognizable of the helicopter remained except the tips of the rotor blades and the end of the tail boom. The two passengers had been thrown clear of the wreckage and lay nearby, naked and hairless. The copilot had tipped over, but the pilot remained sitting bolt upright in his seat, atop a pile of flaming wreckage. The pilot's hands were raised up in front of his burned marshmallow face, as though protecting himself from the blows of an invisible enemy, still holding forth.

I sent the others back to the tanks to get fire extinguishers. This left me alone with the dead. I pulled the two passengers back a little farther. The guys were taking a long time getting back with the extinguishers. The sight of the pilot kept burning in my mind. I knew I had seen it before. Was it another lifetime? Was it really me I was seeing? Total déjà vu on Bad Vibes Hill again. Then it came to me. I had seen it in *Life* magazine. It was the picture of the Buddhist monk burning himself to death on the street in Saigon with that same gesture, in death, which can be interpreted as either anger or genuflection, but is in fact simply referred to by coroners as the pugilist's position. At least I'd figured it out, with this pilot sitting, as though on a throne, on his pile of wreckage, enshrined by flames. It was all here: the sacrifice, the grief, the ugliness, the war.

❖ II ❖

MY FATHER CHOSE THE SEA. He chose it over me, and dreamed of the return of the great sailing ships he remembered seeing as a child. He was lost in the vast emptiness of the ocean, while I am drawn by the river, which is always changing and yet remains the same, moving ahead like a column of men through the jungle, even with the tightening in the groin at the sound of white water up ahead. My favorite time is on the river with my boys. We have everything we need with us in the canoe. Sometimes we run fast, swerving and shouting. Sometimes we just drift, feeling the tug. In the afternoon the wind comes up from the south and swells like sails the silver maples that line the shore, and we eye the sandbars at each island and oxbow, choosing the best one for our camp. Then we land, move to the wood line, check the perimeter and gather sweet ferns for our bed. The beach is patrolled for driftwood. A fire is started, the smoke drifts upward as the sun sets, and my children's voices ring like bells. We eat, we fish, and we wait for the moon to rise. Sometimes, when the moonlight is bright and the water is calm, we go out in the canoe again. You can lose yourself, suspended there between the sky and its mirrored reflection, as though flying.

I came to Vietnam on the night of a full moon. All across the Pacific Ocean, all through the endless night, all around the world, the moon was shining. I had always wanted to fly. I had joined the service because I wanted to fly. And now, here I was, flying high over the Pacific in a yellow Braniff 727 charter along with a couple hundred other guys. I had been just about to graduate from high school on the day, June eleventh of 1963, when Thich Quan Duc seated himself by a busy downtown

Saigon intersection and assumed the lotus position while an assistant doused him with gasoline and set him on fire. The press had been notified beforehand, and the cameras clicked away while the monk's position gradually changed from lotus to pugilist. I remember looking at the color photographs and thinking how bizarre and grotesque and alien it was. Everything I had seen or read about our growing role in Southeast Asia had seemed compelling and uncontestable up till then. It was odd that one flaming monk half a world away should garner such attention. Mine didn't last for long.

This was my summer of freedom, with a freshly minted driver's license and college coming in the fall. After many difficult years I was finally at ease socially, and halfheartedly planning a career in medicine. I worked in the local hospital again that summer, as I had for several summers past, preparing for combat with the cystic fibrosis which held my cousins in a death grip. But there were lots of parties, too, as our class began to disperse. It had been a good class, close-knit and active, where I had finally found myself after years of unhappiness. For most of my time growing up in the metastatic suburbs of New York's Westchester County I had felt excluded, even ostracized, raised by my mother and grandmother in a grandly decrepit house which contrasted vividly with the constant bombardment of television images, Mom and Dad and Buzz and Sis, images which were largely the creation of Westchester's fathers to begin with. Nearly all of them seemed to work in either television or advertising in the city. My mother worked for the *Reader's Digest,* another cornucopia of convention which had its world headquarters on a grassy ridge right next to the high school.

I can see myself now on the kitchen floor. I am three or four, playing with pots and pans while dinner is prepared. The floor is blue-green linoleum, the color of the sea, rising up like the sea in places where it has buckled, with frothy seams of burlap. I miss my father terribly, even though I have not yet met him. I am exploring the blue-green sea looking for myself amid women's ankles. The pots and pans could be ships. This could be a navy of my own, grey metal dented by war, and I was told that the best of them had actually gone to war, been turned in and melted down during scrap drives to make more ships and tanks and airplanes. Among the other utensils, and objects of wonder themselves, are a knife and fork from an army mess kit, with "U.S." sternly engraved. These were left behind by my uncle, or perhaps my grandfather. There is the possibility that the army may come back for them someday.

Meanwhile, I look at them with respect. They are symbols of manhood. Already, I am preparing to go to war.

A few years later, when pressed by schoolmates about what my father did, or where he was, I lied and said that he had been killed in the war. This was more than acceptable, it was heroic in their eyes; but the lie did nothing for my own self-esteem and staved them off only briefly. The truth was too painful; I could hardly bear to look at his photograph on my bedroom dresser, so handsome in his lieutenant commander's dress whites. He had deserted me, abandoned me to schoolyard sharks who sensed my weakness and fear, and circled endlessly day after day. I fingered the insignia in my mother's jewelry box. I pinned them on my shirt, and looked at myself in the mirror, trying to find strength.

I see him more clearly now as I write half a century later. I know of his sexual ambivalence, his anger, his swings between sprees and monastic isolation. But my mother couldn't offer me an explanation at the time, and all I got was a few postcards depicting Saudi oil ports in gaudy colors. He was on tankers, and I longed for his ship to come in. When it did, he was taken to a hospital where I was not allowed to meet him. I had to wait in the car while papers were signed. He had shamed all of us again. I was told he could be dangerous. Later, when a toy tugboat arrived in the mail, I was not impressed, even though he had meticulously carved and painted it himself, down to the details of doors and windows and rails. I abandoned it as he had me, and within days the boat was chewed to pieces by a young puppy we had.

When I finally came to know the man, I was always to carry the weight of the tugboat, a foundered offering, and now as a father myself I understand more what he must have felt. We spent much of our lives angry with each other and afraid of each other and yet loving each other as well. Our relationship was always one of abandonment and rediscovery, like the sea breaking upon a beach, flowing in and flowing out, giving and taking away. Except that my loneliness was unbroken in those early days, with no islands in sight, afraid as I was of men and the man in me. I couldn't play catch, was afraid of the ball, flinching as it hurtled closer. I lost weight and became sickly. Then I gained weight and became obese. My only playmates were my cousins, half of whom were slowly dying. Together we played "army," limping from wounds of one sort or another and finding a special bliss in imaginary combat punctuated by wracking coughs.

What a team we made! I remember finding several pairs of army spats and a doughboy helmet up in the attic. They had belonged to my great-grandfather, who went to war when already a grandfather himself. The spats were a disappointment; it was hard to figure out how to wear them, or even why one would, but we took turns with the helmet, wearing it proudly even though mice had eaten away all the lining. An uncle had left a field jacket behind, and there was also my grandfather's greatcoat, which trailed behind whoever was wearing it like a king's robe. Already we were learning the loneliness of men, finding comfort in marching together for a while, before dying.

On the west side of the ridge topped by the *Reader's Digest* and high school, the land fell away through abandoned meadows, which turned amber in autumn, to green-watered swamps and oak defiles. And behind my cousins' house a forest of primordial hemlocks kept the twilight even at midday. These places were my sanctuary, even though suburbia was steadily bulldozing them, just as the Rome plows would sweep aside the forest a decade later in the Iron Triangle. I felt like a Viet Cong, or an Indian, and began to find strength there. I found more strength when I went off to a boys' camp, learning to canoe and getting the first inklings of leadership. But although my grades and social ease improved in high school, the temptation to play hooky was ever-present, and my memories of stolen moments in the woods are more pleasant than any of academia. One could say I lacked direction. By the time of my graduation I was mainly looking forward to beer parties and sex along with the lesser amenities college had to offer as my social life blossomed. I was not to be disappointed.

The college I had chosen, on the bank of the nearby Hudson River, soon became the setting for a two-year celebration on my part. It was a small and passionately liberal school, with a flamboyant student body juxtaposed with deep, brooding woods and rocky river inlets, the perfect setting for me. I made a lot of friends quickly among the "ban-the-bomb" and folk song crowd, often spending weekends in New York's Greenwich Village. More Buddhist monks had immolated themselves in front of the press, and the death toll of Americans in Vietnam was approaching one hundred by that autumn, but civil rights and voter registration drives down South were bigger issues. The burden of my virginity was quickly lifted, but it was soon followed by a far greater loss of innocence when Kennedy was killed in Dallas. As was true for so many of us, this was a pivotal event which began a swing into disillusionment. I had admired and trusted Kennedy as a leader, a father figure and war hero. He had been much reviled in Westchester during his candidacy, and his victory had seemed like a personal one. His death was personal as well.

I continued to work in the local hospital during the midwinter and summer breaks, clinging to the notion of becoming a doctor, but it was increasingly clear that my cousins were going to die anyway; there was nothing I could do about it. Worse, my last job was as an ambulance driver and we happened to get a succession of calls to fatal accidents involving children. Long before I was to be a parent myself, or go to war, it was a test of my emotional limits. It would happen again but there was no way of talking about it then; the images of dead children followed me everywhere, juxtaposed with the banter of morticians. I knew by then that medicine was not for me, and I began to experience depression again, as I had in my grade school years. I dared not share this with anyone, least of all my father, for although we were spending time together at last, I knew his own wounds were so grievous that I had to maintain my distance by feigning strength.

I traded my white linen jacket for a black leather one, bought a motorcycle and wrote confused poetry. I also spent a lot more time in the woods by the river. Fetid, brackish, rising and falling with the tides, it smelled a little like the waterfront where I had found my father, just sixty miles downstream, but had a wildness to it which was new and fresh and exciting. At one place, a tributary came tumbling over falls and into a secluded bay, and I happened to be there one evening in the spring when some Indians arrived in rusting old automobiles, having come down out of the Catskills as they had for thousands of years, like the water itself. I watched while they silently cut saplings in the woods, then sprung them on big nets and dipped bushels of spawning herring out of the water and into the trunks of their cars. Later, in the summer, I watched as they seemed to materialize out of nowhere again, and waded through marshy shallows nearby, grappling for snapping turtles with hooked poles.

The college expelled me at the end of my sophomore year. I worked as a motorcycle mechanic and hung out in the city. I was not particularly alarmed when the local draft board began to hound me. I burned for a new adventure, something to dispel the demons. A leap from biker to jet fighter pilot seemed romantic enough, but I didn't have enough college credits for the Navy or Air Force aviation programs. That left the much more chancy options of going through a year of training as an Army or Marine officer, and then reapplying for aviation. This still appealed to me, and I was not dissuaded when I heard that an acquaintance from high school had been killed in Vietnam. It was Bill Moss; I'd liked him a lot, he was another rebel, and we used to sneak cigarettes behind the gymnasium together. One could not ask for better company than his, and his death, the first any of us learned of, seemed to draw me in deeper. Trumpets were sounding. The draft board was closing in. The anti-war movement didn't have much to go on yet. Fortunately I still had a vestigial instinct of self-preservation and I chose the Army over the Marines. Besides, if aviation didn't work out, I thought the Special Forces might be interesting. It would put me in the woods again.

So there I was, two years later, high over the Pacific with the crossed rifles of the infantry on my lapels and the gold bars of a second lieutenant on my shoulders. We were off on the adventure of a lifetime, although for many aboard it would also be the terminal event. Everybody had his own reasons for being there. About half had been drafted, and half had joined. Some were running away, some trying to find themselves. Many, like myself, were trying to find their fathers in the military, or kill their fathers, or both. Other than myself, few had witnessed a violent death. We were the first generation to be raised in front of a television, and our perception of the world had been shaped by the glib images of Madison Avenue in the fifties. And that made it so weird, surreal to be in that dim cabin with those stewardesses padding back and forth and the moonlight pouring in, not at all like one's image of going to war.

A lot had happened to me in the two years I had already spent in the army. I had discovered that I liked being an infantry officer and was good at it. I had found strengths inside of myself that I had never known before, and finally felt at ease in the company of men. I had also discovered the joy of leadership for the first time, which is something quite different from flying a jet plane solo, and made aviation seem boring. Other things had changed, too. The war had festered and erupted into something much bigger, and the anti-war movement was growing as well. But most of the time those facts could be pushed aside. Most of the time it was a lot of fun to be in the pipeline with a bunch of other guys, and little thought was given to where that pipeline led.

There was the perky-breasted stewardess in the moonlight again, taking away the dinner trays and offering pillows. Outside the window, miles below and beyond the tornado roar, puffs of cloud glowed like cotton balls and cast shadows in the moonlight on the endless glittering ocean. Now and then I could see a ship, just a black dot followed by a foamy phosphorescence, and a V-shaped wake fanning out for miles behind. I remember wondering if the men on those ships had any idea how big their wake was, how wide it spread across the ocean behind them, and if it ever really stopped. I felt as though I, too, was a ship alone and far at sea. I remember thinking that even if I died, there would still be my wake going on to lap against some distant shore. I had carefully cleaned up my bedroom, putting away the things of my childhood before I left, even throwing away my favorite issues of *Playboy*, knowing that I might never come back.

It had been twilight when we ascended through the fog over San Francisco Bay. It was a few hours before midnight when we landed in Hawaii to refuel. Already I had gone thousands of miles farther than I ever had before, and we were not yet halfway there. My send-off had been less than auspicious, and for the first time nagging doubts kept creeping into my mind as I looked out the window at the moonlit sea far below.

Three things had happened to unnerve me. First, the great Tet Offensive had just taken place. As with all Americans, my previous images and rationalizations of our mission had been profoundly shaken. For the first time, public opinion was beginning to turn against the war. Then, when I had visited my father a few days before departing, he had turned hostile and childish, far too bristly for the embrace I needed. He had always been contemptuous of the war in Vietnam, but at least at this moment he could have kept silent. Instead, he went on about it, and worse, condemning the officer corps as well. He suggested that if I was going to fight at all, it would be far better to do so as a common foot soldier.

I understand now, as I did then, how I had been goading him. I had learned long ago that I was more agile than he, and had learned to slow to his pace and indulge him. In my own struggles, my own agonies, I had found him pretty much useless, although I always hoped for better and remained loyal, sensing that no matter how much pain I was enduring, his pain had been greater, his wounds were deeper. Yet at the same time, in my own pain, my own rage, I also could not help myself from competing with him as men do, even bullying him at times with my agility. It was more than a matter of ignoring the tugboat. I was inviting confrontation by going to war, I was the son turned into a potential assasin, as sons so often are. Still, it was a rude send-off, and the loneliness of earlier days was returning as I drove away during a cold April rain. Then finally, while I drove, I heard on the car radio that Martin Luther King had just been killed. I began to cry, partly for my country and partly for myself. For the first time, I doubted the course I had chosen. I could not rid myself of the feeling that our country had gone wrong in a terrible way, and that the father I was still looking for was crazy, or malevolent, or simply didn't exist at all; or worse, that my father was right and I had suicidally disobeyed him.

At about midnight we crossed the international date line, and today became tomorrow. With every hour we sped over more of the Pacific than my father had crossed in two days, twenty years earlier. We passed Wake, with glowing seas breaking against inky darkness and the ruins of war far below. Then, as we approached the Marianas, the tone of the engines changed. We were going to land at Guam to take on fuel. Guam, the largest island of the chain, was just over a hundred miles south of Saipan, where my father had gone crazy. We banked to the left, banked to the right, with the sky and moonlit sea rising and falling. As we descended, outlying islands passed below, rings of darkness surrounded by rings of phosphorescent surf. A thousand times before and since, I have tried to imagine the moment of landing on those beaches in 1944, felt the sickening motion of the landing craft as it wallowed landward, watched as the ramp lowered to show us the face of death. Would I have had the courage? The most poignant images of war are of those beaches, with waves gently lapping against the corpses of young American men, shattered palms in the background, and those magnificent clouds overhead. I grew up haunted by them, repulsed and fascinated and drawn forward at the same time, just as the men themselves had been.

Now we were passing over the bones of the dead, with our dinner trays put away and seats in the upright position. These were the dead who were so important that the whole town would turn out to celebrate them each May. We hurtled across the beachhead, flaps extended and gear down, just as the B-29s had, returning from Japan. We touched down on the runway, first built by Pan American, then captured by the Japanese, then recaptured by us again. The first B-29s had arrived at Guam just three weeks after I had been born, yet being there made it seem like yesterday. The brakes shuddered, the plane slowed. At first there was nothing to see but darkness and glowing runway lights. But then, as we taxied toward the terminal, we saw the B-52s. There were dozens of them, looking like giant pterodactyls in camouflage paint. Each bomber sat in a pool of light, with tank trucks and bomb carts drawn up alongside. Mechanics, armorers, technicians swarmed over them, ministering to their needs. There was a frenzy to it, a sense of urgent purpose that was palpable even through the Plexiglas windows of our yellow Braniff charter. In another hour, long before dawn, the B-52s would begin to lumber down the runway, their sagging wings heavy with fuel, their bellies engorged with bombs. Just as the B-29s had before them, they would then begin the long take-off roll, rising at last, the beachhead falling behind them. Just as the B-29s had, they would climb high into the cold Pacific skies and fly west with the dawn slowly catching up with them. The crews would nap, or play cards, or eat snacks. Just as the B-29s had before them, they would arrive over their targets at eight or nine in the morning. The bombs would tumble out, the airplane would rise, suddenly unburdened. Then they would turn and fly back towards Guam, with plumes of smoke streaming downwind of craters far below. They would land in the early afternoon, just as the B-29s had before them. Soon I would know the routine more intimately myself, feel the earth shudder beneath my feet while oily clouds surged overhead. But at that moment, seeing the great machinery of war in motion, I was struck by how sinister it was. It seemed as though the Pacific war had never stopped, that bombing missions launched from Guam were always a part of our destiny, kept secret from the folks back home.

Our plane was parked far from the B-52s. We were allowed off to stretch our legs, but there were armed air force police all around to keep us from wandering toward the bombers. More ominous yet, we were also surrounded on three sides by a high chain-link fence topped with barbed wire. It was a little like being a prisoner. Perhaps this was because of the bombs and B-52s, but more likely it was to discourage any of us from changing our minds at the last moment and bolting for the darkness beyond. Had anyone done so, and somehow managed to dodge the bullets of the air force police, climb the wire, drop to the other side and find his way into the thickly jungled crenellations of the interior to hide out, he might have met the last Japanese soldier left there, still hiding out himself. This Japanese soldier would not surrender until 1972, four years later. He must have assumed, as I had, that the war still went on and that the B-52s were bombing his homeland. He would continue to resist as long as he thought his country was at war.

There was nothing else to see at Guam besides the latrines and the liquor store. Liquor, that great elixir of war, was offered for sale at about a third the stateside price. Bombs and booze. A gentle wind came off the sea, smelling of kerosene. It was hot, even at 2:00 A.M. Everyone was excitedly talking about the bombers, and what Vietnam would look like. We got back on the plane, rolled down the runway and lifted off, now within striking distance of Vietnam ourselves. I was even more unnerved. Perhaps it was the urgency, the hugeness, the brutality of it. I could not quite name what I felt, but sensed that what I had found was not just the war, but the great American frontier, and ahead lay Indian country.

Finally I was able to sleep for a while, lulled by the cold rush of air. I awoke again at dawn, when the tone of the engines changed once more. It was announced that we were landing in Manila to take on more fuel. This seemed odd, as we had so recently refueled at Guam, but, as it turned out, the field at Tan Son Nhut, our ultimate destination, was being shelled again. So down we went, weaving above the most beautiful jungled mountains I had ever seen as we began our final approach. Now, here at last, was something to write home about: the rugged, deeply gouged mountainsides of Luzon at sunrise. Like almost everyone else on board, I had never traveled to a foreign country before, and it was pretty exciting. I knew from my days as a training officer that many on the plane had never traveled any farther than the fifty or hundred miles to their nearest draft board before they joined the army.

My grandparents had been to this part of the world in the 20s, though, squandering the last of their inheritance. I had found a picture of them standing in front of the Manila officer's club. There were pictures of Manila harbor filled with tall-stacked steamers and even a few square-rigged sailing ships. We didn't get to see the harbor, we couldn't even get off the airplane. But later my grandparents had gone on to the Annamite Kingdom, which was exactly where I was going. They had brought back photos of naked tribesmen, villages of grass huts, and women in long white dresses, wearing conical hats, pedaling bicycles. There were pictures of misty mountains and winding roads, and a place that looked just like Highway Thirteen, north of An Loc, my yellow brick road. Perhaps I could recapture a bit of their adventure, which I had never tired of hearing about when I was younger.

It was the last bit of romantic fantasy I allowed myself to indulge in. When Vietnam itself actually appeared on the horizon toward noon, the sense of foreboding returned heavily and kept getting worse. A grayish brown haze lay above a flat, gray-green land. We were nearing the end of the pipeline, and it had none of the visual appeal of the Philippines. The passenger cabin, which had been curiously silent for nearly twenty hours, with everyone thinking thoughts like mine, suddenly came to life with murmuring voices. Our descent became startlingly rapid and steep; I hadn't realized that a passenger airplane could fly like that. There was hardly time to ponder the fabric of the place: the paisley-like tendrils of estuaries, the polka dots of bomb craters filled with water. Numerous smoke plumes were visible climbing upward and then trailing off, and I assumed they were burning villages or convoys that had been ambushed, not yet knowing that it was just the rice farmers, burning the straw from the year before in preparation for spring planting. Down we went, dropping like a stone to avoid the anti-aircraft fire from Saigon's sprawling suburbs. Then we skimmed over muddy revetments of sandbags, rusted tangles of barbed wire, and touched down.

This place made Guam look bucolic. The din of our engines reversing thrust was lost amid the din of all the other engines of war. Our brand-new Braniff "yellow bird," (named for the calypso song that promised transport to a warmer climate), stood out like a sore thumb, like the "new guy" in war novels amid the battle veterans. As we taxied past snarling fighter-bombers, transports and gun ships, the sprightly-voiced stewardess welcomed us to Vietnam over the intercom. She continued through the standard spiel, on behalf of Braniff, hoping we had a safe stay and looking forward to serving us again, while our faces were plastered to the windows, trying to absorb the magnitude of the chaos outside. Whether she had to lock herself in the lavatory and chug a handful of liquor bottles in order to get through this I know not. I doubt it, because everything inside the cabin still carried the strange, plastic, unreal, made-for-television quality that had accompanied us from the beginning. I was reminded of the squeaky clean conservative-funded singing group, "Up With People." They were on a tour of military bases stateside, and I had seen them at Fort Benning. Our attendance was mandatory, and they had cheered the troops with the fervor of a born-again Christian toothpaste commercial. Braniff was doing its best to sustain the illusion, but inevitably the airplane stopped and the doors were opened. Going out through the door and breathing the air for the first time was like stepping into the biggest, hottest fart on earth.

We were met by military buses with sturdy iron mesh in the windows to deflect hand grenades. Much had been made in the press about civilian terrorists, even children lobbing bombs, and everyone seemed suspicious as we were driven through the outskirts of Saigon toward Bien Hoa, upstream against a flood of motorbikes and pedicabs, Munchkins with satchel charges and fragmentation grenades. The Tet Offensive was just barely over, and the splatter-marks of stray rockets and machine gun fire marred the walls everywhere. People were still edgy, too. The war had changed, nothing was as safe as it had been just months before, even the U.S. embassy had been invaded and confidence was shaken to the very root. We passed through a part of the city that was in complete ruins, like Dresden or Hamburg, with just the stubs of walls poking up through mounds of rubble, yet still the traffic ebbed and flowed through narrow paths. I was amazed. It seemed impossible that anyone could survive such devastation, not to mention carry on business. I was also still naive enough to assume that the devastation had been caused by the Viet Cong.

By the time we got to Bien Hoa I was so stupefied by the heat and the most horrendous jet lag imaginable that I went through the various replacement processing steps as though suffering a terrible hangover. We were issued jungle fatigues and given an orientation lecture which emphasized, among other things, that we were the guests of the Vietnamese people. I had never thought of it that way, nobody really did. It seemed like one last feeble attempt to put the war into an attractive package. Then, finally, we were assigned a bunk for the night. Throughout the process, the roar of truck convoys outside the flimsy wooden buildings, and the helicopters and jets overhead, had been constant, adding to the sense of hangover. But when the sun set, everything suddenly became still, as though in a darkening theater. Then, before long, the first illumination rounds burst far away, just above the horizon, fired by guns well beyond our range of hearing. The flares floated there, casting light like little stars of Bethlehem, buoys of light moored above a deep dark terror miles and miles away.

I had gotten my orders assigning me to the First Infantry Division over two months before, while I was the executive officer of a basic training company at Fort Polk, Louisiana. I had spent my first year as a commissioned officer there, giving new recruits their first taste of the army. I learned how to use anger creatively, intimidating and then rewarding, just as the drill sergeants had once done with me. I was astonished and disturbed at the results. The men thrived. It was almost too easy. I rode my motorcycle across the rolling sand hills and pine barrens on the weekends. I explored abandoned bombing ranges, picking through the hulks of World War II tanks. These carcasses, used as targets and inhabited by black widow spiders, seemed to speak of the waste of war, but I was not dissuaded.

I was also taking flying lessons at last, civilian lessons at a former World War II bomber base which had been largely deserted. Trees rose through the walls of buildings, and knee-high grass, even shrubs grew in the cracks of the runways. It was wonderful to go there on still evenings, climb up into the sky and look down upon the darkening land. Thousands of men had come there before me, and gone off to war a generation ago. My little Cessna couldn't compare to their B-17s, but I felt their presence in the air and in the echoing emptiness of the base. I was waiting, as they had done, sharpening my skills and surrounded by ghosts. The steady thump of my motorcycle engine brought me ever closer to what they had known, and farther and farther from my father, whose long letters to me about the decline of our civilization, imminent catastrophe and a return to feudal times seemed pathetic. I was finding joy in the sky, and even more in leadership. I began to sing the cadences while my company marched and ran. I learned to run backward, so that I could watch my men and sing to them. I stalked the rifle ranges, inspecting, perfecting, showing them how to slowly squeeze off each round. Then on Wednesday afternoons, the other cadre and I would silently gather in the orderly room, for this was when the army newspaper *Stars and Stripes* came out. In the center pages, they printed the latest casualty list. It kept getting longer as the year went on, and toward the end of my year at Fort Polk, I began to see the names of men I had just trained. I remembered them as pale, inept recruits just off the farm, or city street. This was the one who was overweight, and later excelled as a runner. That was the one who tried to run away. It was hard to imagine them as dead so soon, or that Vietnam could destroy so many so fast, while I flew and motorcycled, waiting for my time.

My own commander, a grizzled and hard-drinking captain who had gotten a battlefield commission while serving in the First Division in Vietnam himself, was very pleased when he heard about my new assignment. The First Infantry was one of the very best. The captain and I had formed a solid respect for each other during our time together; I was unwavering in my loyalty as his lieutenant; in return he often let me lead the company and had even recommended me as aide to the commanding general. My orders came too quickly for that, but it had been a spectacularly successful year nonetheless, captain and lieutenant working well together like father and son, with me finding fulfillment at last, totally secure about the men I was with and the man I had become.

My unofficial duties often continued well into the night. The captain and our first sergeant, who had both been in the army since the Second World War, enjoyed recruiting my company on their nightly drinking bouts. My duties included playing poker and "liar's dice" with them, and losing a substantial portion of my paycheck to those two wizened, drawling professionals. Then I would drive the captain back to his distraught wife and children. He and the "Top Kick," as the first sergeant was known, had in turn become rather protective of me, an innocent about to be abroad.

"Wait 'til you see the bear," slurred the captain one drunken night after my orders came. "You don't know nothing 'til you see the bear."

A long silence followed while those two men remembered the bears they had seen. Then Top added his own late night advice. "Sir," he said, "once you get there, you ain't nothin' but one little fart in a great big tornado."

Those two men, each with three rows of ribbons on their chests, were astonishingly candid about their lack of enthusiasm for combat. The message they gave me was quite different from the message given by the army up until then. The booze made them talk, not of finding glory and virility, but of humiliation. The captain said he'd pull some strings and try to get me assigned to one of the First Division's aviation outfits, like he'd been in. He said that being a platoon leader was the worst job in the world.

I was still clinging to the possibility of an aviation unit assignment when those of us destined for the Big Red One were loaded onto a "deuce-and-a-half," the standard army two-and-a-half-ton truck, for the drive from Bien Hoa to the division headquarters at Di An the following day. The drive took only about half an hour, and introduced me to Highway Thirteen. Down here at its beginning it was paved with asphalt, wide-shouldered and heavily traveled. Military vehicles moved freely instead of in convoys, and our truckload of replacements was vastly outnumbered by civilian trucks and buses. We still didn't have weapons, only the driver had an M-16, stashed under his seat along with tire tools and empty soda cans. Considering the dust and grit in the air everywhere, it probably wouldn't work very well. We were getting closer to Indian country, though. At Di An itself, things were a bit shabbier; there were tents pitched among the wood buildings, and I could see some artillery batteries in the distance. Right after we unloaded I was told by a personnel clerk that I was being sent to the First Battalion, 28th Infantry, one of the finest, hardest-fighting and least restrained outfits in the army, also known as the Black Lions of Cantigny. I meekly mentioned the promise of an aviation unit, and the clerk's reply was simply the wry, pitying smile reserved for asshole officers.

Then it rained. It rained like I had never seen rain before, like it had been waiting ten thousand years to rain. Now at last I understood why the skies had been so dark for two days. I also discovered that ponchos are useless as garments in Vietnam. It quickly became so hot under the poncho that one became equally drenched with sweat. It was more comfortable just to get rained on. Very soon, the base at Di An looked like a vast ocean of tan water with tents and barrack buildings floating on it. Walkways made of shipping pallets weighted down with sandbags helped, but not much. The great monsoon had begun. Then it got dark again, a darker night than my first night in Vietnam had been because of the rain, and also because the base was partly blacked out. It was within the range of Viet Cong artillery. And this time, when the inevitable illumination rounds came, they were closer. You could hear the thump of big guns. Later, orange sprays of tracer bullets fountained up from the horizon. Then more streams of tracers poured down from helicopters, still miles away and out of earshot. And finally, late at night, as I felt my way back to my bunk through the mud and steady rain, I heard the legendary "fuck you" lizard for the first time.

"Hah hah hah hah hah hah," it laughed with a ridiculous falsetto, calling from a nearby bush as I slogged past, "hah hah hah hah hah hah fuck you fuck you fuck you all . . . all . . . all."

It was the most eloquent lizard I had ever met, and it expressed exactly what I had been feeling inside.

The next morning we loaded onto a Chinook helicopter for the long flight up to Quan Loi, headquarters of the first brigade and the northernmost outpost of the First Division. Those big Chinooks have two rotors and carry thirty or forty men in their cavernous interior, but by now our group of replacements was just me, another second lieutenant, and a handful of enlisted men. We were not nearly enough to replace the steady stream of dead and wounded flowing south, a fact which was pointed out to us several times by helpful and encouraging clerks. Our pale skin, bright green newly issued uniforms, and nervous insecurity made us stand out like Braniff's "yellow bird," and we felt as foolish as indeed we were. It would be weeks before any of us would be more than a liability, and as the helicopter lifted off and headed up into the sodden skies I think we all felt the same, like helpless prisoners whose death sentence would soon be carried out. And for many, the worst nightmare would indeed come true. Most casualties were among the fresh replacements, killed during their first few weeks, before their instincts had been sharpened, and while they were still blinded by fear. They would, as the saying goes, zig when they should have zagged, or stand paralyzed like a deer caught by automobile headlights. Their names would appear in *Stars and Stripes*.

Apparently the Army thought this was a tolerable cost. It was a policy which had begun in Vietnam long ago, replacing men instead of units, and it was one of the things that made this war unique. Perhaps it began as a guise, a public relations move designed to make the war more palatable and its escalation less obvious. Perhaps it was an attempt at attractive packaging, like "Up with People" and commercial airline charters, as though we really were just going to a warm place for a year. But like so many other policies in Vietnam, it ignored the human truth of the war. The FNG, (fucking new guy), dragged the whole unit down while he had his learning experience even if he did survive, and what was true of enlisted men was doubly true of officers, whose inexperience put the lives of everyone under their command in jeopardy. This much we already instinctively knew as we beat our way through the sky toward Quan Loi. We had all heard the stories, the lone lieutenant standing up, the private who stepped aside to pee. What we didn't know, could not even dream of, was how bad it could be should we survive, and experience this whole process in reverse going home, without the comfort of the men whom we had grown to love. There would be no parades, no ceremonies, none of the psychological devices that society had evolved over eons to reassimilate men returning from war. Going home was sometimes even worse than the war itself.

I suppose we must have all looked airsick. We'd heard that Quan Loi was the Army's version of the Marines' Khe Sanh, a besieged outpost on the edge of nowhere. I didn't even bother to look out the windows at the murk beyond. Like everyone else, I was confronting an enormous reality. Talk was impossible over the beast's screaming turbines. The two door-gunners, slouched over their M-60s, had the demeanor of executioners. The canvas seats were bright red, to hide the blood that so often flowed upon them. The walls vibrated like the chest of a bellowing monster as we followed Highway Thirteen north for an hour, deeper and deeper into the unknown. Then the helicopter reared up and began to settle down. Welcome to the green latrine.

As I walked down the cargo ramp and onto the steel planking of the runway, my first impression of Quan Loi was that the place was under attack. It was all noise, ugliness and confusion. A line of slicks, the ubiquitous UH1D or "Huey" troop-carrying helicopters, was coming in nearby to pick up some infantrymen for an air assault. A short distance away a giant "Sky Crane" was lowering a rubber fuel bladder to the ground while an armored cavalry outfit topped off their tracked personnel carriers with deisel fuel. Red clay dust covered everything, and it mixed with the spilled fuel on the tracks, running down their sides like blood. At first I thought it was blood. Artillery batteries were firing just a few hundred meters away, too, but the noise of their salvos was lost amid the noise of engines, turbines and men shouting nearby. The stench was unbelievable, too, diesel and kerosene of course, but also gun smoke, rancid latex from the surrounding rubber trees, and most of all stale urine. If this was a war novel, there would also have been some body bags lined up on the runway, but it isn't and there weren't, for the moment.

A sergeant led us off the runway and in under the shade of the rubber trees. The rubber trees were everywhere, right up to the edge of the strip, with sagging green tents pitched beneath them. One of the tents was for replacement officers, and the other lieutenant and I went there to stow our gear. The tent, which was on a wood platform, was riddled with shrapnel holes. Raw latex dripped from shrapnel wounds in the rubber trees overhead. Next to the tent was a damp, dark shelter made of sandbags and steel culvert halves in case of a mortar attack. There were eight bunks inside the tent, and seven of them were empty, with the mattresses rolled up at one end. There were shrapnel holes in the mattresses, with white stuffing oozing out. I assumed the former occupants were dead. The eighth bunk was occupied by what looked like a large pile of worn out and discarded field equipment. Our next stop was the arms room, where we drew our M-16 rifles, fourteen magazines, and two hundred and fifty rounds of ammunition. We were issued the other field equipment we would need, the web gear, canteens and so on. Then we were given the afternoon to rest and acclimate ourselves before starting the five-day orientation course that all replacements had to go through. There was time to wander about and scope the place out a bit, but the other lieutenant seemed even more terrified and confused than I was, so I went on alone while he went back to the tent to sleep.

Quan Loi lay on a long ridge of red laterite clay, with the central runway running down the ridge's spine. At one end of the runway was the French plantation manager's compound, and my first introduction to the cruel ironies of this war. It looked like a movie mogul's estate in Beverly Hills, with a complex of low stucco buildings with red tile roofs set among well-tended lawns and gardens. I assumed that this would be the first target of Viet Cong shells, but it looked spotless, untouched by war, while everything else looked like hell, encircled by the spring-like coils of concertina wire, lines of sandbag bunkers, and lookout towers. Beyond the defensive perimeter the rubber trees had been bulldozed into a no-man's-land, just a jumble of mud and stumps sloping down to the valley floor. Beyond that the land rose again, thickly vegetated, dark and brooding, rolling away toward infinity. Looking into the dark depths of those woods was like looking into the eyes of a wild animal.

I was told that we had to pay the French forty dollars for every rubber tree we destroyed, which made quite an impression on me, but not as much as the talk about ground attacks. There had been another one just two weeks before, so the memory was still fresh. North Vietnamese regulars had broken through the perimeter defenses and come running down the runway, right past our tent. They weren't stopped until the artillery batteries lowered their tubes and fired canister rounds of buckshot directly at them. There were so many dead NVA the next day that the bodies were just piled into cargo nets, picked up by the Chinooks as sling loads, and dumped out over the jungle. And now, a rumor was sweeping the base, a rumor which every petty clerk, every cook and supply sergeant was enthusiastically sharing with me upon seeing my fresh green uniform. Jeane Dixon, who at the time was a well-known clairvoyant with a syndicated newspaper column, had reportedly just predicted that ". . . the little known base of Quan Loi would soon be overrun and destroyed, changing the course of the war for America just as Dien Bien Phu had for the French."

I returned to the tent convinced that I would probably not even survive the orientation course. Then, just as I was settling in, the pile of discarded field equipment on that eighth bunk began to move. Then it grunted, farted and sat up. Two wild eyes blazed out of a filthy, unshaven face, shifting gaze from me to the other lieutenant and back again. Then it began to laugh maniacally as we backed away. It was another lieutenant, and we must have looked as strange to him, with our pale skin and fresh uniforms, as he looked to us, a wild man festooned with fragmentation grenades, smoke grenades, flashlight, watch, compass, bandage packs, ammunition pouches, canteens, flares, claymore mines, a survival knife strapped to one leg, a strobe light on one shoulder, more ammunition draped in bandoliers, maps sticking from some pockets, grease pencils in other pockets, a bleached and battered steel helmet with insect repellent in the camouflage band, and a CAR-15, the shortened, telescoping, stock commando version of the M-16, at his side. He had been sleeping soundly rigged up like that, as though knocked unconscious. Now he was happy, excited, agitated and possibly delirious. He was the Black Lion's reconnaissance platoon leader, and he had just made a quick trip back to the rear to have his ear sewn up. A VC machine gun bullet had gone right through his ear while he was assaulting their position, and he seemed very happy about this, laughing his totally insane laugh again while he told us. Now he was going back to his platoon, and he could hardly wait. It was like he was going back to his lover. Then he was gone, clanking and shuffling off toward the evening supply helicopter, or RON (Remain Overnight) ship, which was waiting out on the runway beyond.

I felt nauseated. It was clear to me that the army had made a terrible mistake, that I was not that kind of person, never could be. At the very least, I had made a terrible mistake. In the unlikely event that Jeane Dixon was wrong, and I survived the next five days, I could no sooner lead an infantry platoon than fly by flapping my arms. How could I have known at that moment that the monster I had seen would soon be myself? The other replacement lieutenant and I were so stricken by heat and fear that we couldn't even eat that evening. Then, as we prepared to attempt sleep, I noticed that he was wearing a full set of long underwear underneath his jungle fatigues. Amazed, I couldn't resist asking him about it and he patiently explained that he was a Mormon, and that he had to wear "the garment" at all times as protection against evil. "Evil is everywhere," I thought to myself, "it's the shrapnel I'm worried about."

Things got worse after dark, of course. With every salvo from the artillery, just a few hundred meters away, my nerves flew apart. Then there were the illumination rounds bursting directly overhead, bathing the tents and rubber trees in an eerie, swaying yellow light. Surely the ground attack had begun. Again and again I reran the scenario of being overrun in my mind. I would crawl under the tent platform, because the NVA would be certain to throw grenades in all the bunkers. From under the tent platform, where I lay perfectly still, I could see their feet padding back and forth, dark tan feet wearing sandals made out of discarded automobile tires.

I finally fell asleep counting sandaled feet. Then: KA-BOOM! A truly horrendous explosion had me sitting bolt upright. I could even feel its shock wave in my chest and sinus cavities. Surely, they had blown up the ammunition dump. But no, it was the eight-inch howitzer. I could hear the huge shell flying through the night with the same cold sucking sound as a jet airplane. Almost a minute later, the distant crash of the shell's impact somewhere in the jungle miles and miles away came echoing back. Eventually I got used to the thump of the mortars or the ripping thunder of the light and medium artillery. But I never got used to that eight-incher, which fortunately seemed to take about twenty minutes to reload and aim again.

Sleep, in intervals of about eighteen minutes, was terminated by the arrival of the first C-130 just after dawn. The four-engine turboprop cargo plane was turning around right outside the tent, and the tent itself was flapping and billowing in the prop wash and exhaust. Then it was time to start the orientation course. We were herded through it by a couple of obviously shell-shocked sergeants with facial twitches who were too frazzled for front line duty. The other officer and I were treated no differently from the rest of the replacements. We were shown how to build the famous First Division Fighting Hole, which was a defensive position adopted from the Viet Cong after some bitter lessons inflicted when the division had first arrived. Wherever we were, except on ambush, as soon as we formed a defensive circle we would dig the holes. There was one hole for each group of three men, shoulder deep, with firing ports angled right and left, and three layers of sandbags forming a roof on top. The First Division never lost an NDP (night defensive position), after the fighting holes were adopted, though they lost parts of lots of them.

Another lesson in defense the frazzled sergeants repeated was the use of the claymore mine. These seemingly innocuous rectangles of green plastic contained a layer of explosive facing a layer of ball bearings. Boldly raised letters on one side said: "This Side Towards Enemy." Still, now and then somebody would get confused and blow himself up. Worse yet, there were instances where the enemy themselves had crawled unnoticed close enough to turn the claymores around. Then they would yell things like: "GI eat shit," trying to provoke a detonation.

We learned the protocols for using smoke, especially important for platoon leaders. Yellow, purple or green smoke was used to mark positions. It was one of the first things done when coming under fire. Supporting units would be radioed: "Contact five zero meters northwest yellow smoke," or "Yellow smoke marks my position." It was a bad idea to use red or white smoke, since the air force used those colors to mark enemy positions. All these lessons had been learned by experience, and were conveyed to us by the instructors with a grim sense of fatality, like it was all useless because we were going to die anyway.

After a few days, I began to calm down a little. And one night I actually got to participate actively in the noisy nervous ritual of mortars and illumination rounds. My name came up as duty officer, in charge of a section of the perimeter. In the early evening, I strutted along my line, familiarizing myself with the positions manned by the cooks and clerks and drivers who kept the base going during the day. My sector ended at the French compound, which was enclosed and kept out of sight from the perimeter by an eight-foot tall bamboo fence. But a tank had been parked beside the fence, and you could see inside by standing on the tank, which I did. It was fantastic, even better than what I had seen from the runway, about ten acres of Eden with various low buildings. There weren't any mortar craters in the lawns, or shrapnel splatters on the walls. The war seemed to stop at the bamboo fence. A swimming pool was close to where the tank was parked, a large, clean turquoise blue swimming pool with a diving board. The tank crew told me that they had parked at this spot mainly because there was a girl living at the compound, a girl of about sixteen who bathed in the pool every morning. She had long blonde hair and always wore a brown bikini. She never acknowledged the presence of the Americans, expressing contempt in every move she made as she resolutely went through her morning routine. Later, I learned from one of the high ranking officers who were occasionally invited to dinner with the family that she went to school in France during most of the year, and was flown back and forth by Air America, the CIA airline that flew in and out of Quan Loi several times a day.

Then darkness slowly came, first with a rosy hue to the curtain of jungle to the east, and then with a pool of darkness filling the valley, rising upward. Darkness flowed out of the jungle, where it had lurked all day, and spilled across the no-man's-land of bulldozed stumps. With the darkness came silence. Then, at about midnight, a team in one of the watchtowers reported over the field telephone that they had some people moving just outside the wire. I went up the tower and borrowed their "starlight scope," a night vision device which amplified ambient light. I flipped on the toggle switch and scanned the luminescent nightscape where the guards said they saw men. I told the guards it looked more like stumps to me. They insisted that the stumps hadn't been there a little while ago. So I called back to headquarters and told them we had stumps on the march. "Whump, whump, whump," the mortars fired back where my fellow replacement officer was trying to sleep. "Crash, crash, crash," the rounds detonated in front of us. Then "whump" again, as one of the mortars fired an illumination round. "Pop, hiss," it ignited overhead, bathing us in the swaying yellow light. It was stumps.

The five days ticked past all too quickly. Our graduation exercise was a real overnight ambush patrol, led by a frazzled sergeant. Near dusk, we filed out through the wire and into the no-man's-land of shrapnel-riddled stumps. We went all the way down the slope, farther and farther from the relative safety of the perimeter, and hid in some brush in the valley floor waiting for dark. Then, on a silent signal, we all rose and sneaked up the opposite slope into the rubber trees. According to the map, according to the plan, we were supposed to set up our ambush beside a dirt road in the plantation. One thing I did know as an officer was maps and plans, and I could tell that we were not really there but I kept my mouth shut and let the sergeant lead. We made a comfortable circle in the rubber, set out our claymores, and waited.

After a few hours the sergeant said he heard a motor scooter coming. I couldn't hear it at all. He decided to call in mortars. After a short wait, the rounds exploded in the tops of the rubber trees a few hundred meters away in the opposite direction. It was quite pretty the way the sparks of shrapnel came showering down, and I was glad he had missed us as well as the phantom scooter.

The next morning it was time to join the battalion in the field. They were way down south, near Di An, where it still hadn't stopped raining. The other guys and I went down on the afternoon RON ship, another big Chinook, along with needed supplies. Once again, the lift-off toward the unknown, which would never get better with time. Once again, the anticipation of something unfathomable. Everyone in Quan Loi had spoken in lowered tones about the relentless fighting and heavy casualties the battalion was facing. I was in over my head, and would soon be exposed, ridiculed and then killed. I should have listened to my father, instead of seducing myself with childhood war games. The gray murk outside and below was like the miasma of death itself. There was plenty of time to think about all of that before the ship finally began to rear and settle. I could see the battalion position slowly materialize below. It was a circle of tan-colored water with bits of green stuff floating in it, and it had all the appeal of dog vomit. As we hovered lower I could see that the green stuff was people. They were angrily waving their fists at us because our rotor blast was blowing their makeshift shelters away. As soon as the helicopter settled, I jumped out into the muddy water. Splat. Welcome to the end of the pipeline.

The battalion sergeant-major led me and the other officer back to the battalion commander's CP, or command post, in the center of the circle. The perimeter itself, which was just a circle of flooded fighting holes only about a hundred and fifty meters across, looked like a nightmare version of World War I trench warfare. Coils of concertina wire stood in the water beyond the fighting holes. Beyond that lay a vast open plain, fading away into gray rain. The men around me were moving like zombies. They cursed the helicopter as they plodded through the mud and water to retrieve their ponchos. Inside the CP tent a handful of men were hunched over maps. A brace of tactical radios hissed in the background. The other lieutenant and I were introduced to Lieutenant Colonel James Rew, commander of the Black Lions, known by his call sign as "Defiant Six." Over the six months to follow he would become my harshest critic, and my mentor as well as my commander. As he turned around to greet me I was surprised by how gaunt he looked for a man in his late thirties. In a few terse sentences he said that the battalion had been through some rough times and was down to half strength. Just a few days before they had lost fourteen men to a booby-trapped artillery shell. He told me I was being assigned to Bravo Company. He told the other lieutenant to get back on the supply helicopter. He was going back to Quan Loi to be our supply officer, and he almost collapsed with relief.

Bravo Six, the commander of my company, entered the tent. I can't remember his name, because he didn't last much longer. He led me back outside to our section of the perimeter where my platoon, the second platoon, lay sprawled in mud and sandbags and torn ponchos, elementally wet and filthy. Bravo Six called them together. They came slowly and reluctantly. They reacted to my introduction with indifference, avoiding my eyes. They were like animals, suspicious, resentful of my intrusion. Finally, one of them spoke. It was Sergeant Dennis, the third squad leader. He looked at me for an instant, then looked away again and said to the mud, "Welcome to Mike Division." Then they all went back to their positions again. It was our turn to go out on ambush, and they needed to get ready.

❖ III ❖

I REMEMBER ONCE BEING TOLD by an old officer that leading a platoon of soldiers in combat was the greatest honor that a man could have. I think it was while I was in officer candidate school, and I remember feeling a bit skeptical. In retrospect, I think he was confusing honor with humility. At any rate, the only thing I felt during my first moments as a platoon leader was my own overwhelming terror and sense of helpless incompetence. It was the same feeling I'd had as a boy in the schoolyard, not knowing what a man should be, or if I belonged there at all. I was naked as a jaybird in the locker room of war. Such is the loneliness of men. This was my father's loneliness as he crossed the Pacific, part of the greatest armada ever assembled, yet with nearly every ship out of sight, fantastic clouds above and the sea rolling below. I suppose this was my father's father's loneliness on the playing field, a star athlete driven forward by the pain of his own wounds to wound others. And such is the loneliness of my two older sons, torn away by divorce; but it is more. It is the elemental loneliness of birth, of death, of soldiers. I had not yet felt the balm of marching together.

And Mike Division was tough. They had won their nickname long before I had arrived, so long ago that nobody could remember just how, but everybody called it that. It was the platoon that could do the work of ten thousand men, the platoon you could count on when things got bad. It was far from being a division, though, and in fact it was hardly even a platoon by the time I joined it. A platoon is supposed to have forty-two men, and Mike Division was down to nineteen, including myself. I shared a fighting hole with my CP group; Mike Five, the platoon sergeant, my "romeo" or radio man, and "Doc," the platoon medic. Mike Five seemed to be the only one who was actually glad to see me. An "old man" of thirty-four, he was really too old to be in the field with us and would only stay on for a few days more while I settled in. He was also the only career man among us, with ten or fifteen years of service behind him; leathery, lanky, hard-drinking and intensely loyal toward the men. Like so many other career non-commissioned officers, he spent most of his time in a supportive, even paternal role, shuttling back and forth between base camps. Also like most of the "old guys" in the rear, he was a bit lost in Vietnam, too old to partake in the daily field operations, rather dismayed by the erosion of the "old army" standards of discipline that was beginning to take place, especially in the rear; and rock hard in his support of us. In return, the platoon loved him, used to quote him, imitating his Southern drawl as he told war stories to the men gathered about him: "Ah saw a man git hit by a 122 millimeter rocket, tore his haid clean off."

During our first hours together, Mike Five kept telling me what a great bunch of guys they were, how it was the best damn platoon in the army. He had helped make it that way, and his words heightened my own sense of responsibility. At the age of twenty-three, I was the oldest except Mike Five; nearly all the rest were nineteen or twenty. All but one were white, most came from rural backgrounds. I assume that when they had taken the battery of army entrance tests, nearly every one had answered the question "Do you like to hunt?" with a resounding "Yes!" Half had been drafted, half had joined, some had a few years of college, and one had a degree. A few had ended up here because of trouble with the law, or trouble at home, or a thirst for adventure, but most just ended up here. And Mike Five was right. I knew from my year as a training officer, from looking at the aptitude tests and performance ratings, that the infantry always got the best of the recruits, and this was the best of the infantry, drawn from civilian ranks before the Tet Offensive, before public opinion had turned against the war.

I remember my fear, I remember the rain. I remember that toward evening the rain let up enough so that I could call the platoon together for a get-acquainted "chat." I asked everybody their names, which I promptly forgot due to my own panic. I asked them where they had been, and what sort of action they had seen. Sergeant Dennis often spoke for the group. With almost eight months behind him, he had been there just about the longest, was tough, smart, and very capable as well. He had seen a lot of men come and go. Others occasionally chimed in as he recited a litany of battles; Song Be Mountain and the Ho Bo Woods were the worst, accompanied by the names of the dead, although sometimes the name was just "that fucking new guy" whose name nobody could remember. Most of the men didn't talk at all. I guess they were trying to figure out if I was going to get them killed or not. I began to feel like I was a very bad nightclub act in front of a hostile audience. I figured it was time to dismiss them before they just walked away. Surely, they had already recognized my weakness, just the way dogs do.

Song Be Mountain and the Ho Bo Woods. You could see Song Be Mountain in the distance sometimes, looming gray above the horizon, shaped like a volcano, the most prominent peak in the war zone. There were cliffs, and caves in its flanks, a natural fortress like Saipan's Mount Tapotchau, with the dead and wounded falling back into the arms of those still climbing. The Ho Bo Woods, down low, held a more miasmic terror. They said the jungle was so dense it was always dark. Air and artillery support were useless, and the Viet Cong moved silently as snakes, striking then fading away. Mike Division had lost twelve men in the Ho Bo Woods.

I could almost make myself sick imagining what it was like in those places, churning the legends over in my mind. Fortunately, we were going out on a company-size ambush that night. Somebody else would be leading and I could just follow along. I was in a daze when I listened to the briefing with the other platoon leaders. Lima Six, the first platoon leader, had been with the unit for about a month. He was a warm, funny, blond-haired ex-surfer from Hawaii. November Six, dark-haired and more silent, had about two weeks under his belt, but to me they both seemed like grizzled veterans. I knew "six" meant leader, but I was having trouble with the rest of the call signs. I was also confused about map coordinates. We were using baseball teams as map reference code: "from Red Socks down three point two, left niner." The average Viet Cong probably knew more about baseball than I did. I nodded my head and tried to look competent, but I was jelly inside, as though a major part of my brain had just packed its bags and split for home.

As twilight descended and the drizzle tapered off to a fine mist, Bravo Company filed out through an opening in the coils of wire and entered the wet gray world beyond. Lima had the point, and we fell in behind with our three squads of infantrymen, each reinforced with a machine gun crew from the weapons squad. I can see them file past now, soaking wet. "Animal" has a machine gun. He's the guy from Wisconsin with a college degree. He has curly blond hair and glasses, and he's also one of those rare souls who is able to remain somewhat overweight in the field. You have to be a big guy to hump an M-60, and the heavy black long-snouted gun rests comfortably against his belly. There goes "Red" Renzel, the weapons squad leader, another of the few survivors of the Ho Bo Woods. He's tall, lean and lanky, red hair and freckles with a wide, generous grin, quick with a joke. Along comes Trent, a Southern boy with a machine gun. Longish blond hair and glasses, sometimes he likes to sing while he walks; with an exaggerated twang: "You-take-a-chicken-and-you-kill-it-and-you-throw-it-in-a-skillet-Southern-cooking, mighty fine!"

The machine guns are the heart of the platoon. They speak the loudest. The rest of the men mainly provide security for the machine guns. Each gunner has an assistant gunner whose job is to feed ammunition to the beast when it is speaking. Then there is the ammo bearer, the third man on the crew, humping four hundred more belted rounds in addition to his own weapon and ammo. Men slowly work their way up through the crew with time and experience, or quickly during combat. There goes Aikens, he's Trent's assistant gunner, still fairly new but very smart and competent. Dark-haired, seeming more urban than the others, his time to move up will come soon.

We crossed the high open plain, crossed fields planted with peanuts, crossed abandoned fields, and passed the tumbled brick ruins of a fort that had been built by the French. Ghosts of French soldiers watched us pass in the twilight. We descended into the valley as the grayness thickened, through shiny wet-leaved groves of banana, past where the booby-trapped shell had been. We slogged through rice paddies where the season's seedlings had just been set out. Over the months to come, I would learn a lot about rice cultivation. Then we ascended the next hill, toward a large gray steel water tower. It was the same kind of water tower you see in the States, lacking only the "Class of '63" spray painted on it to make it perfectly authentic. There were no villages, nothing nearby to explain its being there. It must have been built as some sort of USAID scam.

The landscape was mostly under cultivation, but had become silent and deserted as the magic hour approached, the magic hour when men begin to look like bushes, and bushes begin to move. We hid in a field of cabbages, waiting for the darkness to become complete. I lay there, feeling like a cabbage, watching the hills and the water tower recede behind the thickening veil of drizzle and darkness. I had kept a vegetable garden while I was in high school. While the others had been playing football, or spray painting water towers, I had been planting seeds, pulling weeds, and hauling armloads of zucchinis to the kitchen. I felt really good about gardening, a nurturer not a killer. I would have liked to stay right there with the cabbages, and perhaps help with the weeding. But then it was dark, and the cabbages were up and moving again. I followed the cabbage in front of me up out of the garden and across a dirt road.

At least I had good squad leaders. I could rely on them. Besides Dennis, the most experienced one, there was Overton, a Georgia boy with nearly as much experience, and Paolino. Paolino was from a large and prominent family in Providence, Rhode Island. While less experienced, he was one of the men who had gone through an NCO school, rather like OCS, and emerged as a sergeant E-5. Paul Noonan, from California and for now still a fire team leader, was another. I was relying completely on these men, following blindly. We moved along beside the road for a while, slinking through the bushes, until we reached a graveyard where another road intersected. Just like the French before us, with their brick fort, we were supposedly blocking a major avenue of attack, part of a circle of strong points outside the suburbs of Saigon. Of course, during the Tet Offensive a few months before, all the strongpoints had been bypassed entirely. But that did little to calm my nerves. I imagined battalions of NVA coming down the road toward us, marching double-time.

We set up in the graveyard. Everyone put out two claymore mines facing the road, then uncoiled the detonator wires back to a sheltered spot behind a gravestone. It was the first time I had seen a Vietnamese graveyard. The stones were big, carved out of hard laterite clay, more like statues or icons than gravestones, and the whole thing was enclosed by a low wall. The ground was soft underfoot, and the weirdly shaped stones leaned like snaggle teeth. I chose a low spot near the center of our sector and settled in, shifting the canteens and ammo pouches on my hips. There was a strong, musty damp smell, and after about ten minutes I realized that the low place I had chosen was probably atop a collapsed coffin. I tried shifting to one side, but there was no place else for me to go. I picked up something soft and damp I had been lying on. It was a piece of rotten wood, and it glowed with an eerie purple luminescence. An evil omen for sure.

Then came the rattle of distant gunfire to the west. Sprays of tracer bullets skipped above the horizon, followed by the inevitable illumination rounds. Bravo Six had his radio on the battalion frequency, and the word got passed back to me in whispers. "That's Dagger's AO Delta Company being hit." So it went on my first night in the field, distant firefights were the usual sight, sometimes we would watch two or three in progress at once. At about nine, a team of helicopter gunships showed up, circling over a target a few kilometers away. Their miniguns blazed red streams, liquid fire, accompanied by a moaning sound. Their rockets left trails of sparks through the night and exploded with a flash and thump. Then more tracers spurted upward to the south. More illumination rounds. I kept waiting for the NVA battalion, but they never materialized, and eventually I went to sleep thinking about Chappaqua, the town I had grown up in, and the wonderful house with the windows open and the curtains moving in a summer breeze, and the vegetable garden beyond, and what a misadventure this was, with the ground beneath me about to collapse and dump me into the underworld of rotting corpses below.

When dawn came, with a gradual thinning of the night, it seemed like a miracle. It was always to seem like a miracle. Everyone stood up and urinated. The start of my second day in the field. We coiled up the wires to the claymores and took a zigzag course back to the NDP. The farmers showed up and resumed tending their fields, giving us sidelong glances as we passed by. We ate cold cans of C rations when we got back, and tried to nap in puddles of water. I tried to remember the names of my squad leaders. Then it was time to go out on ambush again. We went with a couple of "duster" forty-millimeter antiaircraft guns mounted on tracks this time. Those relics of Korea were enjoying a comeback as direct-fire weapons in Vietnam.

Then we rotated with Charlie company and joined the daytime routine, going on sweeps during the day and staying in the NDP at night. It rained almost continually. Mike Five went back to Quan Loi, restating his loyalty to the platoon once more. We had some real sharp newer guys coming along. There was Alfano, another Italian, from New York City. He wanted to be a cop when he got back. There was Poovy, another Southern boy, destined to become a squad leader himself. There was Millhouse, from Fairbanks, Alaska. He carried the state flag with him, and flew it above his fighting hole. And there was Redfeather. Redfeather was a full-blooded Sioux from the big Standing Rock reservation in South Dakota. Immensely popular, immensely skilled, he was quickly emerging as one of the most important men in the platoon.

I was still trying to remember the names and call signs. Then, after a few more days, just when my panic was subsiding a little, my feet began to rot. Parts of them were turning black and sloughing off. I showed them to "Doc" Behm. He was sympathetic, but couldn't do much since they had run out of the proper medication for treating it. Doc, as part of my CP group, was seldom more than three meters from my side. Like so many other medics in Vietnam, he had all the attributes of a first-rate infantryman but was nearsighted. Nearsighted medics were our heroes. Nearsighted medics would walk through fire to save us. Doc Behm, bespectacled, thin, sensitive, a newcomer like myself, gave me Darvons to ease the pain and get me through the day. With the Darvons and the numbing fatigue, it got so that I could hardly feel anything at all.

The other person who was always near my side was Roy Wakefield. Roy was my "romeo," the name drawn from the military alphabet for the man humping the PRC 25 field radio. As such, with the whip antenna standing high above, the romeos were a favorite target of snipers. And often, when the platoon leader was hit, it was the romeo who took over the coordination of units and fire support until somebody else arrived. Wakefield, although another new guy, was very smart, personable and capable. It didn't take long for me to grow very fond of both Doc and Wakefield, as we marched, ate, and slept as a threesome. And I knew Mike Five was right about the rest of Mike Division, too. I felt my own loyalty, even awe, growing daily.

A couple of times, but only if it wasn't raining, local Vietnamese units would join us on our sweeps. They were driven out to the NDP by truck, and they'd disembark, laughing like happy campers, and fall in behind our double files as we set off to scout the surrounding hills and valleys. I suppose they were to benefit from this, learning from our example of discipline and aggressiveness. And we were performing what was to have been their job in the first place: providing security in a fairly densely populated area. They supposedly knew the neighborhood; at the very least, they knew the language. But we all knew the stories that had been passed around: they wouldn't fight, couldn't be counted upon. So we slogged up and down the hills in incredible heat carrying fifty pounds of equipment, and they sauntered along behind us carrying old carbines and M-1 Garands, and a couple of bullets in their pockets. But basically we liked them. As a bunch of American kids, we were intrigued by them. During the breaks they tried to speak pidgin English, bumming cigarettes.

I had been in the field for a little over a week. I was still numbed by fatigue and jungle rot and Darvon. My platoon had the point as we traversed a ridge on a company-size sweep. Lima and November platoons were behind us, and a platoon of Vietnamese were sauntering along behind them. We were in broken woods and brush land; the skies were overcast but it wasn't raining. It was four-thirty in the afternoon, and soon we would begin another dogleg back toward the NDP. Redfeather was out to the left, walking flank security, doing his Indian thing. He'd slink ahead, oozing through the bushes silently, then pause, all ten or eleven senses alert, shifting his head up and down, side to side for a while. Then he'd slink ahead again, feeling the vibrations of the earth through the soles of his feet, evaporating and rematerializing somewhere off to my left.

A monumental firefight was about to begin, building slowly, almost like a courtship. Three Viet Cong were ahead of us, in our path of travel. They heard us coming, and fled down a dry stream gully. The point man never saw them, but Redfeather did. He fired a full clip into their backs from where he stood, and heard the thumps and grunts of bullets hitting flesh. Then he hit the ground himself, because several men in our column began to shoot off to the left, too, me among them. We hadn't seen anything; it was just how we reacted. Then Wakefield reminded me that Redfeather was out there, and we all stopped. I was acutely embarrassed. First bit of action, and the lieutenant almost shoots one of his own men. Great.

Redfeather came back in, breathless, and told us what he'd seen. Then we did a quick cloverleaf search of the streambed. There was a good blood trail continuing on down the ridge. All this information was relayed up to Defiant Six, who was overhead in his command and communication (C&C) helicopter. He decided to insert a scout dog team from Saigon. It would take about half an hour to bring them up overhead, so we sat in the shade smoking cigarettes and talking softly, like deer hunters waiting for their prey to bleed out. I worked on my flagging self-esteem. The Vietnamese hung back together, chattering nervously. Somebody borrowed my camera and snapped a picture of me and Doc Behm and Wakefield and Redfeather together. I still have it.

By the time the slick with the scout dog team showed up overhead it was late afternoon. Mike Division showed them the trail, and they were off at a run. The dogs were wagging their tails and dragging their handlers by the leash, down the steep gully. We ran along behind, going toward a dense pocket of vegetation surrounded by abandoned rice paddies on three sides at the valley floor. Then, just a few hundred meters short of that thick, dark place, the dogs stopped dead in their tracks, frozen solid by what they sensed. The handlers understood instantly. VC were in there. The scout team was sent back to the ridge top, where they would be picked up and returned to Saigon. A fire team of gunships came on station overhead, and began to circle along with Defiant Six's C&C ship. Lima platoon was sent into a blocking position across the far side of that island of thick vegetation. When everybody was ready, Mike and November would go in. It was a classic maneuver, going like clockwork. We expected to find three VC, at least one of them seriously wounded, and anyway we had them surrounded.

It was now almost six. November platoon led the way toward the thicket, followed by Bravo Six and his command group, followed by me with my platoon. By this time the Vietnamese were hanging back at an ever greater distance, very nervous, just keeping us in sight so they wouldn't be lost entirely. We were in the paddies now, with each paddy enclosed by a hedge of bamboo growing on the dike. Finally we got to the last paddy, the one beside the thicket. We began to line up for a sweep to the left when the two gunships suddenly veered around, their rotors slapping angrily. They made a run straight over our heads, low and fast, touching off rockets which whooshed and banged into the paddy beyond us. Then they whipped around in what resembled a hammerhead stall, and made a run back again. The rockets were hitting close enough to spatter us with mud, but we still couldn't see anything because of the intervening hedgerow.

A couple of us with radios switched to the fire team's frequency so we could hear what was going on. The fliers were giddy with excitement, whooping like cowboys as they swung around and made more passes. What they had, running out of the thicket ahead of us, was not three wounded VC but about a dozen very healthy ones making a break for it or trying to, across the open paddy land before we closed the trap.

When the helicopters had expended all their rockets, they strafed with the miniguns. Then they just circled for a while, stitching any corpses that still seemed fairly whole with the door-gunner's M-60s.

I watched all this dumbfounded, in a daze of death and Darvon. You could smell the blood and entrails amid the smoke and paddy muck. The Vietnamese soldiers, meanwhile, had entirely disappeared, as though they had been an illusion in the first place. Then it was time for November to go into the thicket. I put two of my machine guns on some high ground across the way to give some supporting fire in case they needed it, and kept the rest of my platoon in reserve with me beside the paddy dike. November platoon walked in as though there was nothing to fear. The lead man had only gone in about ten meters when there was a soft "pop," more like a champagne cork than anything really dangerous. But then somebody started calling "MEDIC," and two or three medics, including Doc Behm, jumped up from behind the dike and ran forward into the thicket. Word came back in a few moments: a man in November's platoon had stepped into a booby trap, and had shrapnel wounds in his legs.

It was now a little after six, and people were getting impatient. Bravo Six, who had been at the paddy dike beside me, decided to see for himself. He got up and entered the thicket, taking along his entire CP group and a squad of my men. His own personal armament was just a .38 revolver which he treasured and wore in a shoulder holster. Nobody bothered to do any clover-leaf searches of the area. Soon there were about fifteen men in a tight group, standing around the one wounded man. What they didn't know was that they were standing in firing lanes which the VC had meticulously cut through the thicket. These were just simple little tunnels cut in the foliage about knee-high; you had to get down on your knees to see them, and nobody had. Each firing lane led back to the firing ports of some exquisitely camouflaged bunkers just ten meters away.

The skies were darkening. It looked like my platoon would be going in next, so I brought my machine guns back in. They left the high ground and came slogging across the knee-deep paddy water. Just as they got down beside me, the whole world seemed to explode in a roar of automatic weapon fire, all VC, sweeping back and forth just inches above the dike. It seemed to go on forever, without letup. The high ground where the machine guns had been erupted with the impact of bullets. Leaves, severed branches, clods of dirt came raining down.

During the few very brief lulls, while the VC changed magazines, the air was filled with human sounds; cries for medics, or cries of pain.

My own brain was tripping out as though on LSD. Everything had a crystalline clarity to it, still does; total awareness, like going through an automobile wreck in slow motion, dreamlike, able to observe but unable to stop it or get away. I looked over at Dennis, and he just looked back at me and shook his head. The bullets kept coming, sweeping back and forth, incredibly loud. A few men, several of them wounded, managed to run back to the shelter of the dike between sweeps of gunfire. Among them was Bravo Six. He quickly rolled over to my side. His teeth were clenched with pain, he was holding his hand and rocking back and forth. He had somehow managed to shoot his own thumb off with his revolver when the VC opened up. He summed up the situation for me. To begin with, I was to take over as company commander. Medevac helicopters were on the way, and he would soon be departing with some others to secure a landing zone a few hundred meters back. But there were still a lot of men down in the fields of fire. They were too close for us to call in air or artillery support. My job was to gather what was left of the company together and organize a ground assault.

This, then, in real life and the most brilliant color imaginable, was the "worst case" scenario I remembered from officer candidate school. Suddenly the terrified and inexperienced young lieutenant finds himself in command of a company pinned down by automatic weapon fire from fortified positions, with wounded down in front. In the classroom, the instructions had always been the same; everyone stands up at once and starts walking toward the enemy, firing on full automatic. But, in the astonishing clarity of the moment, I realized I couldn't do that. Part of it was my own fear, and part was total revulsion at what was taking place around me. Furthermore, I was really pissed off at the captain by now. I had never liked his swaggering about with his .38 revolver in the first place; the fact that he had shot his thumb off seemed only fitting. And it was, after all, a series of blunders on his part that had gotten us into this mess. Now he was telling me to get us out. Why hadn't he appointed November Six, who was senior to me by two weeks, and thus next in command, and right there beside us? It is amazing how quickly the mind can find excuses while under fire.

Reasoning aside, what gripped me was my own terror. I was looking at Bravo Six, and my lips were moving, but I couldn't speak. Then finally, I managed to croak "I can't." He seemed a little stunned.

"What?" he asked.

"I can't," I repeated. Then, like the school kid who had failed to do his homework, I elaborated on my reasons while the gunfire swept back and forth overhead. All I had left of my men was part of Dennis's squad, and anyway November Six was supposed to be in charge. Bravo Six gave me one last accusing glance, then turned to November Six, who also fixed me with his own acrimonious glare upon being given command. November Six and I agreed that we could work something out. Bravo Six said he would put us both in for a bronze star (he didn't), and departed for the landing zone to be evacuated.

November Six, obviously feeling as miserable as I was, crawled off to find and organize the men to our left. For a while, I was nearly alone. There were just five or six soldiers with me, and several of them were wounded. I was already regretting what I had said, and in a daze I began doing the only thing that made sense, which was to tend the wounded. There was a black man from November's platoon beside me who had been shot in the knee. It was extremely painful and he was bleeding a lot. Now this was something I could handle, from the days when I had been interested in medicine. I could talk to him calmly while I applied the bandage, even though he was screaming that the bandage was too tight. And I could look at some of the other guys too, make sure they weren't bleeding too much or going into shock. I could be a medic easily. I just couldn't quite bring myself to be an infantry officer at the moment.

Finally, the company medic showed up. He had been down at the landing zone with the first group of wounded, and he'd had his hands full. He said that as soon as the first medevac helicopter had appeared, the Vietnamese soldiers had come pouring out of the woods where they had been hiding and tried to scramble on board. They had even tried to pull some of the wounded Americans out so they could get in, and he had threatened to shoot them. It was a grim foreshadowing of the fall of Saigon, six years later, and it left us all feeling pretty resentful. Now more helicopters would have to be brought in to lift the Vietnamese out, along with our growing collection of wounded, who were still rolling, crawling or being dragged out of the kill zone, one or two at a time, whenever there was a lull. The medic left for the LZ with a few more men.

More time on my hands. The gunfire from the bunkers was letting up somewhat; I assumed this was because they wanted to conserve ammunition and because there weren't any more targets. Meanwhile, what was left of Mike Division began quietly going to work without me. Some men crawled out into the kill zone to locate wounded and drag them back, drawing more fire themselves. Other men tried to scope out the bunkers. It was now past seven, and the light was beginning to fail. There were no signs of an assault on the part of November's team; in fact there was no sign of them at all. It had helped me a lot to have been doing something, even if it was just first aid, and I began to get a grip on myself. I picked up one of the radios beside me and tried to raise November Six, but to no avail.

Defiant Six quickly broke in. He was glad to hear my voice. He hadn't had any contact with anyone on the ground for some time. He asked me what I had with me and I told him that I had eight men and a whole bunch of rifles and radios abandoned by the wounded. Then he told me that I was once again company commander. Apparently, November Six hadn't wanted the job any more than I did. By now I had regained my composure somewhat and didn't try to talk my way out of it. I set up the radios on the various frequencies we were using, and began trying to figure out where everyone was. My only real concern was the continued safety of the men. I had already seen enough of this war to abandon the primary mission. I wanted Lima Six to get his platoon out of the blocking position, where they might be hit by friendly fire, and I wanted to make sure there were no more wounded men down in front. Then I wanted to deliver the wrath of air power on those bunkers.

I'm fairly certain that somewhere there are tape recordings of what was said on the radio that evening. I know that whenever a nearby unit was in a firefight, we used to tune to their push and listen to the frightened, desperate voices of platoon leaders and company commanders. I know that there were generals in Saigon listening, too. And that tapes were made, and that the excited, shaky, sometimes screaming voices were studied, analyzed, duplicated and edited stateside. Somewhere, deeply classified, (thank goodness), the whole agonizing spectrum of combat in Vietnam exists on tapes. Never before has the instantaneous reality of combat, and combat decisions, reactions and emotions been so well preserved. It is a painful record of men at their most desperate moments, and often at their last moments. My own unique personal contribution to this archive occurred after I had been on the net organizing for about five minutes. A strange voice broke in, identifying himself as Devil Six. He said: "This is Devil Six. Get your men on line and assault." I knew "six" meant commander, but commander of what? And I had already rejected the idea of an assault once that evening. It pissed me off that this guy was breaking in to tell me what to do. So I said: "Get the fuck off the net," which, to his credit, he did. It was Keith Ware, Commanding General of the First Infantry Division, who had joined the growing swarm of helicopters overhead.

It was almost dark now, near eight. Still no contact with November, and still no sounds of our own gunfire. Just occasional bursts from the bunkers. I took another man, named Ellison, who was actually a cook but happened to be along that day, and an extra radio, and together we set off to find November, who had gone around the left corner of the dike with about ten men. I had assumed that they were going to attempt a flanking movement, but had to find out, at least had to find out what they were up to and give them a radio. But as soon as we reached the end of the dike and stuck our heads around, we were met by another blistering burst of gunfire. I guess the surviving VC had moved through a trench to a new bunker so they could cover their flank. Ellison and I looked at each other, and scrambled back to our original position.

Now "Puff the Magic Dragon" was on station overhead. The ancient AC-47, a modified World War II transport, circled lazily, its twin radial engines lending a steady sonorous drone to the scene. As it got darker, the crew chief of the "Puff" began to kick huge parachute flares out the cargo door while I talked to the pilot. The flares lit the place up almost like daylight, drifting lazily under twelve-foot parachutes. The shadows of the trees swayed eerily. There were only intermittent bursts of gunfire from the bunkers now. I assumed that the VC were either running low on ammunition or bleeding to death. They may have been some of the same men Redfeather had hit earlier in the day, who had stayed behind to die while the others fled. Meanwhile, Sergeant Overton had led the effort to get the wounded back, returning to the kill zone again from his position on the left. It was the sort of heroism that he, and the medics, and other men would repeat routinely. When the wounded were finally cleared, Sergeant Paolino and a couple of other guys went to work.

Ten or twelve grenade explosions in a row suddenly rent the air. It was Paolino and the others on the bunkers, tossing grenades into the firing ports. The explosions were followed by a wonderful silence, then shouting voices as our men began to stand up and locate each other. Gradually, everybody came back to my position, including November Six and a lot of other missing men. After the initial burst of gunfire, which had left half of Mike Division cut off from the rest of us, the VC had indeed shifted positions to cover their flanks, and effectively kept November pinned down. I recognized Doc Behm in the swaying yellow light and threw my arms around him. He had been one of the medics who had jumped up and run forward when the first man had stepped on the booby trap, and I hadn't seen him since. I'd figured he was hit.

With everyone back, I tossed some yellow smoke grenades out in front to mark our position and gave the go-ahead to "Puff," even though the fight was really over. The old airplane went into a steep turn, propellers clawing at the sky, and poured a solid red stream of tracers from its bank of miniguns. It was amazingly accurate, and the place where the bunkers had been erupted with a roar. And all around, at other ambush sites and NDPs, men watched and whispered, "That's Defiant's A.O. Bravo company stepped in shit," as we painted the night sky with tracers and parachute flares.

Lima platoon had secured the landing zone, and the rest of us prepared to pull back and be extracted. A counterattack or a mortar attack was a distinct possibility, so we sprayed the jungle behind us with our M-16s as we withdrew. I was carrying six abandoned rifles, and decided to check them out. Each one jammed after expending a magazine or two. A lot of other guys were having the same problem. The last of us slogged down to the landing zone and were preparing to load when Defiant Six asked me if we had our dead. I had remembered the rifles and the radios, but I had forgotten the dead. "We never leave the dead behind," he roared.

Another failure. What a day loaded with failure it had been. Shamed and miserable, a small group of us found our way back to the bunkers and picked up the body of that same luckless man who had first stepped on the booby trap. Another man and I shared his dead weight; it was like chains around my neck. There had been acts of bravery, even heroism that day, but my spirit felt as dead as the man whose weight I bore. We hefted him onto the deck of the slick, and held on to his belt while it lifted off so he wouldn't slide out again.

Back at the NDP, I was suddenly so tired I could hardly walk back to my fighting hole. A couple of jets streaked low overhead, guided by radar toward the bunker complex. Moments later they delivered their load of cluster bombs and the horizon flickered like lightning with the staccato detonations. They missed by over a kilometer. I looked at my watch. It was eleven at night. And I noticed a huge leech clinging to the web of skin between two fingers of my left hand. It must have been there for a long time, because it was about eight inches long. I pulled it off, and a thin, watery fan of blood spread across my hand. It was the only blood I had shed.

❖ IV ❖

WHEN MY FATHER WAS ELEVEN years old, his mother gave him a little one-man scow with which to test the waters of Long Island Sound. This was a turning point for him, something his mother did which changed the direction his life would take, and I like to think of my father out in his scow, nosing about the backwaters of Rye, New York in 1931. There were still some coastal schooners in those days, and he watched them unloading coal and lumber and ice using spruce booms and winches powered by "one-lunger" engines. He found himself, and he lost himself, and was never far from the water after that. He was happy, but he stopped moving forward, as one would do on a river or highway. He continued to do beautiful sketches of those schooners from memory until his death, and on occasion he could be persuaded to do an impersonation of a one-lunger engine. His great chest would heave, his face would contort, and he would huff and pant as the engine took up strain and relaxed. His stories and drawings made the waterfront come alive, you could smell the sulfurous coal smoke and sea salt, and now I wonder about his mother, and if she wished she could have escaped with him, while his father stormed and glowered.

My father began to visit when I was six, one afternoon a month. He had found a job as a deckhand on a New York harbor tugboat, and would arrive by train wearing the khaki work clothes which were his habit. He would walk the mile or so from the station to our house, often stopping at the Catholic church on the way, for his madness had delivered the face of God to him one afternoon, manifested in the shifting sea and clouds while he waited for war. The visits were painful for both of us; I had already learned to be cautious of him, as he was of me; and he was still nursing a grudge about the toy tugboat's demise. The language of boats was the one he was most fluent in, and we cobbled a few crude toy boats together; but it was of little help to me, more embarrassment than asset, I was still so afraid of him, and the him that might lurk inside of me. If he began to share his vision of spirits I would pretend to be listening but was really envisioning my escape routes. Then he would shuffle off toward Brooklyn again, smelling of stale port and tobacco.

When I was eleven, my mother sent me off to a boys' camp for the summer. It was a turning point for me just as the scow had been for my father, but at first I felt as though I had been cast adrift and abandoned. I was terribly homesick, afraid of the other boys and their rough games. I was quite certain I would not survive another day, but another day came, and then another. This camp, on the shore of Lake Dunmore in Vermont, had already seen three generations of boys like me and they began to fill a void just as boats had for my father. We stood inspection, moved in files, saluted the flag and responded to bugle calls. I learned to canoe, hike, work on a team and keep going when I really wanted to quit. With now and then a harsh word, and now and then a gentle hand, this camp was leading me toward manhood and war in ways my father never could, and I responded with unwavering loyalty. My loyalty was such that I began to sing the evening lullaby to the camp every evening after taps were sounded. This honor came as a surprise to me, as would all honors to come. I felt unworthy of it. Then as years passed and my voice changed, my loyalty was such that I was put in charge of the camp cannon. Twice a day, while the camp stood in formation behind me, I would touch off the ten-gauge cannon shell and the flag would go up or down accompanied by a bugle call. I was finding my way into manhood in a cloud of smoke with my ears ringing.

I had found myself at Camp Keewaydin, but lost myself completely again for a while on the plains of Gia Dinh, in the hills of Binh Duong just twelve years later. If this was truly the essence of manhood, then surely I didn't belong at all and wanted no part of it. This had happened in little ways before, so the feeling of hopelessness was vaguely familiar this time, though still overpowering, almost paralyzing as it blended with fatigue. There was no way I could have known that I would survive, and that I would live some day in a house filled with family, even birds nesting under the eaves. I didn't think I could live with my *self*, if I were to find it again, if I lived at all. This is the rite of passage, this is what men are prepared for with the humiliations of basic training and officer candidate school, but magnified here a hundredfold. And this time, the voices yelling at me were not those of drill sergeants but instead all came from within, and the loyalty which had served me so well at camp and Fort Polk was becoming divided, with my mission pitted against common sense and humanity.

Meager rewards were forthcoming, however. We were given a day of rest back at another brigade's base camp at Lai Khe. Bravo Company's first sergeant drove down there from Quan Loi and met us with a jeep trailer filled with beer and cracked ice. The first sip of cold beer was like a breath of fresh air after nearly drowning. Everyone was drinking beer and listening to music on Armed Forces Radio out of Saigon. Then, as we listened, the DJ dedicated a song to Mike Division. It had been called in by the guys in the hospital. I don't remember what the song was, but everyone cheered and laughed and cried and drank more beer than they could have dreamed possible. Peer support was working for them, but as an officer, I felt more isolated than ever. Then the relentless pursuit of the enemy resumed, leapfrogging by helicopter farther north, away from the cultivated land and deeper into their thickly wooded sanctuaries.

We were in the midst of the May Offensive, a period of conflict second only to the Tet Offensive of a few months before. The strategy of the First Division was to be unrelenting, with no time off to regroup or rest. It was a test of endurance, ours against theirs, a test of will. From a military point of view, our firefight had been a great success. Charlie Company had found fourteen dead VC the next morning but there were probably more. From a personal point of view, of course, it had been a great failure. I had not been strong enough to make my own men get up and assault. I had allowed my own fear and revulsion to transcend years of training at considerable taxpayer expense, and ignored the mandate of my profession by placing the welfare of my men, (and myself), ahead of the mission. I had inadvertently almost left a dead GI in the field, and furthermore could not account for the six rifles and three radios which I had hauled down to the LZ and left in the charge of a private whose name I couldn't remember while I went back for the body. The VC had returned in the night and recovered them. But worst of all, I had told the division commander to fuck off. I had failed at man's highest calling. I had failed as a father and failed as a son. A stinking yellow shroud hung over me as we hacked our way through the stinking woods. I assumed that everyone else could see it, not knowing that they, too, could only see their own.

I did not know that the woods would never really end, or that so many ambushes still lay ahead, like the darkening jungles of self-doubt, like the middle-aged ambushes of the heart, a sick child, a divorce, a love affair. I could not even fathom that my actions and their consequences would serve me well enough in time to come. I was disbelieving when Dennis said I was "pretty cool" back there. There was little time for introspection anyway: armies don't like introspection interfering with momentum. We got a new company commander, a first lieutenant who had done his time as a platoon leader. There would be no more blundering into kill zones, or jammed M-16s. I went back to being Mike Six again, but with six men wounded there were only twelve of us left. We began to take the point a lot more because we were as small as a squad, and because we had some real sharp guys like Redfeather, and because the recent firefight had somehow inexplicably enhanced our reputation. It was, after all, Mike Division who had initiated the fight, and Mike Division which finally crawled into the base camp and brought the gruesome fight to a close, with no help from me whatsoever.

With so few men, it was a lot easier for me to know all the names and call signs, but the woods loomed deeper and darker than ever. This was the Iron Triangle, the oldest and traditionally most secure of the enemy's sanctuaries. It was a place that none of our troops had even dared to enter until a few years before, and a place now so pummeled and poisoned and riddled with holes that it seemed impossible for anything human to survive, including us. It was hard to tell what it had looked like before the war. Villages, where there had been any, were mostly deserted and burned to the ground. The villagers and outlying farmers had been killed, or become refugees in the growing slums of Saigon, or joined the resistance. In the well-watered low places, the rice paddies were abandoned and were reverting to swamp. On the gently undulating hills which comprised most of the landscape, a vast deciduous forest with occasional grassy openings was under constant attack by B-52s and defoliants.

Each day would begin with a briefing. Defiant Six would explain the day's operations to the junior officers gathered in a circle at his CP. We would mark the landing zones and the routes on our plastic map cases with a grease pencil. If, at some point, Defiant Six's eyes should meet mine, I would quickly look away. My paranoia was such that I assumed he fully knew the depth of my cowardice. He had been aloft, talking to me on the radio during the firefight. But his executive officer, a captain who was almost always at his side, must have been told. Often, during the briefings, he would fix me with what I perceived as a stony and contemptuous glare. Then we would go back and gather our men. Soon, the fluttering beat of the helicopters would come. It was already hot, just an hour after sunrise, and we were already tired, tired from the day before, and the day before that.

Of the battalion's four line companies, one would be on night ambush duty and often another detached for different duty. So we generally just fielded two under-strength companies plus the headquarters group. Still, it took three or four lifts to get us out. If we were in the first lift, we would scramble on board as soon as the helicopters landed; all that was left of Mike Division could fit inside two of the Hueys. If we were in one of the later lifts, we would sit by the LZ and wait while the others went out; smoking, eating, napping until our time came. Then we would run out as the ships returned, split into "sticks" for each ship, and divided left and right of the landing zone. I would pop smoke to show wind velocity and direction. We would climb aboard just as soon as the skids touched the ground.

In many ways the helicopter rides were the only good part of the day. The thrill of sudden lift and speed was a great counterpoint to the deadening drudgery of foot-soldiering, and as soon as the ship gained a few hundred feet of altitude the air got a lot cooler, with a nice breeze beating in under the rotors. Some guys would sit in the doors with their feet dangling out. Others would sit on the canvas seats. Conversation was difficult over the whine of the turbines, but the view was great, and it didn't take long to figure out that this was a hopeless war. All you had to do was look down at the landscape slowly slipping past your feet. The mission of the infantry is to take and hold ground. We took and held none. Nothing would be gained in the shell-pocked forests, the abandoned farmland, the burned villages below. And everything would be lost.

Then the pitch of the engines would change. We would sink lower toward a clearing. The men would sit up, adjust gear, peer forward. I would try to fathom the countryside, anticipate the difficulties of swollen streams or steep gullies. I would look at my map and rehearse

in my mind what we were to do upon landing: pile out, join the perimeter at three o'clock, fall in line behind Lima in a column of two, start the
long, hot trek back to our NDP. By nine in the morning the temperature
would have reached ninety and still be climbing fast. Two quarts of water, one on each hip, would seldom last the day. Five meters separated
the man ahead from the man following in a column which could, with
the whole battalion out, be almost a mile long. Under the cover of
woodlands it would be a little cooler, but it was often rough going. The
trees here were small, just a foot or less in diameter and fifty to seventy-
five feet tall. But there was often a dense brushy undergrowth: big
greasy-leaved shrubs and the dreaded "wait-a-minute" vines, so named
for their tough, thorny stems that grew in crotch-ripping tangles. Since
it was the rainy season, we often had to wade streams. At least this was
a chance to cool off and refill the canteens. Then it was back to the hot
ridges again. Often, as we traversed the ridges, the Viet Cong would
shadow us, keeping abreast left and right, and crowing back and forth
to each other like roosters.

Twenty-five years later, when I wondered if my memory still served
me well, when it all began to seem like a dream to begin with, I found
our battalion's log book in the National Archives. I took a deep breath,
and began to read the entries, scrawled by a clerk at Defiant Six's side.
At first, it was like walking into a darkened room. The jargon, the code
names made no sense. But then my brain began to readjust. I could see
the wood line, the green shapes of men moving beside me. I was suddenly very tired. There were Viet Cong everywhere, appearing and then
fading away. In this impartial record of twelve platoons maneuvering, I
could see how we all were suffering. I was not alone in my trials by fire.
Although it would be ten days between firefights for Mike Division,
other elements of the Black Lions were in contact and suffering casualties almost every day. The typical day began with a "stand-to" at
five-thirty. Here is the partial record of a typical "seal and search" operation, with Alpha, Bravo and Charlie companies moving toward a
village by seven in the morning.

At 0750 Bravo company received small arms fire from the village,
and called in artillery. Negative U.S. casualties, one wounded woman
was found. At 0755 Vietnamese intelligence reported that the plantations next to the village were mined. By 0846, all elements were in place
and a helicopter began broadcasting a message in Vietnamese to the village. At 0910 Charlie company was fired on, and one man wounded.

At 0920 the search team came under fire while their helicopters approached the landing zone. Additional helicopter fire teams were requested. Additional artillery fire was requested. The search was called off as more gunfire erupted from the village. At 1020 the wounded woman died.

Some companies seemed cursed with bad luck. Charlie Company was one. Early in May, before I arrived, the lead elements of Charlie came into contact with a Viet Cong force of unknown size. The initial roar of heavy gunfire was followed by a deathly silence. The helicopter pilot who arrived overhead reported the grisly scene below.

1042 Report from Apache 10 entire squad all casualties. Probable 10 U.S. KIA.

1045 LOH standing by at Dagger for Defiant 3 (the battalion is preparing to insert by air).

1105 Vulture C&C on station slicks coming, (growing swarm of helicopters overhead, nothing moving below).

1110 Apache counts maybe ten dead VC among the bodies.

1237 Forces of Darkness oriented, moving out at this time. (Almost two hours after the firefight, the appropriately named reaction force is finally on the ground and moving toward the location. There is no contact with the enemy, nothing to do but bring the bodies back.)

Four days later, it was Charlie Company's turn once again to receive small arms and rocket fire. Five men were wounded, the company commander among them. By 1315 the "dust off" of the wounded had been completed, at 1447 came the message from the 93rd evacuation hospital that Charlie Six had died. Grief permeates the terse, shaky notes.

This landscape, this twilight zone where Bravo and Basher and Defiant and the Forces of Darkness maneuvered, this playground of death was still not what the battalion was looking for. The VC, in groups of two or three, harassing us, shadowing us, were small potatoes compared to the main force units lurking somewhere else. We endured the heat. We found bits of abandoned equipment and fortifications. Often we found ourselves in the wretched role of ghoul, excavating recent graves to see what they contained. The corpses were dated according to the rotting of flesh and clothing, and added to the body count. Intelligence reports filtered down, mostly through the Vietnamese and mostly unbelievable, of enemy regiments maneuvering beside us. Long-range reconnaissance patrols, LURPS of five men each, were sent out by Devil, and scout teams of helicopters added to our own intelligence, directing the battalion's movement from checkpoint to checkpoint. But most of all, it seemed as though the woods themselves were the enemy.

Every three hours, while we struggled ahead and the roosters crowed, the B-52s would come. They were like God's avenging dump trucks, unloading their bombs on the woods with a steady thundering roar. The ground would shake beneath our feet even though the bombs were falling ten or twenty kilometers away. Dark brown and gray clouds would slowly billow up thousands of feet, hanging in the sky for half an hour or so. Most of the time the bombs just fell on woods. We would pass through silent moonscapes of craters and broken stubs of trees. But once we found where the bombs had fallen upon tunnels crammed full of people. The bombs had left the dirt and woods and people so thoroughly homogenized that the only recognizable human fragments were the vertebrae. Thousands of vertebrae lay bleaching in the sun and rain, mixed with the dirt so uniformly that it seemed more like a geological phenomenon than anything that had once been human, had once loved or been loved.

The places that had been defoliated were the worst. We didn't know anything about Agent Orange beyond the fact that it was a failure. During the year or two that had elapsed since it had been sprayed on the woods, the "wait-a-minute" vines seemed to have developed a liking for the stuff and taken over like a kudzu horror movie. The long, prickly vines hung in festoons from the stark skeletons of poisoned trees and covered the ground with a shoulder-high thicket. Sometimes it would take an hour to move forward a kilometer, hacking through the vines while the sun beat down unmercifully. Extra water was frequently dropped by helicopter between stream crossings, but men kept collapsing from heat exhaustion nonetheless, and we all had to stop and wait again while they were medevaced out. Once it was Redfeather who collapsed. He was walking flank security again, which was doubly hard because he had to break his own trail. It was bad enough for those of us in the file, almost impossible for those out on flank or point who had to hack their way through, and remain on course and alert at the same time. Down went Redfeather, overheating, red face and dry skin, in a system meltdown which would turn deadly if it were not for quick attention. Then just as he was lifted out and we got going again, Dennis suddenly disappeared. The rotting roof timbers of an abandoned tunnel had given way, and he dropped down through the "wait-a-minute" vines. We had to wait again while he got fished out.

The tunnels and bunker systems were everywhere in this area; obviously it had been a refuge for main force units for a long time, and as the Viet Cong themselves were later to say, they fought the war more with shovels than rifles. It was also obvious that the main force units had departed, gone farther into the hills. All that was left was the security squads, or recon units. While we were entangled in "wait-a-minute" vines they were staying just ahead, crowing like roosters and fading away. We found their little camps, a cooking fire, a lean-to made with scraps of plastic sheeting, a few empty tins of Japanese sardines or mackerel, a pile of feces. But battalions, even regiments had clearly been there once; sometimes we found great piles of empty fish tins, along with American soda cans and, once, a Micky Mouse T-shirt.

Sometimes we would walk all the way back to the NDP along a dog-leg course. Sometimes the helicopters would come back and give us a lift. We would slowly file in through the coils of concertina wire, dog tired. Men would find their way back to their holes, throw their equipment on an engineer stake, and collapse. There might be time for a quick nap. There might be time for a cold can of C rations. We seldom bathed or changed our clothes, any ablutions were performed in a steel helmet. The RON ship would come in, the big Chinook carrying supplies for the next day's operations. The roar of its rotors, the blast of wind was unnoticed, everyone was too exhausted. A few men from battalion supply would unload it as soon as it had settled in our midst. Company commanders would go to the CP for ambush assignments. I would gather my strength enough to check my men's positions. Redfeather came back, and we were glad of that, making jokes about it. The RON ship would lift off again, out well before dark, blasting us with mud or dust, depending upon the weather.

An hour before dark, the ambush patrols would form up and file out through the wire. Scared and tired, dirty and grim, they would trudge slowly into the distant tree line. Then those who remained behind in the perimeter would walk, often painfully, out to the circle of concertina wire and place their claymores. They'd walk slowly back again, uncoiling the detonator wire. Men in the mortar pits would be checking their aiming stakes, squad leaders would make their listening post assignments. Half-light now, the tempo and noise would begin to taper off. No more helicopters overhead. Darkening gray skies, darkening green wood line, everything growing silent. The magic hour: bushes, men, stumps becoming indistinguishable, no talking except in whispers, no smoking except in the concealment of a fighting hole. With darkness complete, the listening posts, each of three or four men, would crawl out beyond the circle of wire to keep watch through the long night. Watches were set, darkness and silence was complete, and the enemy would start to move, hopefully not in our direction. At the CP tent, operations and logistical reports would be encoded and transmitted. The horizon would light up with the first illumination rounds. The man on radio watch at the company CP would periodically check on the listening posts. Battalion radio watch checked on ambushes. In the smallest hours, three or four in the morning, the sergeant major and sometimes Defiant Six himself would walk the line, making sure the watches were still awake, despite the numbing fatigue. They were, most of the time.

So it went, day after day, as though we were being punished for some unspeakable crime. I continued to keep to myself; it would be months before I got close to my fellow officers. In part, this was because of what I perceived as my personal failure. If they knew me well, they would know my cowardice. In part, it was also because we officers tended to be an ambitious, competetive bunch anyway. A number of enlisted men had taken the trouble to point out to me that they could have gone to officer candidate school, too, had they wished. That they didn't wish made all the difference. Getting a commission was like getting an MBA. It was a leg up on the future, and in fact in those early days, before being a Vietnam veteran implied being a spaced-out antiestablishment freak, corporate recruiters were actively seeking freshly discharged lieutenants. As officers, we were watching each other for mistakes and weaknesses, macho junior managers in an environment that was competetive as well as deadly.

Perhaps this was how my father had first begun to falter. He could not bring himself to be a part of such an environment for long. His temperment was too much that of the artist. He had dutifully attended a fashionable private school, as his father had wished, for these things were important, especially for the only son of a man with a seat on the New York Stock Exchange. He then went on to Yale, which was even more important, since his father had been one of the earliest All-American quarterbacks at Yale. Performance on the playing field is a model for performance in life, but he was proving to be a disappointment to his father. My father had no more interest in sports than I had. Instead, he daydreamed and did beautiful sketches, his loyalty divided between two parents. It was not easy for him at Yale, still in his father's shadow, and when the war came along it presented the opportunity to leave short of a degree and enter the navy. There was at least some redemption to be found in a commission, but divided loyalties soon gave way to deeper rifts which I still can't fathom. I still have the sketchbook he carried in those early navy days, though. There are the schooners again, and steam coasters, and cartoons of navy life which sparkle with humor, but there are also pages of darkness and tormented, ghost-like figures. Things began to go more profoundly wrong with my father while on convoy duty in the cold gray North Atlantic; and there was no vision of God as the perfect father, not yet, only demons. At the same age I was in Vietnam, my father was beginning to crack up. His fellow officers on the small and unsteady sub-chaser became so wary of his state of mind they took all his duties away. When he became violent, they locked him in the brig.

My father faced a discharge upon returning to shore. But to his father, this was completely unacceptable, unthinkable, impossible. A classmate during football days was now the Secretary of the Navy, and it took only a little reminiscing together to get my father fully reinstated and off to the Pacific on a new ship. I am reminded of General Ware. You must get up and assault. You must not lie there, wallowing in fear and revulsion. Winning is everything.

I carried all of this with me, too, along with my claymores and smoke grenades. In my heart, though, I already knew that this was the wrong war for an officer to be ambitious. We had not yet heard of "fragging," there were not yet open rebellions or assassinations, but you could see the seeds of these sprouting in the rich soil of disillusionment. I began to know that I had been right, during the firefight, to disobey an order, although I could not yet forgive myself for being afraid. I had cast my lot on the side of my men, and there it would stay.

I listened to them as we moved through this landscape of hopelessness. There was chat about the home towns, or food, or whores. These guys knew each other well, knew the names of each other's girls back home, the cars they'd owned, the jobs their fathers worked, but most of the time they grumbled about the war. And I was evolving too much respect for them, and the truth, to try to separate myself from them and be a champion of victory. I, too, felt that I had been lied to and abandoned. There was nothing heroic here, we were being pushed by old men, with self-serving ideas, pushed to the brink of death just to glorify old men. To falter, or worse, to question the sanity of the whole undertaking was the most threatening thing a man could do. Nothing is safer than a bunch of dead young heroes. Nothing is more scary than an army of potential assassins. The father had turned malevolent, preferring a dead son to a rebellious one, or one who was somehow unfit.

All wars are fought only by a very few, but especially this one. As individuals most of us could have gotten out of it, too. We all had friends who had beaten the draft, but something in us had led us to this place. For some, it may have been a thirst for adventure, for others a pathetic glimmer of patriotism, all of us still trying to fill some void like the missing father or brain or heart or courage. Now one tended to feel gravely deceived. Clearly, the Viet Cong were admirably determined and well trained and had some good points to make as well. The French colonialists were like the British our forefathers had rebelled against; furthermore, the French we encountered were as openly scornful of us as we were of them. As the war in Indochina had escalated, the popular American opinion had tended to characterize the French as effeminate and soft on communism, even to the extreme of tolerating it as a legitimate political entity in their own country. Now the French openly hated us for our belligerant crusade while, as witnessed in our recent firefight and elsewhere, the South Vietnamese soldiers were dangerously corrupt and demoralized, reflecting the fundamental dishonesty of a puppet regime. And clearly, our war, Johnson's war, Westmoreland's war, was destroying a beautiful country, as well as a beautiful race. Few who were there continued to think that if we didn't stop the communists here we'd be fighting them later on the sidewalks of California. We just hoped to live through it and get back to those sidewalks ourselves. Look at what the men have scribbled on their helmets with ballpoint pens as they pass by: Vietnam sucks. The peace symbol. The short-timer's calender, marking off each day.

I certainly wasn't afraid of my men anymore, the way I had been at first. As I walked with them, dug in with them, ate and shat with them, I began to interact with those tough guys in a way that was totally new to me. I admired their strength and courage, and often envied them. I saw how close they were, and how far they would go for each other. As far as death. They wouldn't die for L.B.J. but they would die for each other. Although I didn't know it at the time, I was being seduced in a far more subtle way than by the parades and war glories of my childhood. I was beginning to love my men.

We were coming back into the NDP late one afternoon. It was already getting dark as we passed the observation post and began to head toward the wire. I could see that there was some sort of agitation among the men up ahead. Some guys seemed upset, even crying. "Wasted," I heard that terrible word that summed up so much tragedy, somebody got wasted. More agitation as the word filtered back toward us. Some guy named Kennedy got wasted. I didn't know any Kennedys in our outfit, but he must have been a popular guy. Was it Charlie Company again?

"It was Bobby Kennedy. They fuckin' wasted Bobby Kennedy. They fuckin' blew his brains out."

At first I was so relieved that it wasn't one of "us" that I almost laughed. Later, along with the grief, there was also a grim sense of justice. Now they know what it is like here every day. Every day here guys get wasted, great guys, too, and yet the giant headless beast keeps staggering forward.

It seemed like forever, but only nine days had passed since that first firefight. For nine days we hacked our way through vines, crossed swollen streams, and did cloverleaf searches of the dark parts of the woods while the roosters crowed. Every day the helicopters would come in, pick us up, and lift us out to a new part of the woods. Always, the B-52s were overhead, cutting swaths through the woods. Once, while crossing one of those swaths, we came upon a dead tiger lying in the bottom of a bomb crater. It hadn't been killed by the bomb; it was an old crater half full of blue-green water. The tiger had been dead only for a day or so, and we couldn't see any marks on it. It was huge, seven or eight feet long, glowing, almost luminescent yellow-orange and black, lying on its side halfway in the water, and we just stood in a circle on the crater rim staring at it. None of us had ever seen a tiger before except in zoos or circuses, and a couple of guys wanted to go down into the crater and skin it. But there wasn't time, so we just had to turn our backs and go back into the woods the tiger had come out of. Everyone was kind of quiet after that, like we had seen a part of ourselves lying in that crater, too. Then later, that evening or the next, the word came down. Main force elements had been located. They were in the Ho Bo Woods.

❖ V ❖

WHEN MY COUSIN DOUGGIE was eleven years old, and I was ten, and he knew that he would not live much longer, he built himself a camp in the woods. He built it on a slope among some young hardwoods near his house; his illness made him too short of breath to go any farther and it took him most of the summer. He did it alone, clearing the ground, cutting saplings, assembling a rough lean-to roof like a Viet Cong. The disease had made him wise beyond his years, and I listened closely as he spoke about his private place on earth. I could not enter it, didn't want to, knowing that he was engaged upon a journey that was beyond my comprehension. He spent many hours there during his last year just watching and listening, smelling and feeling. Then he was gone.

I went farther into the woods, up the slope to the top, where the hemlocks grew tall, shutting out the light, and beyond to where the oaks and beeches shed a light of their own. Often, as I started out, I would pass the ruins of Douggie's camp. It lasted for years, an outline of stones, a frame of sticks, as far as he could climb, as much as he could build. Sometimes I would lie awake, terrified, through most of the night, envisioning my own death, trying to envision nothing. There was nobody to talk to about this, no companions close enough, no God, only those same whispering woods. Even now, I go to the woods almost every day, finding resinous balm for cystic fibrosis and the death of children and young men. My three sons often go with me. There was a fourth son, too, who began his journey toward me a decade ago, but was stillborn. The woods remind me of him, meaning nothing and meaning everything, eloquent and mute. I see his peaceful face in the woods, even now, and I hear the sound of gunfire up ahead.

We filled in the fighting holes, emptied the sandbags into them, covered the garbage pits and latrines of our NDP in a daze. It seemed impossible that we were going to the Ho Bo Woods, we were so tired already, but that was the word. The concertina wire was coiled, engineer stakes and sandbags bundled into sling loads. The Chinooks came and shuttled the battalion back to Lai Khe for a chance to change clothes, bathe, and get drunk. Officers were summoned to Defiant Six's temporary CP in Lia Khe that evening. We were given fresh maps and aerial photographs. We were told what to expect; main force NVA units being reinforced by replacements fresh from Hanoi, elite squads of Viet Cong sappers, extensive base camps and tunnel systems, speed trails comparable to the Ho Chi Minh trail itself, all in unusually thick triple canopy jungle broken by occasional savanna-like openings. It was going to be a big operation: three battalions of infantry, a battalion of armored cavalry, artillery units. Expect a hot LZ. Artillery prep would begin at 0600. Aerial prep 0700 with the first lift going in ten minutes after that. Alpha Company would go first.

I felt like this was a death sentence. We all did. There was no celebrating that night, just quiet, deliberate drinking to numb the fear and allow sleep to come. Then dawn arrived, all too soon, with the booming of big guns and the whine of turbines. We sat on the runway in sticks of six or seven men, waiting for our lift. The 155 medium artillery was shifting their fire from one clearing to the next, shelling various LZs so as not to tip our hand. The slicks loaded Alpha Company, then took off fluttering into the distance. We counted them before they disappeared. Eighteen. We waited. The sun began to get hot. In half an hour, the slicks reappeared. There were still eighteen, which was a good sign. Mike Division loaded, just the twelve of us. Then came the louder scream from the turbines, the lift and the pitch forward, the rotor blades thwacking the air, the skids just skimming above the runway as airspeed picked up, then the surge upward with everybody looking like shit.

Even while envisioning what lay ahead, it was better being in the helicopters than anywhere else. Once again, Vietnam slowly glided past our feet. Rubber plantations, rice fields, villages gave way to more and more woods. You could tell the trees were getting bigger, too, with many trees standing much taller than the rest, their trunks shining in the early morning light, casting shadows on the trees below. It was almost like snorkeling over a coral reef, the woods below had such depth and variety, not like any we had seen before. Far ahead, we could see the dappled pattern of the clearings. Gray and tan smoke was puffing up, drifting downwind from some of them as the artillery kept shifting to new targets. I reached into my ammo pouch, took out my Kodak Instamatic, and snapped some pictures of Mike Division riding helicopters to the Ho Bo Woods before we began our descent. I still have them.

These clearings, such as the one toward which we were on final approach, were an essential element in our airmobile operations. I'm still curious about what made them; some must have been natural, others deliberately cleared. In the Ho Bo Woods, nearly all the clearings were surrounded by VC trenches and bunkers, built in anticipation of our arrival. I could see ours ahead. The artillery fire had lifted long ago, but gunships were still working the wood line with their rockets. The slicks formed a straight line and dropped down low, right over the treetops, out of sight and fast. Big trees zipped past, then the opening, a glimpse of troops on the ground firing to the west. The crew chiefs were nervous, motioning for us to jump while the helicopters were still four feet above the ground. All was smoke, dust and confusion. We ran toward our sector of the perimeter. Bursts of gunfire erupted from the woods, cracking high over our heads. They were shooting at the slicks. A team of gunships swooped around and came in low overhead, firing at the trees to our front. I saw a man wearing a white shirt about thirty feet up in a tree. He had an AK-47 but he wasn't using it, he was just looking. I guess we had gotten the jump on them, because he hadn't had time to change his shirt yet. As the helicopters began firing in his direction he dropped to the ground like an over-ripe fruit. We ran to the place where he dropped. There wasn't a trace of him. He had been absorbed by the earth, like magic. The firing stopped. The woods fell silent. There was no sign of anyone, anywhere. Just trenches zigzagging through the wood line.

We argued with Alpha Company about who should get what sector, shifted our perimeter, made more room as the next company got lifted in. Gradually the circle of men enlarged and inched, amoeba-like, across the LZ to a place that seemed best for digging in. There were some huge stumps in the field, so it must have been logged once. Some trees were left standing, one of them was truly enormous, six or eight feet thick. There were also termite mounds everywhere, four to six feet tall and hard as concrete. These obstacles made it difficult to clear fields of fire, and heightened our paranoia. Also, we soon discovered lots of cattle skeletons, a hundred or more. They looked like beef cattle, slaughtered about two years before. Perhaps after this area was logged it was grazed in the same tradition as Brazil. But who killed the cattle? Were they VC cattle? Conjecture was that the sight of a herd of cattle roaming free would have proved irresistible to certain personality types flying gunships, whether they were VC cattle or not.

At least it was easy digging in the sandy soil, all too easy, and once we got the lines of our perimeter established we dug fast, knowing that the enemy had done their digging long ago, and expecting an attack at any minute. I shared the digging with Doc Behm and Wakefield; good, long-handled spades had quickly been flown in along with the sandbags, engineer stakes and concertina wire that always accompanied us. By early afternoon the perimeter was pretty secure. The Chinook, shuttling back and forth, had brought in additional sling loads of ammunition, food, and a water trailer. Then the armored cavalry came bashing out of the woods, having made a long and dangerous cross-country run. We added about two dozen M-48 tanks and armored personnel carriers to our perimeter.

The plan was to keep the initiative, keep the enemy off-balance and unable to react quickly enough. Each battalion NDP was to send out three platoon-size ambushes that night, deep into the jungle, casting a fine net across it. I was called to Defiant Six's CP. Mike Division was to be one of the ambush patrols. Defiant Six explained the situation in a grim, businesslike way. I got the feeling that he really understood what the other lieutenants and I were feeling at that moment, but I could not escape what I perceived to be the cold, accusing glare of this executive officer. Perhaps I had been chosen because this would be a good way of getting rid of me for once and all. Everybody knows that the first night is always the most dangerous one in a new place, and this would also be the first time I had taken my platoon out on ambush alone. There were only twelve of us, we really didn't belong here, I could come up with a hundred more reasons why we shouldn't go. But Defiant Six droned on, explaining the speed trails while the XO glowered, and then offered us the use of his light observation helicopter for an aerial recon. Each of us was given a general area for our ambush, but we would choose the specific site ourselves.

In the late afternoon my turn came to go up. We were using one of those Korean War vintage two-seaters with the round bubble canopy and no armament. I was sufficiently scared and confused that I could barely even fathom the shoulder harness as I climbed into the right hand seat. Then as soon as I had buckled myself in and pulled the green fiberglass flight helmet down over my head, the pilot flipped his radio to the rock station in Saigon, looked over at me, grinning maniacally, and goosed it. We were off in a flash, nearly impaling the concertina wire with our skids, with Janis Joplin wailing and grooving, even ricocheting inside our helmets. We circled higher like a woodcock doing its mating flight in spring, and I looked down at Mike Division, and the rest of the NDP spinning beneath us while the music blared.

The pilot broke in to ask me what I wanted to see. I told him I wanted to see the speed trails to the northwest, I had never seen one before. He banked the ship, and we cut a northwesterly course above the jungle, music reverberating with the beat of the rotors. It seemed like such a different jungle from up high, deeply textured, a tapestry of different foliage types, deceptively friendly and inviting while the music itself spoke of the darker terrors within. I could see the speed trails ahead. They looked like the rights-of-way that utility companies clear for power lines. There was one big one running from east to west, perfectly straight. Others intersected it, crisscrossing the woods in a grid-like pattern. They were used for moving large units very quickly; the trees had been cut away entirely in these avenues, which were ten or twelve meters wide. Like the Ho Chi Minh Trail itself, winding down from the north, their strength lay in their complexity. Different trails would be used each time, and as soon as an aircraft was heard the troops would just duck off into the tree line, out of sight.

I still didn't quite know what I was looking at; the music itself was disorienting, I'd never done a helicopter recon before, and I was terrified at the prospect of actually spending the night in that convoluted green never-never land. The pilot asked me if I'd like a closer look, and I foolishly agreed. Down we went, like a stone, and I braced myself for the impact, music blaring. Next we were racing along the big trail ourselves, the rotor tips barely clearing the vegetation. He boasted that he had once swung around a corner doing this and almost run into a whole bunch of NVA. Other times, he had seen them staring back at him from the wood line, too surprised to get off a shot. I was not impressed. It seemed so insane that anyone could actually enjoy this sort of thing. I quickly picked out a trail intersection amid the blur of gray-green, which I thought we could reach by dark, and we returned. I walked away from the helicopter as quickly as I could. Obviously, the guy was nuts, and while I didn't particularly care if he killed himself, I didn't want to be nearby when it happened.

Late afternoon, then later afternoon with the twilight descending. Everyone was dug in, the helicopters had gone back to their bases. A time which should be tranquil had me churning with fear and self-doubt. I couldn't eat, was numbed by the prospects before me. Then it was time. We assembled, adjusted the gear on our hips and backs, and filed out through the wire and across the field of stumps and termite mounds and dead cows. These were the woods where Mike Division had once lost twelve men, and now there were just twelve of us left. We reached the woods, and they instantly absorbed us, much thicker than I had anticipated, more like diving into a pool of darkness, almost strangling. I could see why the enemy preferred the speed trails here. My mouth felt like somebody had emptied an ashtray in it, and my testicles must have been the size of dried beans. Everything was wet and slimy, and we couldn't hack our way through because it would be too noisy. We had to slink along, leaning on the jungle to break through in places. And it was getting dark too fast. After almost an hour, I realized we weren't going to make it to the intersection. So we cut over to a speed trail we had been paralleling and set up in a tight huddle on its edge, with the jungle dripping all around us. We were extra close to each other this time, within touching distance, enclosed by claymore mines, wet and scared. I had never felt such a bonding with my men as I did now.

The darkness was so thick we could have been in the bowels of a cavern, or sealed in a tomb. We sat upright, listening to the dripping jungle, and keying the mike on the radio every half hour to signal to the duty officer back at the NDP that we were still alive. It didn't take long for the night's action to begin, as we knew it would; we just didn't know where. There was a series of grenade explosions back at the NDP. One of the listening posts had encountered the guy with the white short-sleeved shirt again. This time, he was slinking through the woods carrying a package, like some sort of deliveryman from hell. Again, he vanished with the grenade explosions. Not a trace. Nothing. It was just eight at night and Delta's ambush was still getting into position when two men came down the trail toward them, chatting casually. They blew two claymores on the men, but as it would turn out, they had popped them too soon. They could hear more movement on the trail. They called in mortar fire on the movement. Then they lay still, waiting.

At ten, one of the other NDPs came under ground attack. They were only about six kilometers from us. Tracers came pouring up from the jungle, quickly followed by the sound of gunfire. We listened to the radio, the volume so low it was barely discernable amid the constant whispering dribble of the jungle itself. There were North Vietnamese trying to rush them before they had their fighting holes finished. They were in the wire, entangled in the coils of concertina wire, ripped up by claymores. Illumination rounds went up, and at last we could see each other, or fragments of each other between the shadows of swaying yellow light. Then Tac Air came in, with a brace of fighter-bombers swooping low. There was the sudden ruddy glow of napalm, and then as the jets pulled back up again, we saw the distinctive green glow of North Vietnamese anti-aircraft tracers climbing up after them, trying to reach them. This pattern repeated a few times, red napalm followed by green tracers. Then it was quiet again. The probe had been repelled. The last of the parachute flares sputtered out, and we were plunged into darkness again.

I fully expected we would be next, as the enemy rushed back and forth, reacting to our intrusion, but it was Delta's ambush again, keying their radio mike to signal they had trouble. The duty officer back at the NDP began to ask them yes or no questions.

"Do you have movement?" A steady hiss of squelch in reply meant yes.

"Are there more than five men?" Again, the one hiss in the affirmative. Then the questioning ended with a ripple of explosions. The Delta platoon leader began to whisper excitedly. There were North Vietnamese all around them. They had blown more claymores, but they had also received incoming grenades in return. More mortars were adjusted on the sounds of living and dying. The darkness writhed. With claymores almost expended, with several men wounded and North Vietnamese crawling almost within their ranks, Defiant Six sent some of the M-48 tanks in to extract the patrol. It didn't take long for the tanks to get there, and of course they were impervious to the grenades. These tanks had giant xenon searchlights mounted on the turrets, which they shone around, shooting at some bodies and running over others, until there was no more movement in the muck and body parts,

and the platoon could come out of hiding and climb on board for a welcome ride home.

Surely our turn would come; but it didn't, not yet, and we began to
see the treetops outlined against the purpling sky. When it was fully
light we just said a silent thanks and headed back to the NDP. Recon
went out before we got back and found enough remains at Delta's ambush site to reassemble twenty dead North Vietnamese. These turned
out to be replacements, freshly arrived from the north in crisp kakhi
uniforms, and armed only with grenades. As with our earlier firefight, it
was considered a great victory. But clearly, the men who had been in the
ambush patrol didn't see it that way. They looked sick and disgusted
and ashamed, while other men, from recon or the armor outfit, posed
for photographs amid the corpses. Some men sent the photos home, but
not the men who had been there for the killing.

Mike Division had the day to rest and improve positions at the NDP
while the rest of the company went out on sweeps of the surrounding
countryside. I wasn't certain it would be our turn to go out on ambush
again that evening; in fact I was counting on that uncertainty because
I really didn't think that I could do it two nights in a row. I was even
having trouble napping as moldy old feelings came surging back. I was
unable to participate in gym class because I had forgotten my sneakers
again. I was unable to do my homework because I had brought the
wrong textbook home. My limbs were very heavy and I could barely
keep my eyes open. Maybe some canned pears would help. We had the
whole NDP almost to ourselves, with a week's worth of C ration cases
stacked up. Nobody would miss the canned pears.

Was this what my father felt under the dome of the Pacific sky? Were
we inextricably linked, father and son? As I got to know him, tried hard
to follow him, I found myself leading half the time anyway, because he
seemed stuck going in circles, an outsider, not one of the boys. I really
wanted to be one of the boys myself, anything but a platoon leader surrounded by termite mounds. Mike Division was lazily clearing fields of
fire and camouflaging our fighting holes. Something should be done
about those termite mounds. The canned pears were delicious. I wondered what would happen if I put a shaped charge of plastic explosive
inside the empty pear tin and used it to blow a termite mound. It took
less than a minute to stuff the can full of explosive, mold it into a cone
shape, and insert a claymore detonator. I walked to the nearest mound,
laid the can against it, uncoiled the detonator wire, yelled "Fire in the

hole," and blew it. Half a pound of C-4 just blew a hole in the side the size of a football, but it sure did get the attention of the rest of the platoon. Gradually, they all drifted over to my side and began to offer assistance. Now we were having fun, like playing with boats together. We put a two-pound block of explosive in the hole I had blown, wired it, and stepped back. There was a big explosion this time, and we all cheered as chunks of termite mound hurtled into the air.

There were still lots of termite mounds, and lots of explosive left. It was an easy course for me to take as helmsman. Soon my crew was hard at work, eating all the canned pears and then filling the cans with explosive. It was like the course my father took when we had sailed together on my last leave before going to Vietnam. He had been trying to get me on a cruise for years but I had always managed to back out. I had never liked the idea of being in such close quarters for more than a few hours, was never comfortable on the water for long with somebody else in charge, and as our cruise in a little Bahamian fishing smack progressed I began to realize that he wasn't in charge, either. His hand was on the tiller, he looked great, rather like Hemingway with a handsomely grayed beard, could have even been the old man and the sea except that he had no idea where he was steering, or if he did have an idea, it was wrong. This was me now, blowing up termite mounds. The one-two punch of blowing a hole with the shaped charge, then inserting a larger, bursting charge worked perfectly and everybody was having a great time, but it was leading nowhere, just as our trip to Block Island had. The fog had returned, metaphorically this time, instead of the real pea soup we had encountered at sea. I had my commission by then and had excelled at navigation on dry land. Even my own father could not mislead me, and sure enough, as night fell and we continued through the fog, our whole world defined by the limited extent of our vision, I was certain we had passed Block Island and were headed for Spain while my father, beer in hand, held his course steady and continued to relate his theories about the decline of Western civilization. Could my men see through me now, as I had seen through him? Would the deep sea swells finally bring me back to reality, as they had my father then?

Pretty soon we ran out of our own C-4, but we got more from battalion supply. Then by early afternoon we ran out of termite mounds, so we started working on the tree stumps. We were like kids on a romp, working in teams of three or four, and when one of the squad leaders asked me about ambush I simply pretended I didn't know, like my father, cheerfully bringing the boat around and heading in the opposite direction again at midnight. It is fascinating how easy it is to fool people into thinking that you know what you are doing. It is an art, this feigning of composure and competence. Even when we almost ran aground on Long Island, just as my father really had once while in the navy, even when, at two in the morning, we finally anchored beside what turned out, at dawn, to be a naval bombing target, having completely missed both Block Island and Spain, my father's deportment remained unruffled. Perhaps I could pull this off a while longer as well, knowing all along that I had forgotten my sneakers, and taken the wrong textbooks home.

Meanwhile, without effective supervision, Mike Division was characteristically getting out of control. A really big stump with about ten pounds of C-4 beneath it took off, got up about thirty feet, and came down right on top of a fighting position in Alpha Company's sector, narrowly missing a couple of men. They were really mad at us. Not ten minutes later, some big clods of earth came down on top of Defiant Six's tent. He happened to be in it, too, having returned to go over some maps. He came flying out and growled that the game was over. So once again, I was acutely embarrassed. A few moments later, there was a burst of automatic weapon fire from the woods to the north, which nobody paid much attention to.

We put away our detonators, lay about, and tried to find other diversions. I tried to avoid thinking about going out on ambush again, clinging to the hope of unclear orders. It was June 14th, eight days after Robert Kennedy was killed. Bravo Company emerged from the tree line, returning from their sweep. They looked terrible, haggard, some were crying. The guys in Lima platoon were carrying the bodies of two of their comrades. They had been closing on the NDP in a column of two, and were almost within sight. The point, and most of the point squad, must have walked right over a VC observer in a hole. Then the VC jumped up out of his hole between the columns, killed the two men closest to him with a single burst of fire, and disappeared into the thick jungle before anyone else could even get off a shot.

The guys in Lima platoon were shattered; these had been well-loved men who had been with the unit for a long time. They tenderly wrapped the bodies in ponchos and anointed them with their tears. Then they put them out by the concertina wire to be hauled away by the morning supply ship. And I, in my fear of another night of ambush, felt very small. It was our turn to go out again, but now it was too late for us to pick our own site. Instead of blowing up termite mounds and avoiding reality, I should have been going over maps, doing another recon by air, coordinating artillery fires. Instead, we just ended up joining the recon platoon from battalion headquarters and going out with them.

What humiliation. Recon was the elite outfit, the scouts, the right hand of Defiant Six, commanded by the obviously insane lieutenant I had first met at Quan Loi. They wore camouflage pattern fatigues instead of the plain green ones that everyone else had, and they all carried the folding stock CAR-15, a weapon everyone else coveted. It was beyond my comprehension at the moment, I was so steeped in terror, revulsion and self-doubt, that in five more months Defiant Six would offer the command of Recon to me. It probably would have been incomprehensible to him as well at that moment. But despite the humiliation of that moment, it was also a comfort to go out with them, letting somebody else lead. They were a lot bigger than the other platoons, with about thirty men. It was also somewhat of a revelation, because instead of going about four or five kilometers out into the jungle, they just went out one kilometer, almost within shouting distance, and holed up in a defile where the chances of seeing any VC were about as good as the chances of any VC stumbling upon them. Perhaps their real mission was more that of a reaction force in case the NDP came under attack. Or perhaps they didn't like the idea of going farther into that dark wood any more than we did. At any rate, it was a much better night than the previous one, and everyone slept well but me. I was more ashamed than ever, my shame made all the more poignant by the two men wrapped in ponchos out by the concertina wire.

No tracers skipped along the horizon, no parachute flares drifted down beneath long plumes of smoke. The only sounds were of men softly shifting, and the wild things of the jungle. The next morning we rotated duties with November platoon and went along on the sweeps while they stayed behind and rested for their ambush. These were big battalion-size sweeps which we did with the armor unit. We began by mounting up on the tanks and armored personnel carriers and riding them as they bashed through the jungle for a couple of hours. This would have been almost pleasant were it not for the mines and the fire ants. It was easy for VC sappers to stay just ahead, planting mines in our path, and they were taking out one or two vehicles a day this way. It made the armored cavalry crews into nervous wrecks, but it didn't inflict any casualties on us since we rode on top, immune to the blast. With us, it was the fire ants, which built their nests in the trees overhead. Every time a track we were riding on bashed into a tree with fire ant nests, the red beasts would come pouring down like tracers from a minigun, falling inside our shirt collars and stinging aggressively like bees.

Next, we dismounted and began a long zigzag course on foot. With several hundred men spaced five meters apart, our movement was slow, noisy and awkward. Little was ever accomplished, and it was incredibly tiring as well. Meanwhile, the armor unit maneuvered around into a blocking position, which we gradually moved toward once they were in place, as though the Viet Cong had neither eyes nor ears, and remained unaware of the presence of two dozen tanks and APCs. It is the same sort of "drive" technique used by deer hunters, with the same risk of shooting your own men. Also, deer can't go underground, and underground was clearly where our enemy was. All we found was the places where they had just been; the freshly cut sapling stumps, smeared with mud to make the cuts look old. We never found the tunnels where the saplings were used as roof supports. Oddly, we never found the piles of dirt they had excavated.

It was crushingly hard work, as well as fruitless, often on steep hillsides and with few opportunities to take a break, sit down, and smoke a cigarette. The emotional strain was nothing compared to ambush; there was certainly safety in our numbers. But the physical punishment, humping fifty pounds of equipment through that dark, dank hothouse, was unbelievable. Even now, I can close my eyes and feel the pain of my web gear pulling back and down at my shoulders, the burning sweat in my eyes, and the dizzying fatigue. We got back to the perimeter at six, just as November was going out on their ambush. There was hardly time for a cold meal of C rations, and no time at all to lie back and close your eyes, before we had to put out our listening posts and set up watches for the night. Each platoon was supposed to put out three listening posts of three men each as our early warning system. They would set up in a tight circle outside the wire, surrounded by their claymores as on ambush, and go on watches of two hours on and four off. But how are men to stay awake after a day of sweeps? And while listening post duty isn't too bad with a full-size platoon, once Mike

❖ V ❖

Division's LP's were out, all that was left behind the wire was me, Doc Behm and Wakefield.

At about ten that night, one of my LPs keyed their mike, indicating that they had movement. I quizzed them so they could reply in the standard "yes, no" bursts of squelch noise, and learned from them that there were four strangers out there between them and the next LP to the left. As I whispered into my radio, others in the perimeter gathered at my side and listened, too. Bravo Six was there, and Defiant Six was listening in from his CP tent. I could also hear a ripple of movement traveling down the line of defenses in both directions away from me as the infantrymen there became alert. I assume that if there were VC on the wire, they heard it too. Everyone knew there was movement in Mike's sector, and everyone was jittery.

Often, in the darkness and confusion, listening posts will suddenly see each other and mistake each other for the enemy. Sometimes they even get into a firefight with each other; I've seen that happen twice. Also, it has happened that a platoon leader has blown up his own LP or an LP has become trapped between the gunfire of attackers and defenders. All these scenarios were going through my mind, and once again I was far more concerned about the safety of my own men than I was about the opportunity to kill some enemy. Finally, as we sat there whispering, somebody brought me a starlight scope. I flipped the toggle switch on, heard the high-pitched hum of its tiny television screen, and lifted the scope to my eye. The luminescent screen flickered, glowing yellow-green. I could clearly see the coils of concertina wire, black against a green background of trees. Here and there, a few surviving stumps stood out boldly in the grass. I couldn't see the LPs because they were lying prone. Then, as I continued to scan the wire, I came upon a group of four men wearing floppy hats. They were on their hands and knees, feeling along the wire and gesturing to each other as they worked. I watched, absolutely fascinated. Defiant Six was soon at my side.

I still wanted to be absolutely certain of what I was seeing. It was possible that I was seeing one of my own LPs, but mine were supposed to have three men, not four. Also, they were wearing helmets. At least they were supposed to, but sometimes men on ambush or LP like to wear a jungle hat they've kept stashed away instead. It was against regulations in our unit, but certainly a possibility. These looked like government issue jungle hats, which the VC could easily have bought at the military boutiques which thrived on the streets of Saigon. Clever move. They seemed to be working their way along the wire to the left, so I whispered into the radio for the LPs to move to the right, find the opening in the wire that way, and come in. This they began to do, crawling on their bellies through the grass. We were all very close at this time, a hundred feet from me to the VC, and another hundred to the nearest LP.

As soon as the LPs came in they rushed to my side, breathless and excited. There was no doubt in their minds what they had seen, and they couldn't understand how the VC had gotten past them in the first place. Or was there a tunnel? And what were they up to? We guessed that they were sappers, carrying satchel charges of explosives to blow a hole in the wire and claymore defenses. This would immediately be followed by a ground assault by more forces hiding in the woods, just as they had done at the other NDP a few nights before. I carefully lined up twelve hand grenades on top of my bunker and straightened the pins so they could easily be removed. Defiant Six and Bravo Six told all the other officers that we would be throwing grenades, and that everyone else should hold their fire. We didn't want to give away any of our positions by shooting, nor could we send up illumination for the same reason. When at last I was certain that everybody had gotten the word, and that all my men were in, I took one last look with the starlight scope. There was nothing there, just lumps which could have been anything. Perhaps they had heard us whispering and had lain down. Or gone back in their tunnel. Or sneaked back out however it was that they had sneaked in. Still, one had to be certain. I flipped off the scope and started throwing grenades as fast as I could. I had half of them in the air before the first one exploded.

Of course, the point of using the grenades was to keep our exact position a secret. But we were about to receive our first lesson in the poor discipline of the armor outfit. As soon as the grenades started exploding, a tank to the left began firing its fifty-caliber machine gun. Of course, when the other tanks and APC crews saw that, they began firing, too. Well, with all the armored cavalry shooting, the infantrymen were bound to join in. Within a few seconds, our side of the perimeter had erupted into a "mad minute" with everybody on full auto. Defiant Six, Bravo Six and I all ran up and down the line yelling "Check fire, check fire." There were still other LPs out, and recon platoon was somewhere out there as well. It took almost a minute to get the tracks to stop firing, they were so wired. Fortunately, their aim was as bad as their fire control, characteristically high, and no friendlies were hit. Meanwhile, the radios were crackling. The other battalions at the neighboring NDPs had seen our fountains of tracers and wanted to know if we were under attack. The recon platoon, safe in that same wisely chosen defile, wanted to know why we were attacking them.

Since we had given everything away, there was no harm in sending up some illumination. I could hear Oscar Five, our mortar platoon leader, giving the charge and fuse settings to his crews. Moments later came the "whump," then the "pop" high overhead, and the swaying yellow light. I hoped that the light would authenticate my vision of four men in floppy hats, and so did Defiant Six. The other battalion commanders were bound to chide him about the fireworks display. But there weren't any floppy hats or body parts hanging in the wire. Defiant Six seemed to be looking at me strangely. His XO was looking at me accusingly again. I sent a squad out to search the area, sweeping back and forth in the yellow light, looking for blood trails, equipment, anything. They came back empty-handed. Now Defiant Six was angry. He told me to send them out again. After a very diligent search, they came back with the shredded remains of a poncho liner one of the LPs had left behind.

The last of the parachute flares sputtered out and we were in darkness again. I suppose it was naive to think that any sappers skilled enough to get past our LPs in the first place wouldn't be tipped off by our bustling and rustling and the LPs trying to sneak back inside. As soon as I had the LPs in place again, Defiant Six summoned me to his tent. He was very tired; it was almost midnight and the dim kerosene lamp exaggerated the lines in his face. Again and again, he asked me what I had seen, and again and again I told him I had seen four men in floppy hats fooling around with the wire. Once again, I felt responsible for the whole debacle, causing embarrassment all the way to brigade level. With my self-esteem at its lowest ebb, I suddenly began to unburden myself in a way that men usually reserve only for their wives or lovers. The agony, disgust and shame which had accumulated for a month welled up and overflowed, my defenses all were breached, and I was bleeding to death. It didn't matter to me that there were several others in the tent, including the scornful executive officer. I said that I thought the war was wrong, stupid and futile. I further stated that

I could not ask my men to do things that I didn't have the courage to do myself. I finally told him that I wanted to resign my commission and fight alongside my men as a common soldier. I was utterly lost in the woods, and with my confession I bestowed upon him my complete trust. Of course, to resign was what my father had wanted me to do all along. He had always been scornful of my commission. Beyond its being an affront to him personally, it was a betrayal of humanity.

Defiant Six was silent for a while. Nobody else in the tent made a sound. There was only the soft hissing of the kerosene lamp. Then at last Defiant Six spoke. He said that I should take some time to think about my decision; that whatever I did, it would be something I would have to live with for the rest of my life. He paused for a moment, and then added that we were both very tired, and should get some sleep. He was right.

❖ VI ❖

I USED TO TAKE MY SONS to the woods with me nearly every day, starting almost when they were newborn. I would carry them on my shoulders, holding their little hands when they were too small to sit up there on their own. We would follow hidden footpaths, and I would name the trees, or just talk, knowing they could understand my voice, if not my words, and sometimes I would be silent, giving the silence of the woods to them. They were a platoon I could hold in my hands.

My firstborn son was four months and eight days old when the NVA drove their tanks into Saigon. And when Saigon fell it seemed as though everything else might follow, as my father had long predicted, like a house of cards. I plowed the vegetable garden that day, turning sod and revealing the rich, sweet-scented soil below. I dug a trench for the asparagus which was as wide and deep as the ones the Viet Cong dug, and even considered roofing it over with logs cut in the woods, smearing the stumps with mud so the cuts would not look fresh, then covering the roof with several feet of soil and camouflaging the whole thing if times got really rough. I knew the woods and the soil well, and I carried my sons on my back, just as I had carried the radio when my own radio man got tired, still anticipating ambush.

Being so tired was the worst part, worse than the fear, because sometimes you got so tired that you didn't care anymore. I had not yet learned about fatherhood in Vietnam, I was still trying to be a son and knew only my own pain. Then morning came, another gray-green dawn with lumps of men rising, stretching, urinating. The listening posts came in and threw their soaking poncho liners on the engineer stake racks to dry. Little fires were made here and there out of the C-4 plastic explosive left over from blowing the termite mounds. It would burn like a candle, enough to heat a tin cup of water or C ration can. The ambush patrols came back in, weaving their way through the openings in the concertina wire, and the tankers began warming up the engines, spewing clouds of exhaust into the motionless humid air.

I felt numb, removed, as though I was watching all this through a window, or as though in a dream that I could not wake up out of. What good had my confession the night before done? Would I be deemed unfit and removed? I tried not to think about it, which was easier because there was not much time. The sweeps were beginning again. I adjusted the straps on my web gear, checked my maps, and started walking again. This time the tanks went off to the left, following the ridges, while we slogged through the lowland to the east. I watched the sweat-soaked back of the man ahead of me, and tried to imagine myself as one of them. I felt that I was strong enough to carry almost anything in this heat except the burden of leadership.

Now and then through the day I would come across Defiant Six, and if our eyes should happen to meet I quickly looked away, and so did he. Then the next evening, just to rub salt in my wounds, we were treated to a visit from Devil Six himself. He wanted personally to award decorations to those men who had distinguished themselves during the firefight of a few weeks before. As his helicopter approached overhead everyone was called out into formation to greet him, and as usual there was a lot of grumbling in the ranks. Even the men getting the medals saw this as an arbitrary thing designed to boost morale in a war that had no meaning. We were too tired to care. The memory of our dead lying outside the wire, waiting to be hauled away like trash, even the memory of the enemy dead was too repulsive. Besides, infantrymen tend not to be fond of generals anyway. Acts of heroism, and there were many, were performed for each other, not them.

All I remember, as Devil Six worked his way through the ranks of Mike Division toward me, is those two silver stars on his peaked cap. I was certain he was going to say something to me, as I had told him to fuck off and disobeyed his direct order. And now of course I was in an even more awkward position, having just placed myself on the brink of resigning my commission entirely. But not a word passed between me and Devil Six. The two silver stars hovered briefly in front of me, but there was no meeting of eyes, although certainly he knew exactly who I was and what I had failed to do. It was gracious of him; of course he knew far more about combat and what it does to men than I did at the time. All I felt was my own sense of failure under the glint of two-star authority, and I suppose he knew that, too. Paolino was awarded a silver star for heroism. Overton got a bronze star, so did Dennis, even though he hadn't done much that time. I had put him in for it because of all the other stuff he had done for so long and so well, without any reward at all. Poovy and a couple of other guys got Purple Hearts. Then Devil Six got back into his helicopter and was gone.

I had sunk mighty low since those days at Fort Polk when I had been nominated as general's aide. But stress was taking a heavy toll on all of us; I certainly wasn't the only one. There were guys collapsing from exhaustion. There were guys seeing things or hearing things that weren't there. Then one morning Doc Behm just couldn't get up. He was stuck lying on his side, his back muscles locked in painful spasms. He had been at my side all along, except during the firefight when I thought he was dead. He was always first to jump up and risk his own life when somebody called: "Medic." Now he had to be rolled onto a stretcher and medevaced out himself. I never saw him again.

I could not possibly leave my platoon in such dire straits now. Perhaps in a few weeks, when we had gotten some replacements, when we were out of the woods. Perhaps then. Meanwhile, my mind drifted aimlessly while we walked, like I was drugged. For a while I really believed it would be over for me soon, that I would find myself exiled to a position in some rear area, like my father was, that I would be appointed Fire Safety Compliance Officer for the 199th Replacement Depot in Long Binh, or something like that. Hot meals, clean clothes, blow jobs from *mamasans* and an enormous stigma. I think about that while humping up and down the hills, crouching at the sound of gunfire up ahead, trying to keep a cigarette going through the streams of sweat on my face. Or how about Mike Six the rebel, the war protester who lies down in front of an M-48 tank in order to bring the world's attention to this inhumanity. I already knew enough about the armor outfit not to want to try that; they wouldn't even notice.

Get up, get down. Move ahead, stop. Sometimes I would start to fall asleep while walking; the suspenders of the man in front of me turned into green serpents, writhing on his back. I lurch forward to warn him, then stumble back into consciousness. Cool hiss of the radio, and somewhere overhead the constant pulse of helicopters. On Saipan, on beautiful Saipan with the puffs of Pacific clouds overhead, with Mount Topotchau overlooking the serene harbor and rolling sugar cane fields, on Saipan when the order to stand up and assault was given to the Japanese, it was obeyed to a man, good sons all. So far as I know, nobody told the general to fuck off. In the middle of the night, they all stood up. Even the ambulatory wounded stood up, and hobbled from the aid stations on crutches to join what would become the greatest banzai charge in history. Singing, screaming, blowing bizarre bugle calls, sounding "like New Year's Eve at the zoo," the good sons of Japan ran forward into the American machine guns and certain death with such momentum that it carried them through the lines of defense and into the ranks of terrified clerks and cooks and truck drivers before the last of them was killed. And when at last the sun rose, and fantastic cloud shadows moved across the land once again, and bulldozers were put to work pushing the dead sons of Japan into windrows and then burying them instead of building runways, the Americans heard the screaming again and paused to witness, not another banzai charge, but civilians pouring out of their hiding places amid the cliff caves, whole families running toward the seaside Morubi Bluffs, not just hundreds, but thousands, hurling their own children off the cliffs first, to drop three hundred feet to the rocks and surging seas below, then leaping to their deaths themselves, mothers and daughters, fathers and sons. There was nothing the Americans could do but watch and listen, horrified, keeping the sight and sound alive inside forever. Surely this still echoed from the brooding cliffs when my father arrived a year later, resonating like the atomic boom, tainting the placid harbor, the dappled hills. But compassion and humanity lead to strength, not weakness. It was entirely from within that his vision of The Father was gathering strength, preparing to rise from the sea.

It was an enormous explosion somewhere up ahead that had us all down again. Then a heavy machine gun was sweeping back and forth overhead, the rounds sounding like supersonic boxcars, smashing the jungle, raining leaves and branches down upon us. Alpha Company had the point, and it was toward the end of the day. We had been slogging uphill toward the ridge line where the tanks were. We were almost there, and we were looking forward to riding the tanks back to our NDP. But then one of the tanks had hit a mine. When the tank blew up, the men on the other tanks and APCs reacted by firing their heavy machine guns into the woods to the left and right. This was their custom. It was just like a few nights before, when I had thrown the hand grenades. So we just lay there while those fifties chopped up the woods. A distinct lack of communication. Luckily, they seemed still to be bad shots, firing high again. Pretty soon, with lots of yelling, the word got through and the shooting stopped.

We were told to take the point for Alpha Company, which puzzled me because we only had a few hundred meters left to go. Then as we began to move ahead I saw that Alpha Company had not been so lucky after all. In a small clearing four soul brothers were sitting with the headless corpse of their black buddy. One of them was cradling the corpse in his arms and rocking back and forth. They were all wailing with grief, not caring about anything else, just sitting there and rocking and crying in a small clearing spattered with blood and brain tissue. Now, as I watch the resurgence of racism, as the gap between haves and have nots widens, I will always remember those four men and most of a fifth, and their sacrifice which was so disproportionate, and their loss, which was only beginning.

Defiant Six was in the clearing, too, and our eyes met again. He was crying. It was all you could do. And those soul brothers had been in Alpha's mortar platoon. Normally they wouldn't be going out on sweeps with us, but somebody had decided they needed the exercise or something. So I looked at Defiant Six and this time he was the one to turn away, and for the first time I began to understand his pain, his anguish, his burden, and knew that I was not alone.

We climbed the last hundred meters to the armored column. Infantrymen and tankers were no longer on speaking terms. There were even violent threats. We passed the blown up tank. Those were really big mines the VC were using, and the tank lay in the blast crater like a giant dead beetle, an eviscerated shell with four dead men inside. Spam in a can. I very seldom saw armor fight effectively in Vietnam. Their main function seemed to be as targets for mines and rockets, and mostly they just fucked up or blew up.

The next morning we abandoned the battalion NDP, filled the holes, burned the garbage, and dispersed into three smaller company-size NDPs nearby, casting a finer net across the jungle while the doubly disgraced armor unit slunk and clanked away. Bravo Company took the most easterly position, in another open field. It was nice to be on our own again, although we felt more vulnerable. And we had to dig in again, spending most of the day going down shoulder deep in the firm sandy soil. It was the easiest digging I have ever encountered anywhere: the shovel would sink in like a warm knife in butter, yet the sides of the hole held their shape perfectly. I like to imagine the labyrinthine Viet Cong tunnels that surely existed all around and below us. Digging must have been a pleasure for them, as it was a pleasure for me to share the task with my men, and it helped me to keep my mind off the fact that I was to lead an ambush again at dusk.

By late afternoon we were pretty well dug in, and were just touching up the positions with transplanted shrubs and grass as camouflage. It was very quiet without the armor, except when Oscar Five fired a few rounds from his mortar emplacements to settle the base plates into the loose soil. Oscar Five, now there was a character; red hair and handlebar moustache, ruddy complexion and ready grin. Oscar Five had joined the Marine Reserves in order to beat the draft, only to have his unit called up and sent to Vietnam. After that, he was so disgusted with both Vietnam and the Marines, he managed to wangle a transfer to an Army Reserve unit to complete his obligation. But then that unit got called up and sent to Vietnam, and somehow he ended up with us. He had hated the war all along, really hated it, and led one of the best mortar sections in the country. There should have been an officer in charge, but we didn't have enough to go around so Oscar Five, Sergeant Owens, was really doing a six's job and was one of us. Now his boys, mostly black or Hispanic, were digging in, settling base plates, and rechecking their aiming stakes and sight levels.

With the tableau of the headless man fresh in my mind, I was beginning to know that I couldn't trust anyone else to lead my platoon. What if my replacement were deadly incompetent, or worse, deadly ambitious? I was responsible for the lives of my men, above anything else, and the idea of abdication began to seem pretty selfish. I could keep my men from stumbling into an ambush. I could keep them from being hit by friendly fire. I just had to learn how to control my own fear and self-doubt. We had to hang together, the twelve of us. Now Behm was gone. Paolino had been transferred to November. But Poovy was back, and a sergeant from Quan Loi had been brought in to lend a hand. I can't remember his name, but I'm sure he hasn't forgotten the night which lay ahead of us.

Our ambush was to go out extra far, six kilometers, deep into new territory on the first night. I was extra careful to pre-plan mortar fires with Oscar Five, plotting them at four coordinates, surrounding our ambush site in a box. This way, if there was trouble, I could make a quick adjustment from one of the pre-planned fires, and Oscar Five, having already calculated charge, deflection and elevation, would quickly deliver. And, knowing how dense the jungle was, I also resolved to leave earlier than usual. I was learning. It was like when I first took my children canoeing. I made plenty of sandwiches. I buckled up their life jackets. I listened to the weather forecasts, watched the skies, and reassured them when we drifted over the dark places.

The sun was still shining brightly when we left the perimeter, left the relative safety and companionship, and headed across about two hundred meters of grasslands toward brush land, then thickening jungle beyond. I guess all of us were a little spaced and woozy with fear. It seemed suicidal to go this deep into the jungle, especially on the first night in a new place. Dennis's squad, which was only four men including himself, had the lead. They were the best at navigation, and again Redfeather was walking point. Millhouse, who was one of the newer men but was already proving to be real sharp, was walking behind Redfeather with a compass. Dennis and I were both counting paces and checking azimuths.

We had only gone a few hundred meters into the brush when Redfeather opened up with his M-16 and all of us hit the dirt. Then there was silence. I crawled up to Dennis and Millhouse; I couldn't believe it, we had only gone a few hundred meters and already we had contact. This patrol was off to a bad start. The guys back at the NDP heard the firing too, and were calling on the radio to see what was up. Dennis said Redfeather had seen some VC, but it didn't seem right somehow. At any rate, they seemed to have fled, so we spent some time cloverleafing around in the brush. Noonan, who was second in command of the first squad, showed up with a red smear on his hand which he said was a blood trail he had found. I looked hard at the smear. It looked too thin and watery to be blood. Then I spent a lot of time looking all around myself, but couldn't find anything that could be followed. Weeks later, when we were all feeling mellow, Noonan confessed that the red stuff was sap from a bush Redfeather had wasted, but all I knew at the time was that the guys in the squad were acting kind of secretive.

I reached the point where it seemed better not to ask any more questions. I radioed back that we had found a possible blood trail, but were continuing on to our ambush site. I did not yet know the extent to which the guys were covering for Redfeather. They knew him very well, and whatever it was that was taking place inside of him, they had seen it before and were accustomed to handling it this way. They reassured me that everything was fine, but we had lost a lot of valuable time. The sun was down now, and we were in some very thick vegetation, cutting our way through as quietly as we could. I was determined to succeed at reaching our ambush site. I wanted to redeem myself as a platoon leader, and we had to reach the safety of that grid of pre-planned mortar fires. Oscar Five's mortars were the only fire support within range of us, since we were beyond the reach of any artillery batteries.

I can see that place in the jungle now as clearly as though it was yesterday, with big wet leaves in my face, but with breaks in the canopy overhead here and there so that I could also see the darkening sky. We moved in a tighter column than usual because the growth was so thick, weaving from the direct course in the thickest places. One of the machine gunners was in front of me, his "pig" slung at his side with eight or ten rounds in the feed. He was just two or three paces ahead, but still he would disappear now and then behind the vegetation and gathering gloom. Redfeather still had the point, and Dennis, following right behind, increasingly had his hands full.

Something was wrong with the incredible sensory apparatus which Redfeather carried with him, and which saved us so many other times. It was as though a part of him had dropped down to another frequency, tuned to a strange and distant rhythm. He kept banking off to the left, toward a mysterious land in the Sioux imagination, obeying the magnetism of a drumbeat only he could hear. Dennis and the other guys in the squad had been hoping the problem would correct itself; it usually did, but not this time. Redfeather kept plunging ahead, going faster, pulling the rest of us along behind. The realization that something was terribly wrong broke over me like a tidal wave. Millhouse, Dennis and Noonan were now struggling just to keep him in sight, while the rest of us desperately tried to keep up. Finally they were able to get him to stop, and I could bring Overton's squad up to take point, but by then it was too late. In the gathering gloom I could see a big hill looming up ahead where there wasn't supposed to be a hill at all. For the first time in my life, I was truly lost in the woods.

I gathered my platoon close around me, like my own children. I told them what the situation was, where I thought we were, and how we had gotten there. I could hardly even whisper, it looked so bad. I figured we were about two kilometers from our ambush site, uncertain of our real location, with one guy having some sort of nervous breakdown and the rest of us pretty close to it. I explained that we had to go fast and as far as we could in another direction so that we could get back under the protective umbrella of those mortars. The only way to navigate now with the light failing was by contour lines, which is the worst and most unreliable way, crossing slopes and hoping for landmarks. I had Overton cut an easterly course along the foot of the hillside ahead. We were in deep trouble, foundering in the jungle, and it was getting dark so fast, a lot faster than usual, as though somebody was just gradually fading us out. It was hard to breathe, too, the air was so thick and wet. This could only come to a bad end; nobody could come to help us, we didn't know where we were. It was hopeless. We were making too much noise, in danger of getting separated. We had only gone about half a kilometer on our new course when it became clear that it was too dark to move any farther. So we did what we had done before, made a tight circle. Put out the claymores. Huddled together for the night. Prayed for dawn.

The undergrowth was very thick in this place we had stumbled into. You could lie down only by gently pushing aside the leaves and branches and then slowly, quietly squatting lower and making a nest for yourself. Of course everyone was too scared even to think about sleeping. I listened while my platoon settled in, pushing aside vegetation with a sound as soft as breathing. It took about half an hour before everyone had stopped moving, and then we just listened intently. For a while it was quiet, but then the soft, whispery shifting sounds began again. They began to our front, in the direction we had been moving, but soon the soft, whispery shifting sounds were all around us. One after another, the men on my left and right reached out to touch me, pushing their fingers into my side as a signal that they had movement in front. I could hear it myself, sometimes to the left, sometimes to the right. It reminded me of being in the hardwood forest at home in the winter at night, when there was no snow and the forest floor was littered with crisp fallen leaves. Under the leaves everywhere was the rustle of rodents, mice, shrews, voles. For a while I desperately clung to the ridiculous hope that we had set up in a part of the jungle that happened to be infested with rodents.

The platoon sergeant started yanking on my ankle from behind. The rodents were very close, perhaps just fifteen meters away. They were almost close enough to turn our claymores around so that they faced us, an old rodent trick. Then, if we decide to pop the claymores, we blow ourselves up. We were obviously being probed, felt out, sized up. They were getting a lot bolder, too. It was possible to track their movement as they went around us in the brush. Then we began to hear the whispers, real whispers this time. Whispers in Vietnamese. Rodents don't speak Vietnamese.

The platoon sergeant almost yanked my leg off. I was supposed to do something. I knew, we all knew, that we had only a few minutes left before the first grenades would come tumbling in among us, so I held down the talk button on my handset, sending one long hiss of squelch noise back to the NDP. When they answered, I desperately whispered our predicament into the radio, knowing full well that if I could hear the Vietnamese whispering, they could surely hear me. They would also know that I was the platoon leader, and that I was in the middle. They would have the solid fix on us that they had been searching for in this terrifying stew of men and vegetation. I called for Oscar Five to shoot a round on one of the pre-planned fires.

"Shot, over," came his quick, crisp response. I waited while the slender round, shaped like a large soda bottle, hurtled upward, arched over in a perfect parabola, and started plunging downward again.

I could barely hear the explosion far off in the jungle. It was much farther than I had hoped, like a distant sneeze, even allowing for the muffling effect of the dense, wet vegetation. Bad news; there was not much time left for us at all. The VC would be listening to my voice intently. Perhaps they smiled when they, too, heard that hopelessly distant crash of one mortar round.

"Drop two thousand," I whispered again, adjusting on an azimuth from Oscar Five's position, since I didn't know my own.

There was a moment of silence on the other end while they puzzled over such an enormous adjustment. Oscar Five, Bravo Six, and a growing circle of others crouched around the radio back at the NDP. Oscar Five's voice came back; "Reaffirm, Mike Six, you want drop two thousand."

I reaffirmed and added that we had gooks up the yin-yang and they better hurry up.

For a while the jungle fell mysteriously silent. Back at the NDP Oscar Five's crews quickly calculated the new data on their plotting boards, readjusted the sights of their mortars on the dimly lit aiming stakes, shifted the bipod legs, turned the elevation and deflection knobs, and removed the right number of charge bags from the round. Everyone knew that with an adjustment that big there was a good chance this next round would land right on top of our own position, but there wasn't any time to slowly creep the mortar fire closer. No time at all. Finally it all came down to that one slender but weighty round, with bright aluminum fins and an olive drab body, that an assistant gunner held in his hands. If it, too, landed fairly far away, the VC would instantly know that I was adjusting fire toward them, that I wasn't doing well at it at all, and that they should attack quickly. Of course, if it landed on top of us it would all be over anyway, Mike Six having blown himself and the others to pieces in the consummate fuckup of his short-lived career. When the data had been recomputed and everything was ready, the assistant gunner held the round over the open end of the mortar tube and whispered, "Hanging."

"Fire," said Oscar Five, and the assistant gunner let the round go. It slid down the tube with a hollow metallic whoosh, encountered the firing pin protruding from the bottom of the tube, and came shooting out the muzzle ahead of a blue flame with a chest-pounding, ground-shaking thump. "Shot, over," said Oscar Five on the radio. Now it was decided, the wheel of fortune spun, everything depended upon that slender, tear-shaped piece of steel and TNT. My men knew it, too. They knew their lives depended upon what happened in the next few moments. And, I suppose, so did the VC.

The fates arrived with a blue lightning flash and white noise, a punch in the chest and sinus cavities, and bright streaks of shrapnel overhead. It took a moment to realize we weren't hit. The round had landed just seventy-five meters away. Bingo. I knew where we were. Now about those VC . . .

Right fifty, fire for effect," I said. Again, the guys back at the NDP thought I was crazy, but they heard the terror in my whispering voice and pretty soon nine rounds came raining down in rapid succession, even closer, just in front, shattering the night. We were as low as we could get, wriggling into the moldy jungle floor while shrapnel whizzed by just overhead.

"Drop one hundred, right fifty, fire for effect."

Nine more rounds took flight. The rest of the company was on its feet back at the NDP, watching the pink and blue muzzle flashes of the mortars or crowding close to a radio. The mortar platoon was really working up a sweat shooting for us; I like to think of their black bodies glistening as they saved our white asses. I put those nine rounds on the other side of our circle, right behind us. I had our location nailed down to within twenty-five meters, and Oscar's boys were shooting beautifully. If I had stuck my hand up, it probably would have been hit by shrapnel. Branches and clods of earth were raining down upon us. Now I was able to walk the rounds right around our circle.

"Add fifty, left fifty, fire for effect."

Later, some of the guys in my platoon told me they thought I was killing them. They had never experienced mortar fire that close. Neither had I, of course, but at least I was in control. All they could do was squirm in the dirt and think of home. After thirty rounds I quit for a while. The air was thick with smoke. Reaching out to touch the men beside us, we soon realized that everybody was OK. There was a ripple of whispered expletives, all good solid Anglo-Saxon. Otherwise the jungle was silent. Almost totally silent.

There was a soft noise to the front, almost like a breathing sound, a sucking sound, like somebody with asthma.

"Add fifty, left fifty, fire for effect."

Nine more rounds, no more noise. We lay there for about half an hour and there was total silence. Then the noises came back again, to our front, in the direction we had been moving when we had decided to stop. With our position assured and the mortar crews standing by, I could afford the luxury of just listening for a while. These were not the sneaky whispering twig-snapping noises of before. These were the noises of men in deep shit. These were slumping, dragging, scuffling noises.

"Add fifty, fire for effect."

Again, the hot blue flashes and hammer blows of sound. Then silence, and the sweet smell of high explosive smoke. Another smell, too, which I remembered from our previous firefight, the slaughteryard smell. I wished I could put some artillery in there, too. Oscar Five was dipping deep into his reserve of ammunition, and my fear was replaced with anger at those who had made me so afraid.

It was a little after midnight. There was no more noise at all, nothing. Then, at about two in the morning, the jungle bugs and frogs and lizards began to sing. From all around us came the sweet trilling and peeping and twanging, and we knew that the enemy had gone. The songs rose and fell like waves on a beach, building to crescendos, tapering off, coming back again. It was the most beautiful music I had ever heard. I listened for two hours. Then I could see the silhouettes of shattered tree tops against the sky to the east. As the music gradually subsided, I began to be able to see us, too, for the first time since we had fallen into this black hole. Then the dawn birds were starting to call out. A new kind of music. Colors came back. Slowly, one by one, we stood up and urinated.

We rolled up the claymore mines, moved ahead about twenty-five meters, and found ourselves in a Viet Cong base camp. It was just the sort of thing the whole battalion had been searching for over the past week. It was platoon-size, with eight or ten bunkers connected by trenches or tunnels. All the undergrowth had been cleared away and the ground was polished smooth by activity. So we had set up for the night on the edge of a base camp. The carefully cleared firing lanes led directly toward our ambush position. If we had just stumbled forward a few more meters, they would have taken us. It would have been terrible, the end. Instead, they had heard us coming, waited, and then puzzled over why we had stopped. This, then, was an even greater stroke of luck than the mortar adjustment. Maybe Redfeather had been tuned to the right frequency after all. Maybe it was all good medicine, with distant drums sending him veering off to the left.

A lot of mortar rounds had landed right in the base camp, blowing shallow holes and leaving their aluminum fins lying all around. There was clothing, too, and various papers scattered about. There were also quite a few loose hand grenades, perhaps the ones intended for us. Of course the thick-roofed bunkers were impervious to the mortar rounds, but not everyone had been in the bunkers. There were no bodies, but there was blood, big, unsurvivable coagulated pools of blood, and thinner drag marks smeared with blood.

We couldn't stay. Recon was already on its way to the site and we were ordered back in. I protested that this was our fucking base camp. We wanted to stay, check out the bunkers and cloverleaf for bodies after all that we had been through, but the answer was "No." So we came back, cursing that Recon always got to have all the fun.

Everything was different after that. I still felt inadequate, I still felt the accusing stare of the executive officer whenever I met him, we were never given a body count and no medals were handed out. What had happened that night was something only the twelve of us really knew about, and it wasn't worth trying to explain. But we were bonded together inseparably, and from then on, everything was different.

⟡ VII ⟡

THERE WERE TIMES, later in my life, when I felt surrounded by enemies. There were times, like when I found out that my firstborn son had cystic fibrosis just as my cousins had, like when I felt that my first wife was tunneling beneath my positions just as the Viet Cong had, that I felt lost in the woods. Echoes of the darkness would return. In my marriage, which I had entered into as though trying to save a drowning person, and then was being pulled under myself, in the disease which was stalking again, my position seemed untenable at times, yet it was different from before. There was an unfailing nugget inside of me, good medicine, and there was the river which didn't care. This was something my father could never understand, in his loneliness, and that I could never share with him. I would gather my sons, I would gather my maps and grease pencils. I would mark our course and checkpoints, and off to the river we would go: gliding, splashing, finding hidden pathways, claiming beachheads, and establishing a perimeter for the night, and at last, dusk would be a time of joy instead of terror.

"Is this what Vietnam was like?"

Each of my three sons has asked me that at one time or another on the river, and I would reply, "Yes, kind of," trying to give what I could to them without the support of mortars. It is the closeness, the love, more than the river, more than the head-high thickets of ostrich ferns and silver maples arching overhead that makes it kind of like Vietnam.

I often fly over the river these days in connection with my work, sometimes in a helicopter with a video camera mounted in the nose instead of machine guns, sometimes doing a fixed-wing aerial recon.

The woods and the river wheel beneath me, and I look in the shadows for campsites, base camps, telltale footpaths. Later I may return on foot, feeling at one with the woods and the river and Mike Division, maps and grease pencils still in hand. This too is mine, along with the sons and the love.

The woods over there were so different. They never belonged to us; we always just took the clearings, and then tried to make the clearings bigger with our defoliants, our B-52s and the Rome plow. As the war evolved, from little police-like raids to division-size sweeps, so did our means of dealing with the woods, and the Rome plow was to be the ultimate weapon. It was named after the place where it was invented, Rome, Georgia, and all it is really is just a big D-9 Caterpillar bulldozer with a pointed, hardened steel "stinger" securely welded to one corner of the dozer blade, and a very strong overhead cage to protect the operator. The stinger made it a lot easier to tip big trees over, by first impaling them and either splitting them or lifting them. The Rome plow was going to win the war for us.

In the eastern parts of the Iron Triangle, near where we were, there were battalions of Rome plows in echelon formations flattening mile after mile of woods, day after day. It was something to see from the air; like battalions of tornadoes had just passed through leaving nothing but a shattered tangle of mud and tree trunks and root masses. It was one of the stupidest acts of the war, but at the time was highly regarded, one more light at the end of the tunnel. To Mike Division, it was a bad joke. Imagine chasing after Viet Cong with a bulldozer. And imagine, upon hearing the bulldozers coming, how easy it was to put mines in their paths, either big ones buried in the soil, or little ones hanging in the trees. The fact that the engineers who ran the bulldozers were taking such high casualties was seen as a sign of success. "Boy, Charlie sure is mad now," was what one would hear. "We must really be hurting him."

Forty Rome plows were hard at work in our area of operations, being resupplied along a convoy route which grew longer and longer every day. The daily losses were averaging a couple of Rome plows and a couple of tanks or trucks on the convoy route, plus a dozen men. This, then, was a certain sign of success given the mood of the times, but nonetheless it was felt that an additional battalion of ground troops would help. So not long after our night of mortars by the base camp, we abandoned the Ho Bo Woods, gave those woods back to the termites and fire ants and main force units of Viet Cong and North Vietnamese, and got lifted out to the Rome Plow Shitpile.

It was pouring rain on the day we arrived. The helicopters couldn't land because of all the wreckage left by the Rome plows, couldn't even get close. They had to hover six or eight feet up because of the shattered limbs and root masses sticking up in the air. So we jumped into the tangle of logs and muck, almost got pushed out because the VC in the nearby unplowed wood line loved to shoot at hovering helicopters. There were a lot of sprained ankles and barked shins among us; I have a knee which has never been quite the same since that day, having landed upon a log slick with rain and mud. But, like the others, as long as I could still walk, I did. Then we had to start digging in. That is the policy under the best of circumstances, and an imminent ground attack or mortar attack was touted as a strong possibility here.

Digging in was all but impossible, but we did the best we could in the pouring rain. The ground was covered everywhere with a mat of logs and branches, all interwoven and compacted, three to five feet thick and mixed with gummy gray clay. Surely, America had triumphed over the woods at last, and created a place that was impossible for anyone to hide in. Now, we were trying to hide in it, while the Viet Cong watched from the dark woods just meters away on both sides of the swath. We didn't have any chain saws. All we had were a couple of flimsy folding hand saws like the ones in an L. L. Bean catalog, perfect around the campfire but inappropriate for a combat unit on jungle operations. This was the first glimmer of an awareness dawning over me, an awareness that nobody in the rear really gave a damn about us. The sergeants back at Quan Loi cared, our own supply staff cared, but it seemed as though a terrible corruption and indolence had set in among the thousands of men between Quan Loi and Saigon that was as impenetrable as the jungle itself.

On into the night we worked while the rain continued to fall, lifting out logs, taking out a few shovels full of clay, uncovering more logs. We worked on our CP group hole for two hours, got two feet down, and discovered a log too enormous to cope with. So we moved to another spot, dug for three hours, and finally got a hole that was three feet deep and promptly filled with water. Where were the chain saws? I never found out, but it became a cause for me for months afterward. I hounded the supply officers, the engineers. Here we are, fighting in a jungle. Why can't we get chain saws? I finally got some, lowered by helicopter so I could clear an LZ toward the end of my tour. There were three of them and none of them worked.

As my own personal terror had begun to subside into something that was more manageable, it was the anger that slowly grew. This anger, like the steady rain, focused upon chain saws, and the "Rear Echelon Mother Fuckers," (REMFS), who didn't care about us. It focused upon the French and their rubber trees. It focused upon the Viet Cong, who had made me so afraid. We were a platoon, a battalion, an army of angry men. Such is the stuff that wars are made of. My father suffered the anger of his father as he wallowed across the Pacific toward war. Male anger rises like the clouds, malevolently, cruising above the seascape, spitting lightning. The ship he was assigned to, in the resurrection of his career, was as noncombative as you can get: it was an LSD, a landing ship dock, designed as a floating repair facility for the thousands of beachhead-bound landing craft. The largest armada ever assembled by mankind was slowly working its way across the Pacific, yet often my father's ship seemed entirely alone with the sea and sky and clouds billowing overhead, alone with the anger. But then something entirely unexpected happened. A lone silver bomber took off from Tinian, the little island between Guam and Saipan, and six hours later a cloud billowed higher than any cloud had before, rising forty thousand feet into the early morning sky over Hiroshima, and by the time my father's ship reached Saipan the war was over.

There was no such resurrection for us. There was just the rain and the mud and the anger in the Rome Plow Shitpile. It was amazingly easy to sleep on a pile of logs in the pouring rain that night. All you had to do was sit down and sure enough, you were out like a light in a minute or two. With morning, the rain had stopped, and we went out to sweep the resupply road for mines. We had gotten only a few hundred meters from the NDP when we started seeing the fresh VC footprints in the wet clay. They really had been all around us the night before. They were wearing what we called "Ho Chi Minh freedom sandals," made out of old automobile tires. Pretty resourceful, those VC, and the funny part was that you could see the different tread patterns in the footprints, and identify the individual VC that way. This appeared to be a team of four or five very skilled sappers, and over the days that followed we became quite familiar with their nightly activities. "There goes Firestone Freddy again, with his friend Michelin Mike." For the first time, they emerged as personalities, and having spent the night of mortars so close to them, I was now fascinated and wanted to know more. It was getting personal. And I was feeling stronger, just as Mike Division was in fact getting stronger again with fourteen, then sixteen, then twenty men. The pipeline of replacements was finally catching up with the pipeline of dead and wounded going the other way. We assimilated the new guys, made them part of the team as best we could. And we were learning to live with the woods, while the clouds billowed overhead.

This was something my father never knew. Day after day, his ship lay at anchor in Tanapag harbor. Day after day, the clouds drifted over the shattered ruins of the sugar mill, the rolling sugar cane fields, shell-pocked Mount Tapotchau and the Morubi Bluffs. It had been a year since the landings and the banzai charge and the mass suicides, plenty of time for the wreckage of war to rust, for flesh to be stripped from the bone. Silence was what spoke the loudest now on Saipan.

As his only child, I was taking my first steps in a home he did not want to return to, yet there was nothing for him to do but stare at the sea and the clouds. The war had ended with such awful suddenness that not everybody could go home at once. The officers around my father were allowed passage back based upon the number of "points" they had accumulated. Points were awarded for time in combat, and my father had none. Slowly, slowly, as the days in Tanapag harbor rolled past, as the ship swung at her anchor gathering seaweeds on her hull, as the sea birds screamed and wheeled below the endless clouds, all the senior officers went home and my father, shamed and emasculated, was finally given the ship's command. In a sense, our paths converged for a moment, his command and mine, and in a sense we were both at war, but his war was by then entirely inner. I have asked myself what fatherhood means, what a father should be, and my answer is "loyal and strong." Given these, all else will follow; but my father could be neither, as his father had been disloyal to him.

My father was going insane again while we swept the road for mines. I didn't find out for another year that his demons had returned, had chased him back to the state hospital while we were sweeping down the road every morning; one squad with minesweepers going down the road itself looking for the innocuous-seeming little detonators that barely protruded from the road surface, and the other squads sweeping through the bushes and bulldozed wreckage on both sides. A hundred meters back from the road the jungle still stood, somber and perfectly intact, waiting, while the Rome plows worked elsewhere, stupid beasts, day after endless day.

The sun came out. Moisture was drawn from the jungle and wet clay, and rose invisibly to form clouds again. We found plenty of mines, but we didn't always find all of them. The mine detectors didn't work very well because the only part of the mine that was metal was the detonator, and it was just the size of a cigarette butt. The detonator was placed close to one side of the road, in the path of wheels or tracks, while the body of the mine itself was buried three feet away in the center of the road, where it would do the most damage. These mines used seventy pounds of TNT, which had been carefully heated and poured from unexploded American bombs. For three days in a row, our battalion declared the road safe for traffic at about eleven in the morning, and started back toward the NDP for some chow and rest. For three days in a row we had almost gotten there when an enormous BOOM would resound through the jungle. We would just look at each other and shrug our shoulders.

It was amazing to see how skilled these VC were, with a focused determination exceeding even that of the Japanese on Saipan. This road was made of laterite clay, compacted until it was like concrete. Yet they managed to dig their mines in every night and leave no trace, not even a teaspoon of dirt appearing out of place, while their footprints were everywhere as part of the ruse, boldly marching up and down, back and forth in the dark, virtually retracing the steps we had taken during the day. Feeling challenged, I took to setting up little ambushes at night, just a squad here or there, but the VC were always watching from the wood line because what the Rome plows had really done was to expose us to them. The little footprints would come close during the night. You could see where they then paused, skirted around the ambush, and placed the mine elsewhere. Every day, a couple of more trucks or tanks or Rome plows would blow up. These booms were like the thunder of men's anger, like the storms that developed toward the day's end above Vietnam and Saipan.

Then one evening Defiant Six summoned his officers to his CP and grimly announced to us that there would be a change in policy. He made it clear, too, that the change was ordered by the brigade commander to him. On this operation we were attached to the second brigade, operating out of Lai Khe, not our own brigade, as part of the special

Rome Plow Shitpile detail. And the second brigade commander could not tolerate the high losses due to mines any longer. His solution was to order the platoon leaders to walk in front of everyone else while looking for mines. We were, of course, incredulous as we listened to this. Why were we to blame? It is true that when searching for mines it is common for an infantryman to walk ahead of the men with minesweepers. This is because mines are generally easier to detect visually than magnetically, and the man with the minesweeper is concentrating too much on listening for tones in his headset to really keep an eye out. And it was true that none other than Bravo Six himself had recently demonstrated an amazing ability to locate mines visually in the Ho Bo Woods. He had spotted four or five in a row the way some people can find a four-leaf clover in a lawn without even bending over. It was his thing, but as platoon leaders we had until now escaped the invaluable lessons of locating mines visually. Was this, then, designed to be a quick learning experience for us? Or had the brigade commander decided we needed more motivation?

It was an incredibly stupid, vengeful order, which polarized the junior officers and further inflamed the anger and contempt for authority which was beginning to characterize us. This particular colonel already had a reputation for ruthless ambition combined with deadly ineptitude. I personally felt deeply betrayed. I suppose the colonel must have felt that we had betrayed him. This was so often the case, during this unusual war, a war which had paranoia and delusion as its foundations. When things went poorly the blame had to be laid somewhere. And the growing distrust worked both ways. Every day, there were more potential assassins in the ranks. Strength and loyalty were at odds. In Vietnam, fathers and sons had turned against each other.

In Saipan, below the burning sky, my father's loyalties had long been divided, and it was the strengths that were sapped away. In command in name only, he began to build things with the tons of plywood and steel his ship carried, just as he had done with me. It was how he found shreds of sanity amid the clouds and sea. He put his crew to work more to dispel the demons than the boredom, first erecting shaded porches on the superstructure to defend against the merciless tropical sunshine and downpours. If he had stopped himself there it would have been OK but he couldn't stop. His ship was loaded with stuff for building as well as craftsmen, and clearly they had all been abandoned in the rush to return home from war. Soon the simple porches became ornate verandas. Mansard-roofed towers began to rise, and balconies and gazebos. Even this would have been OK, if not really funny, as brilliant as his finest sketches, a parody on navy life, had he not seen God and felt such surges of anger. I can see him now, the same age as me in my command, staying up far into the tropical night to complete the design specifications, putting the men to work the next day, but it was God that had the last word, as the ultimate father, confiding in His son a special vision which transcended Saipan and the United States Navy and its only Queen Anne Victorian ship and all other fathers, and left my father a senseless casualty, inner lightning lashing out.

There were no visions of God in the Rome Plow Shitpile. There was just the vision of impending and instantaneous death as the other lieutenants and I walked down the road ahead of the minesweepers. It was very scary, something we talked about a lot, and we walked very carefully, sensing full well just how alone we were. The men didn't like it much, either. These mines were big enough to take out a whole bunch of guys besides the platoon leader, and the men would prefer someone with more experience up front, too. Anyway, off we went, not at all happy. Mike Division was sweeping south down the road. There was a platoon leader from Delta Company sweeping north toward us. I knew the platoon leader slightly; Lieutenant Konz had actually come to Vietnam as an officer in the engineers, but he couldn't stand being back in the rear while his fellow officers were going out every day, making incredible sacrifices. So he managed to wangle a transfer, got a platoon in Delta, and had evolved into a highly respected platoon leader.

Of course, the radio man had to walk beside the platoon leader. The radio man always has to be within easy reach, and Wakefield was no happier about this than I was. The life expectancy among both platoon leaders and radio men was short enough anyway; that antenna was more like a lightning rod at times, sure sign of a CP group and thus a prime target. Wakefield and I really liked each other. We'd gotten to be good friends after almost two months of being within arm's reach. As I recall, we were both muttering expletives with every tender step we took. I guess that Konz was doing the same thing with his radio man when, on the second day of this new tactic, his radio man stepped on a detonator. The mine itself was pretty much directly underneath Konz, and he simply vanished in a pinkish brown cloud. His radio man had both legs blown off, and lived for just a few more moments in blinking wonderment.

We returned to our original marching order the next day but it was too late, the damage had already been done. A lot more had been blown to pieces besides a lieutenant and his radio man. Often, over the days that followed, I would come across more pieces of him. It was mostly just vertebrae again, like after the B-52s, just vertebrae and pieces of his 1/28 battalion kerchief. I considered saving them at first, putting them in a plastic bag, but then what would I do with them? A lot of pieces had been sent back already, it wasn't like he was missing or anything. Anyway, it was the kerchief that really got to me, the kerchief that we were so proud of, with the Defiant black lion embroidered upon it. I remember the day Defiant Six handed me mine. My loyalty toward him was unswerving, and I had dismissed any thought of resigning long ago. He, too, had been betrayed by his commander, for the same rules of fatherhood, strength and loyalty, apply to leadership as well, flowing from the top down.

And every night, those same four or five VC would return and plant more mines. Every day, we would find some and not find others. Over the days that followed, I would pause for a moment over additional bone fragments as I noticed them, the fragments already bleaching in the sun and the rain. I'm still looking for the brigade commander.

The success of the Rome plows continued to be punctuated by daily BOOMs. More and more eviscerated tanks and flipped two-and-a-half-ton trucks littered the roadside. Then at last we were rotated out, replaced by Charlie Company, 2nd of the 28th, our sister battalion. Charlie 2/28 has been the subject of several books and documentaries, having been singled out by army public information officers as an exemplary unit early in the war. It was commanded at this time by a Lieutenant Lightle, whom I had first met while he was a Tac officer in officer candidate school, and I was a candidate. Tac officers in OCS were hard-line and scary instructors who made the most rabid drill sergeants look like pansies. But when I ran into him at Quan Loi one day he seemed like a totally different man. He wasn't the snarling tough guy anymore; he was quiet and gentle and very tired, and seemed sorry to see me in Vietnam. He told me the place sucked.

I missed a chance to see him again as we got lifted out; he had his hands full getting his company deployed anyway. Then we went on to do eagle flights for a few days, being lifted from one place to another by helicopter for short patrols. Eagle flights were more fun: lots of rides in the sky, sometimes four or five in a day, and the area we were in, back closer to Di An, wasn't too bad. All we found was about a hundred French army canteens, buried in a shallow grave for some inexplicable reason. We were on one of those leisurely patrols, midmorning, when the word came down that Charlie Company was being hit bad. The slicks came back and lifted us out to the Rome Plow Shitpile as a reaction force.

Within half an hour we were there, jumping into the tangle of mud and logs, with bullets snapping just a few hundred meters up ahead. Once again, the helicopter pilots were in a big hurry to get out, doing pedal turns and zipping away in the same direction they had come, since there was firing up ahead. As was becoming customary, Mike Division was given the point, with the rest of Bravo Company, Defiant Six and his CP group, and a second company of infantry, falling in behind. Apparently Michelin Mike and the tire tread squad had brought in reinforcements. We passed the survivors of Charlie Company sprawled in some bomb craters, waiting for medevacs. I saw Lightle there. He had been shot in both legs and had shrapnel wounds in his chest, but it looked like he would make it. He had remained in command despite his wounds, making sure the rest of his men were OK. This was not so much courage as pure love. Then it was our turn to plunge into those woods.

I put Dennis's squad in front again, because there was no doubt about what lay ahead and Dennis and his men were the best. I don't remember for certain who was walking point for Dennis; it was probably Redfeather again but it may have been Millhouse. Whoever it was, he moved silently and watchfully, the most important man among us at that moment, the man our lives depended upon. He took a step. He froze. He moved his eyes, scanning the jungle. He moved his head. He listened. He took a step ahead. It was like feeling one's way into a darkened room filled with booby traps. We all moved ahead very slowly, just a few meters at a time, doing cloverleafs. We had learned well. Dennis's point and a second man would move ahead about fifty meters. They'd circle around and come back. Then my other two squads would send teams out to the left and right. When all three teams had come back and reported everything clear, Mike Division would move ahead about fifty meters and we'd repeat the process, with about two hundred men following patiently behind.

We had been told by Charlie Company that we were moving against a fortified base camp again, and we knew the VC would be expecting us, having seen the helicopters. Surely they were hoping to inflict the same damage they had earlier in the day. So we were being real careful and nobody was complaining. The point man was doing his cloverleaf, moving through the foliage in slow motion, when he gently parted the leaves and saw four VC sitting on top of a bunker, waiting for us with AK-47s and rocket launchers. But they were looking off in the wrong direction, to their right. Perhaps they had heard a twig snap when one of the other squads did a cloverleaf to the left flank. At any rate, we had them cold and the point man emptied his clip into them.

Boy, were they mad, and there were a lot more than four VC in there. We had been told that it was a company-size unit, and it sure sounded that way when they opened up with an incredible barrage of automatic weapon fire and antitank rockets. But we were all lying flat on the ground by then, and they still didn't know exactly where we were. Everything was going over our heads by a few feet, but now and then a rocket would hit a tree above us and although there isn't much shrapnel from them, Aikens was slightly wounded but mobile. With no wounded down in front, and with their position known but ours pretty much a mystery, we still had them cold.

Wakefield and I were huddled together; I was on the horn. Defiant Six had Tac Air, an air force team of fighter-bombers coming in from Bien Hoa. Dennis's man joined us and said that the base camp was indeed more to our left. We decided to move forward, searching for its flank, feeling it out. Part of my mission was to mark the base camp with a smoke grenade. We got about fifty meters by crawling this time, when another blistering barrage was loosed on us. Again, no serious casualties, but this was a major base camp. No talk of getting on line and assaulting, with AK-47 fire sweeping back and forth and rockets exploding among us. An artillery officer had recently joined our company, George Snow, call sign Niner Two. Over the months to follow we were to become good friends, but this was the first time we had worked together as we began to adjust fire from a nearby battery of 105mm light howitzers. The fire was slow in coming and the first round landed way long, off by five hundred meters. I began to make an adjustment from there when I got the word to pull back. Tac Air was coming up over-head. So I popped a colored smoke grenade as a marker and we withdrew, first on our bellies, then in a crawl, and finally in a crouch as the VC gunfire behind us gradually dribbled to a stop.

We had to pull back a couple of hundred meters because the air force was coming in with heavy stuff for the bunkers. It was kind of difficult to get two hundred men into reverse, and about ten minutes had elapsed since we had first made contact. By this time Defiant Six was beside my position handling the airstrike. This was my first experience with Tac Air close in, and it was quite interesting. An enormous explo-sion suddenly heaved the ground and hit us with a shock wave. Tac Air had arrived; the deafening roar of an after-burner cutting in followed right on the heels of the explosion as a dappled green and brown F-100 pulled out of his dive and climbed back up for another pass. Mean-while, the second F-100 was coming in with more 750- or 1000-pound low-drag iron bombs. What was memorable, besides the fact that the ordnance arrived before we heard the aircraft, was seeing the shock waves ripping through the jungle toward us, green waves, stripping the leaves from the trees. Next came the napalm, once they had blown the canopy open and exposed the bunkers. We could instantly feel the flashes of heat from where we were, several hundred meters back, and orange balls of flame billowed upward. Finally, they made a few passes with their 20mm cannons, strafing any bunkers they could see. The ex-ploding cannon shells beat a strange, arrhythmic tattoo on the ground, then came the haunting, groaning noise of the guns firing 2,000 rounds per minute. This was the way to go against a hardened position. Find it, mark it, pull back and blow it to pieces. Fortunately, I was never again to hear those words, "Get on line and assault," requesting an immedi-ate sacrifice upon the alter of war.

We had to wait another fifteen minutes for the place to cool down before going back in. That was when somebody noticed that Renzel's ass was bleeding. He, too, had taken a couple of fragments in the butt from a rocket, but he had been so excited that he hadn't noticed. I told him he should get a Purple fucking Heart but he shrugged it off, joked that it was probably just hemorrhoids. It actually took a lot of convinc-ing from the medics before he finally accepted the fact that the metal probably would have to come out. He reluctantly allowed himself to be evacuated, and I think he got his Purple Heart despite his protests.

Then we got up and began to move back toward the base camp. I was fully prepared for entrails hanging in the trees and burned corpses on the ground, but there were none. It was a big base camp, fifty bunkers in a circle. The bombs had blown up about a third, but the rest were intact. In the middle of the circle the VC had constructed elaborate chairs and tables out of sticks. Gobs of napalm were still burning here and there. There were no signs of any VC. They had apparently been smart enough to figure out what was coming next after we fired on them, popped smoke and withdrew. They had withdrawn as well, taking with them whatever dead or wounded we may have inflicted. They didn't leave any equipment, either. The only stuff we found lying around was some shattered M-16s and helmets from Charlie Company which the VC had collected as souvenirs. Recon was coming in to check out the bunkers and tunnels before blowing them up. I argued that this was two times in a row now, that we had taken a base camp and Recon got to blow it up, but I got nowhere.

If only I had been able to adjust the artillery faster. If only I had laid down a base of fire, kept them pinned down until just moments before Tac Air came up overhead. If only I had not been so afraid. Although everything had in fact gone well, I again felt like I couldn't face Defiant Six. I again felt the contemptuous glare of his XO. I again felt failure as a son, and saw a body count as the only hope for redemption. This, too, is the stuff wars are made of. Then later that afternoon, the helicopters returned and took us down south again.

It is interesting that such a large base camp had gone unnoticed for weeks and weeks, with the occupants lounging about in their own version of Adirondack furniture while the Rome plows smashed through the jungle nearby. It was just four kilometers from our own Shitpile NDP, and within one kilometer of the cleared swaths. But the mines had kept everyone so preoccupied that there was never any time to search the woods nearby until Charlie 2/28 stumbled upon it. Meanwhile, one might think that we could get a chance to go back to a base camp of our own for a while, at Di An or Lai Khe or Quan Loi. We had been in the field for more than two months without a break. Most of the other battalions got to operate out of the big bases when they were doing eagle flights, returning to hot meals and bunks at night, but not us. Once again, the helicopters dumped us at a muddy NDP, and it wasn't until later that I began to realize why. The people at Di An and Lai Khe and Quan Loi didn't like it when the Black Lions of Cantigny showed up. Our celebrations tended to get out of control.

We went back to the area near Di An again, doing daily sweeps as part of one of the rings of defense of Saigon. We were in the same area where we had been hit so seriously during my first week. One day we came across a cluster bomb pod that an air force jet had accidentally dropped, or had deployed improperly. The pod had a bundle of about twenty long tubes inside. There were hundreds of softball-size cluster bombs inside the tubes. They were supposed to have been expelled over the target. As soon as the bombs leave the tube, little spring-loaded fins pop out and the bombs are armed. The detonators are extremely sensitive. The bombs slowly flutter downward, an avenging flock of angels from hell. Most explode on contact, sending out shrapnel like a claymore. If they don't explode on contact, they explode later if disturbed.

The VC loved to use cluster bombs as mines and booby traps. They had somehow learned how to handle them, and this was what they used to hang in the trees ahead of the Rome plows. So here was a pod filled with hundreds of potential booby traps. The pod had smashed on contact, of course. Bombs still in the tubes were unarmed. Armed ones lay scattered all over the place. Nobody really wanted to wade in among the armed ones so that we could place charges around the rest. Where is Recon when you need them? I decided to do it myself. It was a path toward redemption. It should make a really good explosion.

"Hey, Wakefield," I said, "I want you to take my picture while I set the charges."

"Fuck you, man, I don't want to be anywhere near you."

"Come on, asshole, take my fucking picture. You'll have something to remember me by if this doesn't work out."

"I don't want your stinking guts all over me, man."

I still have the picture.

We crossed and recrossed the same open ridges, day after day, the sun beating down upon us, the clouds rising like bomb explosions. There weren't even any roosters this time. One day we ran out of water. This had happened before of course, and helicopters had dropped bags of fresh water down to us. But on this day the helicopters were unavailable as there was some intense action elsewhere. So we were really burning, ready to drop from heat exhaustion when we finally made it down out of the woods along the ridge and entered some abandoned paddy land. I waded out into the knee-deep tea-colored water. Christ, it stank worse than any paddy water I'd smelled before. But still, I plunged my canteen into the tea-colored water, filled it, dropped two iodine tablets in, shook it for a few seconds, and drank it.

God, it tasted even worse than it smelled. It was the worst, most putrid, tepid brown stuff imaginable. But I drank it.

Then somebody pointed out the corpse floating in the water nearby. It was the head, arms and upper torso of a dead VC. It may have even been one that the helicopters had killed during our big fight, as we were real close to that spot. I didn't puke, I just shivered with disgust, feeling as though I had partaken of some sort of morbid communion. It all made sense somehow. I was fully a soldier now, light-years beyond what my father could even fathom. And my taste for the war was comparable to the taste in my mouth.

I had been in the field nearly ten weeks. It had been longer than that for most of the rest of the battalion. The heat, the fear, the fatigue were unrelenting. Sometimes we had gone for weeks wearing the same slimy fatigues, day and night. When helicopters dropped us bales of fresh clothing it was hard to part with the old stuff. The fatigues had sentimental value.

We went back down close to Saigon again. We were in the suburbs; at times so close we could see the "freedom birds" landing and taking off from Tan Son Nhut. We called the chartered airliners that would take us back "freedom birds." Saigon and Tan Son Nhut were still getting shelled at night, and VC units were still managing attacks inside the city. We walked down French colonial streets which could have been in Europe. The streets were deserted. We walked through suburban backyards, deserted pig farms, graveyards of French soldiers. We picked hot sweet prickly pineapples from hastily deserted gardens and ate them. We found VC campsites along the muddy sloughs of the Song Be river, but they had left an hour before. We didn't know it yet, but the war was changing. The May-June offensive was over. Peace talks had begun in Paris, although in an apocryphal way with debates over the shape of the table. Walter Cronkite reported that only thirty-five percent of polled Americans still supported the war, a complete reversal of public opinion from just the year before. We ran out of cigarettes, and I tried smoking pipe tobacco rolled in toilet paper. Finally a resupply helicopter came out, with cigarettes and cases of soda and a hundred-pound block of ice. And we were told we were going back to Di An, back to the base itself, and not just for the night, but for a good, long stand-down. Everybody went wild.

A Chinook took us back to Di An and we poured out the back still loaded with combat gear, having trashed the back of the ship with mud and litter and cigarette butts. The older NCOs were waiting for us, having been lifted down from Quan Loi, and they led us to the trucks which would take us to a remote corner of the base where the barracks and the beer were waiting. The men were screaming, pounding each other on the backs, yelling epithets at REMFS as we passed by. Beer first, showers could wait. I had to get the taste of that corpse out of my mouth. Cases and cases of beer, all iced down, awaited us in garbage cans. Boy, was it good. Guys were pouring it down, one after another. Guys were pouring it on each other, getting louder and louder, totally out of control. Niner Two started razzing me about the most recent base camp.

"Hey Mike Six, did you know that you blew up a Rome plow?"

"Fuck you, Niner Two, I don't go around blowing up Rome plows."

"You did, man. Engineers say you blew up a Rome plow when we hit that base camp."

"He hit a mine."

"Engineers say it was a 105 round."

"I didn't blow up any fucking Rome plows. VC blow up Rome plows. And anyway, if I did, it was your fucking fault. You're the artillery officer."

"Fuck you, man, you call 'em and I shoot 'em. You blew up a fucking Rome plow."

"Fuck you."

Niner Two and I were getting to be good friends. He was an older guy, too, almost thirty, from Boston, with a wife and kids. I still don't know what happened to the Rome plow.

You couldn't help getting close to people, even though a lot of us tried to fight it off at first, because in a war you never know who will be hit, or what you may have to ask someone to do. But we had all become family by now. For me, and I suspect many others, it was the closest, most loving family we had ever known. The loneliness which is so much a part of being a man, which stalks us men from the cradle to the grave, was gone now. We only wanted to be with each other. This, too, is something my father never knew, in his madness, in his vision of God.

After an hour or so of intense drinking, the company officers drifted away to our own barracks where we could dump our combat gear. Other groups of men, already half-drunk, set off for the Post Exchange to look over the cameras and tape decks. Some began to wander around looking for the legendary steam baths so they could get laid.

And wherever Mike Division encountered some REMFS, they would stare contemptuously at them, rattle the hand grenades and ammo pouches, and try to scare the shit out of them. REMFS were the lowest kind of scum. REMFS had been drinking beer and getting laid all the time we were in the field. REMFS had taken our chain saws. And we liked the way people stared back at us, and backed away. We liked the way they gawked at our filthy uniforms, our strong and deeply tanned arms, our lean faces with the deeply penetrating eyes.

Later, after a short nap on a real cot with a real mattress, the officers of Bravo Company were ready for more beer. First we went back over to the enlisted men's quarters, where the drinking had been going on steadily. Some men lay on their cots playing with the equipment they had just bought at the PX; we were loaded with cash, having been paid regularly in the field, with nothing to spend it on. Other men were playing cards, or just drinking and shouting and pushing each other around. We stayed with them there, missing dinner, drinking steadily for several more hours. Then the officers of Bravo company, minus Bravo Six who had to join the other company sixes, decided it was time to check out the local officers' club and see what kind of assholes we could find there.

This turned out to be a real officers' club, the likes of which we hadn't seen since we had left the states. Not just a tent with ammo crates for furniture, this was a wood building with a wood floor, even a long bar with stools and mirror, some tables out on the floor and a jukebox in the corner. We walked in there stinking and filthy and drunk, and found that a birthday party for the brigade commander was in progress. This was the Third Brigade commander, not ours, and not the one who had made us do the mine walk, but it didn't matter. Colorful crepe hung in garlands around the room. All heads turned to stare at us as we clumped in and ordered drinks. These were clean, well-scrubbed heads. These were fucking REMF officers. And they were high ranking officers, too, all majors and colonels. Primo.

At first we made an effort to behave ourselves. We took a table in a back corner and resumed drinking, November Six, Lima Six, Niner Two and myself. But it got harder and harder to contain our contempt for the rest of the men in the club, like men at a country club, with their clean, starched, and ironed uniforms. Along with everything else, the war had put poison in our veins. We had become so bonded to each other that almost anyone else was the enemy. In the same sort of black-and-white, good and evil judgmental thinking that had gotten us into this war in the first place, Colonel Rew was a good guy, but all other colonels were bad. REMFS were bad. They made us walk on mines and wouldn't give us chain saws. It didn't matter that this was the wrong brigade commander; to us, he and his cronies represented the deadly self-serving ambition that was killing us and the men we loved.

I don't recall the exact order of events perfectly, but at some point we began mixing and moving around the place, trying to engage the REMFS in conversation so that we could then start a fight. I clearly recall Lima Six drinking shots at the bar. These were shots of brandy, which he first set on fire with his Zippo. Then he'd tilt his head back and pour the flaming liquid down his throat. Soon the whole room was filled with the ominous smell of his burning mustache. We got louder and started making abusive remarks.

Several officers of high rank told us that if we could not manage to behave like officers and gentlemen ourselves we'd have to leave. I guess that was the signal some of us were waiting for, like coiled springs. Niner Two politely asked me for my survival knife, which I wore in a sheath strapped to my thigh. I politely handed it to him. Then he jumped up, let out a blood curdling scream, waved the knife around in a circle, and plunged it deep into the lovely polished mahogany of the bar. Having thus gained the attention of everyone, he began to recite the litany of shit we'd been in while the REMFS were in their club, with the rest of us shouting commentaries and encouragement.

Things were on the verge of violence, and there was a feeble effort underway to disarm us. I was trying to talk the bartender into giving me back my survival knife when the military police arrived. They were somewhat self-conscious about invading this officers' sanctuary, and had to be guided over to us by some very relieved majors. Now that he had reinforcements to back him up, the brigade commander whose birthday party we had so utterly devastated finally spoke to us directly. He said we were filthy and disgusting and a discredit to the officer corps. We took it as a compliment. But feeling a bit more contrite ourselves, with an MP holding each of us by the arm, we repeated in softer tones that we had just gotten back from months in the field, we didn't have any clean uniforms, and his fucking party pissed us off. And I think that at this point our anger could have easily turned to tears.

Maybe this brigade commander wasn't so bad after all. He said the MPs were to take us back to our barracks, where we were to take a shower and wait. He told one of the MPs to write down our names, ranks and uniform sizes. He said we would be welcomed back at the club once we had cleaned ourselves up and decided to act respectably.

Well, we sure made a hero's entrance back at the barracks when we showed up under arrest, escorted by MPs. Everyone went wild with cheers and applause. They were all ripped out of their minds, all mayhem had broken loose, and the MPs quickly let us go and disappeared before they were drawn farther still into this unruly mob. We went inside to tell our war stories, and what a mess. Some men had passed out in strange positions, some were throwing up, others were dancing or singing, most were just yelling as loudly as they could. As I stood there, swaying, Redfeather suddenly came at me in a blind rage. He jumped on me and started pounding me with his fists, screaming that I was a fucking white man and he wanted to kill me. A couple of other guys pulled him away and apologized to me on behalf of their crazy Indian friend, who wouldn't remember it the next day. But of course I still remember it with great sadness, Redfeather my friend. He was doing the same thing we had just done at the birthday party, but with much more reason. He was the one I put in front when I suspected trouble ahead. He was the one we depended upon. And he was the cavalry scout in this white man's war, walking point day after day in what we so often called "Indian country."

We went back to our own barracks next door and took wonderful showers. About half an hour later the MP jeep showed up again. In the back were four sets of beautiful, sweet smelling uniforms, complete with rank and even name tags sewn on. Quite an accomplishment at that hour. I'd like to find that colonel again, too, to thank him once more. He understood our anger and our contempt, and was not threatened by such unruly sons.

We returned to the club, apologized, and behaved better. I don't remember the rest of the evening much. I know that I somehow managed to get back to my bunk very late and lit one last cigarette so that I could reflect upon the recent events before retiring. Then, a little while later, the first sergeant noticed that both I and my mattress were on fire. It took two pints of Budweiser to extinguish us, and I slept right through it.

❖ VIII ❖

YEARS LATER, WHEN I WAS ALONE again after ten years of marriage, when I was feeling besieged, with Viet Cong lurking in the woodpile, I went looking for Mike Division again. I needed their tough, raw, funny companionship, needed to know that what had happened was real, not just a dream that I couldn't even articulate inside myself, let alone share with others. The first step was a phone call from a friend when the American hostages were released by Iran. She knew that I was a Vietnam veteran, and she called just to let me know how bad she felt for those of us who had sacrificed so much, and come home to a country that didn't care, while now the country was going wild celebrating with yellow ribbons and ticker tape parades.

The next step was when the Vietnam Memorial was built. I was going to Washington on business now and then, but the first two times I set off toward the memorial I just couldn't go all the way. I was with other people, civilians, making glib talk. I needed to go alone, or with fellow vets, and I still didn't even know any fellow vets. None of us had kept in touch; we had just wanted to put the war behind us. Then I finally made it on the third try, alone, on a sunny day in the early spring. The grass on the mall was green, but the trees were still bare. The Washington Monument loomed high over my left shoulder and from the distance the memorial seemed so small, almost hidden like a VC bunker. But when I got closer and saw the bronze statue, I immediately recognized myself and my men. That was us, looking at the names on the wall. Only then did I feel that I could keep going, find names that are in this book, and go back to the woods feeling stronger than before.

There was a bar in the nearest town to me, a country bar where people who were adrift could gather on Friday nights. I had hoped at first it might be like Di An, with lots of companionship, but it takes a while for people to warm up here in northern Vermont. Gradually, though, I began to find Mike Division there. First there was a guy named Chip Troiano, another Italian guy from New York, like Alfano. He'd been in the infantry, too, in the Eleventh Cavalry, in our same area at the same time. Later he was a door-gunner on a helicopter. Now he was working in a law office. We talked about the war. Billy Joel had just come out with his song, "Goodnight, Saigon." We went out to Chip's Saab, smoked, put the tape in his player and drove around weeping and laughing.

Gradually, other guys began to come forward. They'd been there all along, of course, but in hiding, more or less. There was a helicopter pilot who had no interest in ever flying again. Now he was growing organic carrots. There were several infantrymen who had emigrated to Vermont as I had, trusting themselves and the woods more than the society. Now they were homesteaders, loggers, keeping close to their families of barefoot children and tolerant wives. There were guys who just didn't want to talk about it, walked away, got angry. There were guys who were totally crazy, more like Viet Cong, fighting guerilla wars of their own. There were two fellow infantry officers; one was a local businessman, the other had just done time for armed robbery.

It was pretty clear to Chip and me that we had all been wounded in some way, and some of the wounds had become truly grotesque with time and neglect. Knowing that we never abandoned the wounded, remembering the men who jumped up and ran forward at the cry, "Medic," we formed a veterans' group which met Thursday evenings in a third-floor office on Railroad Street. Other veterans, all across America, had started doing the same thing. It was suddenly OK to talk about it, and everybody really needed to talk. Some of it was very hard to listen to, violent, hateful, abusive. Most of it was simply sad; still limping from old wounds, still grieving for what was lost there.

There is a big bridge in town, big for this town anyway, vaulting over the river and a brace of railroad tracks, and when it was rebuilt that year they decided to rededicate it as the Memorial Bridge, for all our U.S. veterans. A big Veterans' Day parade and dedication ceremony was scheduled, and Chip and I wanted to march in it, but none of the other vets in our group did, and none of the other groups, the VFW and the American Legion, wanted to have anything to do with us. So we marched alone, the two of us, down Main Street, down Eastern Avenue, down Railroad Street to the bridge, leadership and fatherhood out on a limb. It was very cold and windy that day, unusually cold even for northern Vermont, and the only compensation at the time was that we got to stand next to the cheerleaders and the wind kept blowing their skirts up in the air during the endless dedication speeches, which neglected to mention Vietnam.

Under cover of darkness, the veterans continued to meet through that winter, moving aside typewriters and putting the chairs in a circle while the snow sifted down on empty streets outside. Inside, it became the sweating jungle again, or the convoy route to Quang Tri, or the walled city of Hue. You could smell the smoke and dust and diesel fuel. Memories came back, jargon came back, nervous twitches came back. At ten at night the westbound freight would come in and begin shunting boxcars beneath our window. The steel wheel-flanges shrieked as a line of heavily laden boxcars rumbled through the switches, and when they slammed together hard it sounded like artillery.

Then when spring came, and it got warm, everyone just drifted away, back to the woods again, and our group disbanded. How did this happen to us? How could Vietnam have changed us so?

I can see the faces of Mike Division clearly now, as they emerge from the steam baths of Di An. These are such young faces, faces with shit-eating grins, not much older than my own boys are now. They have just gotten a shower, a massage, and a blow job after ten weeks in the field. They are very, very happy.

A lot of guys lost their virginity in Vietnam, both literally and figuratively. It would be the figurative loss which would prove the greater in the long term, but for now give them whores and give them beer, let them wallow in the spoils of manhood, having so abruptly left childhood behind. A year ago these kids might have been trying to whisk a can of beer out of the refrigerator behind their parent's back, or trying to figure out how to unhook a bra with one hand. Especially take the kids who like to test the limits, drive too fast, walk the thin line between life and death, and commit that most revealing act of vandalism, tipping over gravestones. Put them in the infantry. Give them big guns and hard dicks and send them to Mike Division. Start a children's crusade, use them while they are still too young to ask questions, before they are changed by having families, before they have developed much reverence for their own lives or the lives of others. Fly them to Vietnam in a "yellow bird."

Maybe that was the theory, at least, but it was working less well with time. These guys were young, yes, but they were not stupid.

The Tet Offensive was still being touted as a great American victory in Vietnam, but not even the military believed it. The Black Lions were on the outskirts of Saigon so much now because the general staff was terrified that it might happen again, and the Vietnamese army was in hiding. But in the U.S., the offensive had proven to be a catastrophic rout, with everybody deserting the cause, not just Walter Cronkite. The selective service system, which had once been so democratic, was disintegrating into favoritism and racial bias. Young men with the means were usually able to "dodge" the draft. Blacks and Hispanics made up an ever larger proportion of inductees. Secretary of Defense Robert McNamara dropped the minimum intelligence standards in order to induct an additional hundred thousand men.

Those of us already "in country" knew all about the public's turning against the war, and to us it was good news. We wanted to come home. We knew firsthand that the war sucked, and not just the way that all wars suck, but in its own special way. The war had evolved out of naive misconceptions and cynical misrepresentation of facts. Then, in order to keep this truly monstrous machine the U.S. had created going, the very same deceptions and miscalculations which had gotten us into Vietnam in the first place had to be kept up, just like the POW/MIA myth of more recent times, originally invented as a political ploy during peace negotiations, but which then grew out of anyone's control, like Frankenstein's monster. As is always true in such situations, this brought bad leadership to the fore, particularly among senior officers whose careers rested upon a "successful" tour of duty in Vietnam. Those who were unwilling or unable to speak the truth, those who routinely doctored casualty and intelligence reports, for example, were successful.

In this murderous "emperor-has-no-clothes" environment, soldiers made up their own rules, designed their own parameters of good and bad so that they could navigate through the jungle of conflicting experiences. Individual leadership, strength, courage and humanity were more important than in any other war, because there was no guiding vision, no goal, no leadership at the top. In many units with poor leadership it was OK to massacre civilians. This is how My Lai and other atrocities happened. In other units with ambitious or incompetent leadership, the leaders themselves were subject to assassination. Low morale and bad leadership, the inevitable consequences of an ill-conceived war, were spreading like cancer through the ranks. We had come to resemble the most corrupt elements of the country we had come to save. Peace talks, or at least the pretense of peace talks, absolutely had to begin before the United States military disintegrated entirely from within.

And yet another even more ominous thing had happened besides Tet. Martin Luther King had been assassinated that spring. The promise of the Civil Rights Movement, the Great Society, was disintegrating as well. Increasingly, blacks in the military correctly saw themselves as being disproportionately sacrificed in this war which had been conceived by white intellectuals. The Army, which I had loved, which had been in the vanguard of integration, which had rightfully prided itself on its true equality of opportunity, was becoming a hotbed of racism in Vietnam. The army was divided in half, the Chucks and the Souls. We would be together in the field, working well together, respecting each other. But when we came back to Di An for stand-down, the Chucks went one way and the Souls another. And this was becoming much more sinister than a matter of mere cultural differences.

I felt good about who I was in Di An. For the first time, I was beginning to trust myself and my instincts in Vietnam. I was feeling good about being an officer, if not about the war, when on our second or third day there I decided to take a shortcut through one of the few remaining patches of brush on the huge sprawling base. I was moving quickly, but silently, along a sandy path on my way to the movie theater when I nearly stumbled over four black REMFS crouched down together smoking dope. They were as surprised as I was, and for a moment we all just froze. Then in less than a second their expressions changed into something I hadn't seen before, welling up with smouldering anger and resentment. I was not Mike Six anymore. I was a white officer, the enemy, and my combat instincts told me they were thinking about killing me. I quickly turned and continued on my way, thoroughly unnerved.

Our months in the field had been bad, but they had also isolated us, insulated us from some awful truths. In the rear, amid the support troops which made up the overwhelming majority of troops in

Vietnam, the troubles went beyond an inability to provide chain saws. I could understand the anger and resentment to a certain degree myself, having just played a part in trashing the colonel's birthday party. But what I sensed in the bushes that day went much deeper, and spoke in unsettling terms not only of our army, and our war, but also of the society we had created and would have to live with when we got back home. At that moment, more than any other, I realized that not only had we lost the war, but we had also lost ourselves.

Chucks and Souls, grunts and REMFS, there were fights breaking out in Di An every day. We were actually relieved when our stand-down came to an end and we got to be off on our own again. I had expected that we would go back to some hellhole like the Ho Bo Woods, or the Rome Plow Shitpile again. But instead we just went up Highway Thirteen about a dozen clicks, almost exactly where we had been when I had first joined Mike Division. And whereas then we had been in hot pursuit of large bands of VC, now our mission had changed, although we didn't know it yet.

We were assigned to dig our company-size NDP in a circle around a single, stark, bombed-out pagoda which stood conspicuously above the surrounding plains of farm fields. It certainly wasn't the sort of site we would have chosen from a tactical standpoint: the perfect target for mortars or direct-fire weapons. But in terms of creature comforts it was great. Even though more than half the roof had been blown away, you could still find shelter there from the sun and rain. The smooth tile floors were soon swept clear of debris. Bravo Six hung his big rebel flag in the doorway, and made it his CP. Bravo Six didn't mean anything by it, he was from the South. There were rebel flags flying all over Vietnam. The black guys in Oscar platoon just glanced at the flag and looked away.

Our new job was to do what the local Vietnamese troops were supposed to be doing all along, but weren't. This area of open, cultivated land was a major infiltration route, a corridor between the deep wooded sanctuaries to the north and the strategic targets around Saigon. Our job was to intercept the infiltrators. But there was also a sizable civilian population, which made it a difficult situation for us. They were mostly farmers, mostly displaced from their outlying settlements by the fighting which had been going on there for more than twenty years already. They lived in the relative safety and control of central villages, and often had to travel quite far to reach their fields or their markets. They also had to obey curfews, which varied from place to place in inexplicable ways.

We didn't speak Vietnamese, didn't have any interpreters. We didn't know the customs, the local patterns of village life. We didn't understand the structure of the village, the family, or the history. The local Vietnamese soldiers did, of course, and they watched with amusement from their café tables in the local villages when we arrived. At least the time of burning villages was pretty much over. It was no longer customary for Americans to set fire to every thatched roof they saw. And by now we had been told not to throw hand grenades into the underground shelters we so often found inside houses. These were family bomb shelters, where families took refuge whenever danger was near, and I can't imagine how many innocent families died before we figured that out.

It was November's turn to go out on ambush on our first night at the bombed-out pagoda, and they set up on one of the many dirt lanes that connected villages and farm fields. Just before dawn, they heard something coming down the road toward them. They didn't hear voices, or footsteps. What they heard was an ominous creaking, shuffling sound drawing steadily closer. It was so weird that November Six called in to the Defiant CP to describe it. Defiant Six checked with the local Vietnamese authorities, and assured November Six that the curfew was still in effect. The thing, whatever it was, drew steadily closer. It sounded like a team with a heavy crew-served weapon, something like a 20mm gun or recoilless rifle on wheels, being trundled toward Saigon. That was what everyone figured, and November Six was told to pop his ambush when the object was in his kill zone.

In the blinding flash of exploding claymores, some of the men saw for an instant an old man in a heavy wooden cart being drawn by a team of oxen. In the utter blackness that followed, as the blasts of the claymores resounded through the countryside, the wounded oxen began to bellow and thrash about, dragging themselves and the shattered cart off the road and out into an adjacent field. Out of fear, confusion, and the desire to stop that horrible bellowing, November called in a barrage of mortar fire on them. Yet even after nine rounds of 81mm, the oxen were still alive. And they could hear a person crying, too. When a second barrage of mortars came, the crying person got up and moved a little farther away.

Finally it began to get light enough to see a little. They could see the farmer, sitting about a hundred meters away, badly stunned and wounded, wailing for himself and his oxen. The blasts had thrown him quite a distance, but apparently the high, thick wooden sides of the cart had protected him from the shrapnel. They could see the cart, too, on its side, with its load of peanuts strewn about, and the claymored, mortared oxen, still alive and bellowing. Some of the guys began to throw hand grenades at the oxen when they saw the most terrible sight of all. They saw that they were being watched by a crowd of about a hundred people. The local peasants had gathered, utterly silent, a safe distance away.

The guys in November platoon just couldn't stand it. Finally one guy got up with his machine gun and finished off the oxen, while the farmer cried, and the crowd watched. Then, with more light, the platoon medic was able to look at the farmer, who would survive. They called in a medevac helicopter to take him to the Vietnamese hospital in Saigon. Then, upon seeing all the Americans up and out of their hiding place, the crowd suddenly began to rush forward. But they weren't rushing toward the Americans, they were rushing toward the oxen. They quickly began cutting them up and running home with the meat.

Defiant Six himself came out to the ambush site, too. He accepted full responsibility for the incident, which was in fact due to the confusion of curfew times created by the Vietnamese as much as to our own inexperience. A few weeks later, when he had some time one afternoon, Defiant Six went down to the hospital in Saigon himself to visit with the farmer and assure himself that he was OK. This seems unbelievable now, twenty-five years later, in the face of the long list of atrocities perpetrated in Vietnam, but this, too, was the truth about 1/28, the Black Lions, one of the finest outfits in Vietnam. I saw that Defiant Six had a conscience, a humanity just as I did, and my admiration and loyalty toward him was redoubled.

But still, we were being asked to do the impossible and here, amid the local civilians, leadership was more important than ever. We hadn't heard of the My Lai massacre yet, although it had taken place long before. But we knew other stories, stories of units out of control and of needless civilian deaths. And I knew, as an officer, how easy it could be for my men, under slightly different circumstances, to run amok. Stressed-out, heavily armed teenage boys are dangerous. But in our battalion the standard was to treat the civilians with respect. By now we knew that all the peasants wore black pajamas, not just the VC, and the fact that they tended to flee when they saw us coming was not an excuse to shoot them. And by now the VC themselves were less inclined to take refuge in the villages.

I liked the Vietnamese. I think most Americans did; and while the nature of our new mission remained mysterious, this open plain was a great place to be. We named the pagoda the "Dragon House," for the countless fuck-you lizards that inhabited it, silent now that their courtship season had ended. The soil was soft and sandy again, perfect for digging, and of course everybody continued to live in fighting holes, with sandbagged sleeping positions built behind, because the Dragon House itself was such a perfect target and offered no protection. The rainy season was ending, and we were beginning to dry out at last. We were surrounded by a vast expanse of cropland, some fallow and some under cultivation. This plain was largely unbroken except for an abandoned outlying settlement just five hundred meters to the east, which was enclosed by trees. Generally, the view was unobstructed for more than a kilometer in all directions before the land began to slope gently downward. In the lowlands there were rice paddies and again, open land, while there were patches of woods and wild places on the intervening slopes, providing plenty of cover and concealment. A network of dirt lanes, oxcart paths, footpaths ran all through this hidden wild area. We spent about a week getting familiar with the landscape, doing local sweeps during the day and setting up platoon-size ambushes at night.

The scars of war were everywhere. Once, while doing a platoon recon of the brushy slopes a few kilometers from Dragon House, we came across four skeletons huddled together on the dirt floor of a hut which had been napalmed. The skeletons were quite clean; they must have lain there for a year or more. They were all full-size, or close enough, and some of the guys wanted to take the skulls back with us. It was, they argued, the sort of thing other units were doing. Some of the 11th Cavalry's tracks had human skulls mounted on front. Death was always stalking anyway, they wanted to laugh in its face.

I said "No" quite firmly, and there were howls of protest. These were such perfect skeletons, a real find, a great opportunity, not at all like the stinking, oozing corpses we had so often disinterred in the past. We had the sort of heated argument that was becoming characteristic of Mike Division, with me acting as moderator while everybody sounded off.

I was in the minority but in the end I held my ground, pulled rank, and the bones remained as we had found them.

I can still see those skeletons today, as I write, four sets of yellowed bones, slight, small, the way Vietnamese are. Were they Viet Cong? I doubt it. Viet Cong didn't tend to die huddled together on the floor of a hut, the way Vietnamese families would tend to huddle together when we passed through their villages. And there was no evidence of weapons, no cooked-off ammunition, web gear, equipment of any sort. These could have just as easily been school girls clinging to each other in terror. And whatever it was they had been, the war had so thoroughly destroyed their family, or their village, or their unit that nobody was able to come back for them. They lay waiting for us, to prod and gawk. They lay waiting forever. What a glorious war this was.

It was a real eye-opener to be among the people for the first time. It was adding an extraordinary and poignant depth to the way we viewed the war, after so much time in the jungle. Again, coming back from one of our familiarization patrols, we were late so we decided to take a shortcut through the nearby central village. This particular village was more isolated than the rest; it wasn't beside one of the major convoy routes. It was in a beautiful setting, surrounded by trees. It was late evening, the sun had just set, and as we approached we could hear the usual wonderful village sounds: dogs barking, ducks quacking, children playing, mothers scolding. But as we drew closer, the village suddenly became still except for a few last minute cries from the children. Even the ducks were silent. We walked down the middle of the street in the twilight, smelling the smoke of cooking fires, the *nuoc mam* fish sauce and the incense. The soft orange glow of kerosene lamps was visible inside the houses, but the families had all hidden from us. Did this mean it was a VC village, with VC children and VC ducks?

After we had passed through, and left the village behind, the sounds of life began gradually to return again.

On my first ambush at the Dragon House NDP I decided to set up inside the old French fort I had noticed on my first night in the field nearly three months before. I was curious about it. It was a triangular fort, small, the brick walls were each about fifty feet long. It had been built at a trail intersection; obviously this had been a trouble spot for a long, long time, and the tactical situation had only gotten worse over the years. The fort had been blown up quite thoroughly, either by the VC or by the French themselves, and during the dozen or so years that had elapsed since the French had given up, vines had all but covered the brick, with a tenacity comparable to the Viet Cong themselves.

It turned out to be a bad choice on my part. Brick rubble covered the ground everywhere and it was impossible to get comfortable. Then it began to rain, a steady cold rain. It was, without a doubt, one of the worst nights I have spent in terms of discomfort, lying on a pile of bricks, shivering and soaked. Sleep was out of the question. I thought a lot about the French soldiers who had been here before us. Did the bones of a few still molder beneath the bricks? They, too, had been disenchanted by this war. The French colonial government in Indochina was Vichy, had sided with the Nazis, had happily kept on producing rubber for the Axis during the Japanese occupation. Then French soldiers were sent to defend this indefensible regime, just a few scant years after the Nazis had finally been driven from Paris. Next, as the fighting turned more against them, it was the Americans who insisted that the French keep fighting, picking up a portion, then half, and finally ninety percent of the cost of the war. No wonder the French in Vietnam hated us at least as much as we hated them.

But this was so much more stupid, so arrogant to be doing it again, with so many more dying this time. And it was more than just my own personal fear and discomfort, more than the Vietnamese soldiers who waved to us from the roadside cafés, more than the rubber trees endlessly dripping into the pockets of the French. It was the old farmer, trying to be the first on the market with his peanuts. It was the four skeletons huddled together. It was the children whose voices I heard so briefly before they were silenced. Already I had come so far, farther than my father could ever understand, farther than I could have dreamed of, yet my tour was not yet even one third over and the hardest part, emotionally, was yet to come. I wondered what I might say about this war myself, twenty years hence, should I live. Would I become another potbellied patriot, embellishing my war with glory? I took a solemn vow to myself on that cold and rainy night that I wouldn't, that I would always remember the truth. This has not always been an easy vow to keep, especially with three sons of my own who enjoy playing "army," especially the part about the potbelly.

It is too easy, and a part of the healing process, to look back with a sense of victory when all I really felt at the time was defeat. It is too easy to forget the incredible suffering inflicted upon so many. It is too easy for fathers and sons to goad each other into war. Now, as I write, a quarter century later, gray-haired and forty pounds heavier, my fellow veterans are drifting into the VFW and American Legion halls that they once scorned, and that had in turn heaped scorn upon them. Now they sit drinking beer and picking at the scabs on old wounds, forgetting how the wounds got there, reinventing the war and themselves, because the truth is too terrible to face. Our children speak to each other in hushed tones about the war, and what it did to us. There is talk of redemption, of honor, of returning to Vietnam and finding something there, something beyond the shattered bone fragments and vertebrae, something that perhaps might even still be alive, that could even speak and say, "Thank God you came back for me, now there can be peace, now justice is done." Bit by bit, reality is eclipsed by boozy Hollywood images.

For my father, whose shame was such that he hardly mentioned his war except with humorous anecdotes, it was easiest to remain the gadfly, the artist-at-large, delivering social commentary while working as a deckhand. For many years I would visit him in New York, exploring the waterfront, which itself was in precipitous decline although there were still ship's chandleries and Irish bars that would serve you dinner for seventy-five cents. Sometimes we would take the Circle Line cruise around Manhattan, and I would ponder the incredible number of condoms in the water while he went on about the glorious days of steam and sail. We would see warships in the distance. A few times we boarded visiting cruisers and destroyers at my request, and when he began to work as a welder in the Brooklyn Navy Yard I walked on the deck of an aircraft carrier aborning with him; yet he had nothing to say about his war, his silence saying everything. Now my own children are watching me. I am drifting into war again. The river becomes Highway Thirteen, red as blood, red as the sunset with the smoke rising from our campfire, with the smoke rising from Bad Vibes Hill.

"Dad? . . . Dad? . . ."

The voice, like a bell ringing, brings me back. I stir the fire. I sip the beer. I am broody and withdrawn. I buy my sons "GI Joe" action figures.

"Dad? . . . Dad? . . ."

It is the sweetest sound I know. It brings me back from the film I am watching on television. It was old footage, sixteen millimeter, the emulsions fading with time, so much time has passed since the moment when a soldier was dying and the medic was leaning over him saying:

"Don't go to sleep. Sleep is bad."

"I'm so sleepy," says the dying soldier.

"Dad? . . . Dad? . . ."

The voices are older now, changing like the film's emulsions, growing awkwardly deeper. I am wearing an army shirt, and showing them how to load a magazine. I am trying not to be like my father but there are things I cannot hide, like the gray hair and the potbelly. They are learning of war's charisma, and I am drifting away again, back to the French fort and the intersection of footpaths, with my platoon gathered around me like children.

"Dad? . . . Dad? . . ."

At about four in the morning the rain finally stopped. Then, just before dawn, I saw lights appear in the wood line about three hundred meters away. At first there were just a few, bobbing about like fireflies, but more kept joining. Of course my first thought was that this was the enemy unit we had all been dreading. There were intelligence reports indicating that another mass attack, like Tet, was coming and would include tanks this time. We had all been issued extra antitank weapons. But there was no grumble of tanks, no sound at all, and it was too close to dawn for a mass attack; midnight would have been the preferred hour. And why the lights? If they were bold enough to use lights, this must be the advance party for an NVA regiment. Soon there must have been a hundred lights bobbing about in the trees. The possibility of calling in mortar or artillery fire crossed my mind early on, but I decided to wait and see what happened next.

Then the lights assembled into a single file, and began bobbing and weaving down the road towards us. And instead of tanks I heard ducks. As they drew closer I could hear singing, too, high-pitched Vietnamese women's voices singing those funny, sad, discordant melodies. Women on their way to the market, carrying baskets of produce and poultry on their *chogie* sticks. They had known we were there. The Viet Cong had told them. They had waited, gathering, afraid. Now they were walking right into our kill zone, right past the claymore mines we had placed by the road. Each woman carried a small lantern, and each lantern lit each face with a soft, amber glow. There were old faces, and young faces, harsh faces and soft faces, but they were all beautiful faces and they were really scared. They were singing prayers that we would not kill them. A couple of guys suggested that there could easily be some Viet Cong hiding among them, or that they could have grenades and mines and mortar rounds in the baskets, and they were right. This could have been the entire Seventh North Vietnamese Construction Battalion marching past us. But we let them pass anyway, mesmerized by the sheer beauty of it.

❖ IX ❖

WE WERE DEEP IN THE LAND of Oz, a place so strange that only a cosmic tornado could have brought us there, a place where even the trees could move and speak, and magic spells lurked everywhere. We got up and urinated and rolled up the claymore detonators and started the walk back to Dragon House. We had come, each of us, feeling somehow incomplete. We had found each other, and in each other we found strength, even though it was clear by now that the man behind the curtain was an incompetent fake, and that even Kansas would never be the same, should we be so lucky as to make it back. Nonetheless, we kept trying to kill Munchkins.

After months of fighting deep in the sanctuaries, we were witnessing what Vietnam really was for the first time. Every morning, just before sunrise, women would gather for the long trek to the marketplace. Later, with the sun fully up, farmers would show up in the fields which surrounded the Dragon House and begin cultivating their crops, feigning ignorance of our presence. Between midday sweeps of the countryside, there was sometimes an opportunity for a quick trip back into Di An, riding with the armored cavalry to the post exchange. As we rode through the villages, the Vietnamese army continued to wave cheerfully. What on earth were we doing here? Finally, after a week of "orientation," we got an answer.

One morning a couple of "deuce-and-a-half" trucks showed up at Dragon House carrying two pale, nervous REMF technicians from Saigon, some construction engineers, cases of equipment and piles of lumber. At first, the "thing" they were unloading was so secret that we were shooed away if we gathered around, were told to pretend that nothing was going on, just as the farmers nearby were doing. Soon the sounds of carpentry could be heard coming from within our bombed-out pagoda. Two-by-four lumber and sheets of plywood were carried inside, while we kept cleaning our weapons or working on fortifications, and the farmers kept cultivating their crops. It was not until later that evening, when the trucks and technicians and farmers had gone home that we were at last invited, in small groups, to see the centerpiece of our mysterious and experimental new mission.

A sturdy wooden platform had been built under a part of the pagoda roof where an aerial rocket had blown a huge hole. From that vantage point one could look out over the high flat plains for a great distance. And hidden under a remaining portion of the roof, to be trundled out only after darkness was complete, we had one of the very first "NOD"s, or Night Observation Devices, to be deployed in Vietnam. What it was, really, was a huge starlight scope, using the same solid-state television technology to amplify the ambient nighttime light. Even the smaller scopes we were accustomed to were still secret enough to prohibit our taking them along on ambushes, lest they should fall into enemy hands. This version was mighty secret indeed. It was about the size of a duffel bag and mounted on a rugged tripod. Included in the adjustable eyepiece were grids for ranging targets precisely, and its performance was very impressive. You could clearly see a person several kilometers away at night, and you could even read the name tags of the guys out on listening posts.

Our mission, then, was to employ American technology as the ultimate solution where all others had failed. We were part of a ring of outposts, replacing the Vietnamese army, and this open place was perfect for trying out the NOD. We spent many hours, night after night, playing with it. All we ever saw was each other. Of course, there were a few places in our area of responsibility which the NOD couldn't see. One was the abandoned settlement to the east. The lines of trees and shattered buildings there obscured our view of the fields beyond, so every night one platoon would go out on ambush there. Another was the brushy valley slope a few kilometers to the northwest. We were given other special devices to monitor activity there. These devices were camouflage-green metal boxes and cylinders the size of bread loaves with antennas sticking out of them. They were the same things that scout teams placed and aircraft dropped along the Ho Chi Minh Trail.

Some were simply microphones and transmitters, listening devices in case an NVA battalion came along singing the "Internationale." Others were metal detectors, transmitting an alarm signal if anything metallic, like the Tin Woodsman, wandered past.

Of course, the VC were on to us from the start. Nobody sets up an NDP around a vacant building like that, presenting such an easy target. And there were always the farmers working in the fields around us, bent over their hoes, occasionally giving us sidelong glances. As soon as the trucks with the equipment had arrived, the farmers had all inched a little closer while the rest of us were shooed away. As a matter of fact, there were more farmers around our NDP than anywhere else. As soon as one farmer left, another would replace him. They were the ones who were keeping us under surveillance, instead of the other way around. After a few more days we noticed that the fields around our Dragon House were virtually weed free, the envy of any garden club, while just a few hundred meters farther out the weeds ran rampant.

Things were no better with the little boxes. We had to place them ourselves, going out on short patrols, carrying them concealed under our clothing. No matter how far we went, no matter how convoluted we made our route, sooner or later a farmer would show up, hoe in hand. We had to invent elaborate ruses in order to plant the boxes without "Uncle Hoe" seeing. Usually a team of two men would drop away from our patrol and slip into the bushes while the column continued on. They'd plant the thing, camouflage it, and then slip back into our ranks again when we swung around on the return trip. But this was awkward and often obvious, and worse, half the time we would get back to our NDP only to find out the thing wasn't working. Either it was faulty or the team had forgotten to turn it on. Sometimes Uncle Hoe himself turned it off. At any rate, back we'd go again, executing the same ruse in front of the same farmer. Once we returned only an hour later to find that the device had disappeared entirely.

Finally, to round out our experimental arsenal, we were given a third, decidedly low-tech device. We got a dog. Devil Six was always big on dogs. He was the one who had sent us the scout dog team months before, and he had his own German shepherd mascot that even rode in his helicopter with him every day. This dog came to us on loan; he came with a handler of course, these dogs and handlers had trained together, lived together for almost a year before they came to Vietnam. This was an absolutely great dog, too. He was half black Labrador and half Newfoundland; big and warm and slobbery, and his handler was just like him, a big guy with curly black hair. They made a perfect team, sweating and panting, tongues hanging out, friendly, open, innocence abroad.

We really loved having this dog with us. It was the kind of dog guys fall in love with anyway, and he elicited all sorts of dog story reminiscences. Clearly, the dog and the handler had fallen in love with each other a long time ago. They spent hours back at the NDP just looking into each other's eyes. Then, toward dusk, we would take them out on ambush. These dog ambushes were always set up downwind of an area the VC were expected to cross, behind the abandoned settlement or near the brushy slopes. We'd go through the usual routine of putting out claymores and setting up watches for the night. The dog and the handler would just lie down together, with the handler using his dog as a great, warm, heaving furry pillow. Within minutes, both were asleep. Within a few more minutes, they were both snoring. They would snore all night in unison, great sonorous snores that the VC could have heard half a kilometer away. A couple of guys in Mike Division asked the handler if they could sleep with his dog, too, but he wouldn't let them.

This dog meant a lot to us. He was the most real, loving thing we had seen in Vietnam besides each other. And he symbolized our own innocence and trust, so far from home and the dogs who waited for us there. One day the handler told us a story. Another handler he knew had been assigned up in the Central Highlands. While out on patrol his unit got hit badly, with a number of casualties which included the handler. In the confusion of battle and evacuation, the dog got left behind in the jungle. And the handler, due to the serious nature of his wounds, was flown first to the brigade aid station, then transferred to a second helicopter and flown all the way to the hospital in Saigon, eighty miles away. Two weeks later the dog showed up at his bedside.

Mike Division listened transfixed. That story meant so much to us for a number of reasons. It spoke not only of boys and dogs, it spoke of other things we were feeling as well. It spoke of the intense loyalty we felt toward each other, and it spoke of our own growing sense of mysticism. Our trust of instincts was growing into a worship and we had formed a family tribe where anything was possible.

"What happens to the dog when you go home?" somebody asked.

"He'll be shot."

Shouts of outrage from Mike Division.

"Why can't you keep him. Take him with you."

"Army property."

"Why can't some other handler get him?"

"Too highly trained. One-man dog."

There followed a discussion of various plots and methods for sneaking the handler and the dog out together, but they were pretty unrealistic and the sense of betrayal deepened. It was more than the fact that we still clung to the hope for a happy ending, it was the thought that if the army could betray such loyalty and trust in a dog, they could do it to us, too.

The war was changing us in ways the army itself couldn't understand. The dog and his handler didn't stay with us long; obviously they didn't like working the night shift. But then the army sent us a dog biscuit of sorts in the form of a USO show. This was one of the perks of being so close to Saigon, and it was also one of the most grotesque sights we had ever witnessed. Two men and a woman arrived by helicopter one afternoon and dragged themselves and their instruments over to the pagoda. They really looked terrible, very tired and heavy lidded, and while they offered the explanation that they were exhausted from playing nonstop at one fire base after another, what they really seemed to our jaded eyes was very stoned on the local drugs.

Then she began to sing, emaciated and sexless, almost falling over, while one man, barely awake, forlornly beat his drums, and another flailed the guitar. I only remember one of the songs, but I remember it as clearly as I remember our own music: the black music, the white music, the rock and soul and country sounds that meant so much to us. They did "The Girl From Ipanema." And it was a joke with us for weeks afterward. Their agent must have booked them in Vietnam just to get rid of them.

Maybe we were wrong. Maybe this trio had come to us with hearts as pure as fresh-fallen snow, and had sacrificed their health and spirit to boost our morale. Maybe we ourselves were at fault, having become so antisocial, so cynical and distrusting that we couldn't accept what they were offering us. What I remember personally was that this was the first "round-eyed" woman I had seen in months, yet I found her repulsive. It was a cruel tease, and we were relieved when they dragged themselves back to the helicopter again and fluttered away into the gathering dusk. Soon we would go out on ambush again. Soon we would lie together in the moonlight, dreaming of home.

For the first time, we had spare time on our hands. For the first time, we were not afraid. For the first time, we got to know our mess sergeant, and got hot meals every day. Our mess sergeant was one of us, he cared about us and made certain we liked the food and got enough, and in return we adored him, wagging our tails loyally. I have always enjoyed cooking myself, and with Mike Division I began preparing our own dinners while out on sweeps, pillaging fresh vegetables from the surrounding farm fields, mixing them with C rations and cooking them over plastic explosive in a steel helmet. Upon hearing about this, the mess sergeant joined in with helpful suggestions and would scrounge cheese and onions for us to take into the field. Then one day I lost my survival knife while out on a sweep. It fell from the sheath on my thigh while I was jumping a swift running creek, and I returned to the NDP devastated. One becomes inordinantly fond of personal possessions in the field. Upon hearing of my loss, the mess sergeant gave me his own knife. That was the kind of man he was.

There was time to make our positions truly sumptuous and comfortable. There was time to take photographs of each other, and listen to music. There was time for letters from home. Like the USO show, sometimes they seemed like voices from a past life. My mother wrote of her job, what friends were doing, adventures the dog had with skunks. My grandmother wrote of the weather, her daughter, more about the skunk. My father wrote of progress on the pram. He had made a few design changes, moving the wheelhouse to the starboard a little.

The pram was central to our relationship, and he saw in it the promise of a life together, father and son, when I returned from my war. We had begun work on it before I got thrown out of college, building it in the workshop he had bought, just down the street from the house he had bought in Stonington, Connecticut after his parents had died. He had remarried, too, after nearly twenty years of bachelorhood, and I felt safer, soon even encouraged to visit. Those early years of his second marriage were golden; I liked his wife, a woman from one of the local Portuguese fishing families with two daughters just a little older than me. The life they made there was a welcome respite from the one carved out by two spinster women in Westchester, and there were moments when I held hope of capturing what I had always longed for; a relationship, father and son, like the ones seen in movies.

Compromises had to be made: I had to learn to like boats, which he loved, and he had to learn to fish, which I loved. I would visit for a week at a time, and we would rise each morning to march down Water Street with buckets and hand lines to the local market, where we would pick up grinders and the inevitable six-pack of beer. Then we would head over to the Monsanto plant, which manufactured Clorox bottles and dominated the waterfront. Very often, it was acutely embarrassing to be with my father because of his many eccentricities, but in his gadfly way he had discovered the riparian rights of the townspeople and forced Monsanto to give him a key to the chain-link fence which surrounded the factory. Then, in the shadow of this great farting, hissing Clorox bottle factory we would walk out onto the breakwater, haul in his dory, bail it, cast off, and set sail. I can feel the midsummer sun reflecting off greasy water. I can hear the drone of distant outboards. I can taste the beer, warm as bilge water. As long as we pretended the fishing was work and not recreation, my father loved it.

All this seemed so strange and distant as we prepared for ambush, as we wandered toward the abandoned settlement to the east, the sun setting behind us. Even back then, in Stonington, as we fished, I could feel the tug of life like a big fish on my line, pulling me away. Even then, I was just pretending that fishing could be an occupation, a survival strategy for the inevitable hard times ahead, and would listen patiently to the same dire prognostications I had heard a hundred times before: economic and social collapse, the return of feudalism. I was fishing for wisdom amid what was, much of the time, pretty irrational stuff, while the dory rocked and the clouds towered overhead. I found it, too, like the key to the Monsanto plant, but you had to work hard to get it and now, as we entered the darkened interior of the tile-roofed building we had dubbed "The Whorehouse" to wait for complete darkness, I knew that an even greater distance than the vast Pacific lay between my father and me. My eyes slowly adjusted to the dim interior. The huge round clay pots that had once held a year's harvest of rice slowly materialized in the gloom. We moved about silently in the building. A few crouched down and lit a last cigarette, cupping the glow. Posts and beams and braces rose above us, and you could see the sky through holes in the roof here and there. A machine gunner stood silhouetted in the doorway. Beyond lay the tiled courtyard, the intricately carved garden gate. I was more at home in this strange land than I had ever been before.

In the late afternoon when the beer was gone, my father and I would haul anchor and set sail for Stonington again. He had rigged his dory with a rust-colored lug sail, while the hull itself sported the red and yel-

low and green stripes that were typical of the Portuguese fleet. Often as
we headed toward our mooring the setting sun would surround us with
an orange glow as well, the boat and the man among the village's most
colorful characters. I knew that I had captured something more than
just a dozen or so flounder, having found my father, getting to know
him at last. It wasn't always easy; when he trundled loads of seaweed
back to his garden in a baby carriage, for example, right past the houses
of girls I was interested in, I tended to lag behind a bit with my bucket
of fish. But his wife Mary, in particular, did her best to create a second
family for me, putting up with us and my father's friends who tended to
show up at dinnertime with more beer, the artists and Bohemians and
rich kids gone to seed in Stonington.

After dinner and still more beer the sketchpad would come out, and
the pram began to take shape. It would be eighteen feet long, as long as
the shop would accommodate, and it would be square-ended. It would
have a small engine, a wheelhouse, and bunk space for two down below. Always, in the sketches, there would be two men on deck working
together, long-lining for dogfish or setting lobster traps. We laid the keel
together about the time I started college. I helped him saw out ribs and
paint them with green Cuprinol. But progress had been slow even then,
while my own life raced ahead. I offered constant encouragement,
helped bend planks on while home on leave. The deck was on by the
time I went to Vietnam, but this pram had been a-building for five years
already and even though it was the closest my father and I ever got, we
were both still holding back from each other at the same time, and not
all that much had changed since the time of the toy tugboat. We never
did completely trust each other, and even the mess sergeant had given
me more than my father ever could, without asking for anything in return.

Now the darkness was complete. With a hand signal from me, we
got up as one and moved through the blackened interior of the building
toward the door. Moonlight filled the courtyard. We stayed in the shadows of a long porch, carefully avoiding the broken tiles and shards of
rice crocks. We stepped off the porch and followed the shadow of a
hedge beside the courtyard and out into the overgrown gardens beyond. This settlement must have belonged to a wealthy family once; the
cemetery off to our right was filled with ornate laterite monuments and
the house itself was far bigger and better built than most. Later, as we
radioed back to Dragon House through the night, we would embellish

our sit reps with pornographic fantasies. The girl from Ipanema had been waiting for us in the whorehouse.

We would file into our final positions where two hedgerows intersected. We would wait until the moon was in shadow before setting out the claymores. The clouds, drifting in from the sea, were immense. The moon, emerging, fading, emerging again, was the brightest I had ever seen. I would take the first watch, and often the second one, too, staying up past midnight and letting the rest of my CP group sleep longer, just as I sometimes stand watch over my sleeping children now. It was great to be there as the moon waxed toward full. I was jazzed up, wide awake, listening to the rise and fall of insect sounds as the moon drifted in and out of cloud.

Sometimes, if the clouds were moving fast, the moon shadows would race across the fields so quickly the whole world seemed to pulsate. And the clouds themselves, aglow with moonlight, were something you could reach out and touch, climb, and ascend to the stars. But then somebody was pulling my leg and I fell back into reality. There was a little guy running across the fields in the moonlight, trying to stay in cloud shadow but clearly visible just the same. It was just one little guy running obliquely toward us from the opposite wood line across the open field, obviously unaware of our presence. When he reached the hedgerow we were in, just about a hundred and fifty meters away, we could still see him even though he was in the dense shadows. Was he a midnight gardener, trying to get a leg up on the weeding? Either he didn't know we were there, or he knew us better than we thought, knew we wouldn't shoot him.

It would have been easy to shoot him, and we had another of our usual Mike Division discussions because I didn't want to. My argument was that we should see what he was up to, see if more men appeared. But deep inside, even though a part of me needed the vindication of a body count, there was another, more powerful part of me that was still revolted at the prospect of actually killing somebody. There was no personal honor in it, so why spoil an otherwise perfect evening? We waited for a good ten minutes, moonlight dancing with clouds and shadows, night sounds rising and falling. The little guy, when we got a glimpse of him, appeared to be busy unpacking a suitcase. Then he started crawling toward the Dragon House in the shadows, very carefully, and still totally unaware of our presence. We lost sight of him after a while but we knew where he was because there wasn't much cover. We radioed back to the NDP that there was a little guy crawling toward them, but they couldn't see him with the NOD. Obviously, this guy understood the NOD and what it could do perfectly. Even though he was a thousand meters from the Dragon House, he was taking particular care with concealment from them.

Then there was this curious sound coming from the low brushy area to the north, like corks being pulled from a couple dozen jugs in astonishingly rapid succession. I puzzled for a split second before realizing it was mortars, it was a whole mortar section firing for effect. I held down the mike key and desperately whispered "Incoming-incoming-incoming," and almost immediately the rounds began to crash down on the Dragon House while we watched, transfixed. Boy, those guys were really good. Uncle Hoe had paced off the range perfectly. All around the pagoda there were flashes of light, tongues of flame, the crunch of shrapnel tearing through the air, two or three rounds a second. There was a pause of about five seconds, a minor correction was made, and then the mortars fired a second barrage. This answered the question about what the little guy was up to. He was the forward observer, with a radio, and great waves of anxiety and guilt swept through me once again. I was afraid my cowardice, my hesitancy to kill, was being paid for with the lives of my friends.

We had a fix on the forward observer, and we had a rough fix on the mortar position which could be triangulated by the guys at Dragon House. There were two 40mm "duster" tracks at the NDP at the time, and they opened up on the mortar position with counterfire, six rounds a second streaming out over the farm fields like red embers, thumping and flashing in the valley. Oscar Five was shooting, too, first with nine rounds out there, then nine more where we thought the forward observer was. But I guess he had the sense to split as soon as his crews had fired their last round, because there wasn't a trace of him the next morning. The dusters didn't do much good either, beyond making a lot of bright lights and noise. And of course the surveillance devices we had placed in the defile, almost exactly where the VC mortars had been, remained mute throughout.

Thankfully, there were no cries for medic back at the Dragon House, no illumination rounds drifting languidly overhead, no death beat of medevac ships headed in. Our alert had everyone prepared, and the

First Division Fighting Holes had done their job well, too, with three layers of sandbags on top, enough to stop an 82mm mortar round. The only injuries were a few scratches, even though thirty rounds had landed inside the perimeter in fifteen seconds. It could have turned out differently, leaving me a different man, but my time in Vietnam was taking a peculiar turn. I didn't want to break the rapture of the moonlight and as things turned out it was really cool watching a VC mortar attack from behind the scenes, watching that FO out there in the moonlight with what we mistook to be a suitcase. It was still commonly assumed, with characteristic misjudgement, that the VC had very few radios and never used them tactically. But we had seen it, and felt somehow privileged.

We stayed there in the hedgerow, wide awake, for the rest of the night, waiting to see if there would be a ground attack. But the attack never came, and after a while the bugs and lizards regained their composure and resumed singing in the moonlight. It seemed as though we were blessed to be in this place, slightly removed from the war. And every day the enemy was becoming more real, more human, an entity you could almost be conversant with. I was still trying to live with my own fear, my own sense of failure. I was still trying to be the good son, and the months that had elapsed since those earlier terrible times had not erased the bitter taste, like the taste of the corpse-tainted water. But I was also learning to be a leader, a father, myself. With no vision of God to hide behind, no holy crusade, I was left with the clouds and the earth and my men.

We continued to get replacements during the quiet times at Dragon House, and Mike Division's strength kept growing: twenty-two, twenty-six, twenty-eight men. It was a good time to get them. The day patrols were easy most of the time, the night ambushes blissfully quiet and comfortable as long as it didn't rain, and the only VC we saw were carrying hoes or radios. These new guys were lucky they didn't have to jump right into combat. They were scared enough already. One day we were out on a sweep in high brushy country when a withdrawing VC fired a clip off over our heads, either to cover a withdrawal or to bait us forward. It was the sort of thing that happened so often that it was hardly worth notice, but everyone had hit the dirt. Then a second clip went snapping overhead, but one quickly learns by the quality of the cracks and thumps, the sound of the bullets going faster than sound overhead and the thump of gasses exploding from the gun's muzzle, where the bullets came from and where they are going, and in this case it was clear the bullets were a good twenty feet above us and the guy wasn't even aiming, so we all got up and resumed our forward movement. Then I almost stumbled over a couple of FNGs still hugging the dirt. Their fatigues were still bright green. They looked up at me with amazement. How could anyone survive such a hail of bullets? I almost had to pull them to their feet. I felt sorry for them. In time, their fatigues would fade with the sun and rain. In time their faces would turn leathery and dark, and they would learn to gauge the accuracy of enemy fire. But the war, and the army, had turned against them by now, and they already knew it. They were already casualties of circumstance.

The days at Dragon House wore on and on. What we had expected to last a week lasted another week, then another. There were still sweeps, and occasional airlifts out on battalion-size operations in the deserted Saigon suburbs. There was also boredom, long periods of time with nothing to do. Our emplacements became ever more elaborate, with chairs and tables built out of ammo boxes. We bought two baby ducks as platoon mascots, and named them Tu Duc, which was the name of one of those deserted Saigon suburbs. Then one of the ammo box tables collapsed on a duck. Tu Duc became one duck. We captured fuck-you lizards and attempted to tame them. They would have nothing of it. We captured scorpions. We put fuck-you lizards and scorpions together in army helmets to see what would happen. Nothing happened. Malaise was setting in. It was easy to imagine what was going on in the rear among the support troops.

Like the men in the rear, we too were getting more familiar with the Vietnamese themselves. One day a couple of us rode into Di An on one of those 40mm dusters and on the way back, while roaring through a village, we threw a track. This was no big deal, but it meant we had to wait for an hour or so while the crew fitted the heavy track back on again. Pretty soon a sizable crowd of Vietnamese kids and soldiers had gathered around us, bumming cigarettes and candy. These happened also to be soldiers from the same unit which had turned and run when we came under fire months before, and tried to escape on the medevac ships. So far as I could tell, they mainly were accustomed to hanging out in cafés. They certainly couldn't be taken seriously as soldiers, and had proved to be a definite liability in a fight. But, as with most Americans, we didn't really hold this against them. Perhaps this was partly because of their stature, and because they, too, begged candy and cigarettes, that we tended to think of them as children.

The soldiers beckoned for us to join them at their tables, and we did. We bought bottles of the local beer, *Ba Moui Ba.* For most of us, this was a new experience. We couldn't understand a word they were saying, but the soldiers and the café's owner continued to lavish us with attention. Their humor and friendliness was irresistible. When they recognized me as the leader, I was ushered into a dark inner room for what seemed to be evolving into a real party. I stifled my paranoia about VC being everywhere and began to relax. A few shots of *bac si de,* the local white lightning, helped. I was given chopsticks. A strange dish of food was set before me. Great gales of laughter swept through the room as I attempted to use the chopsticks, followed by torrents of mile-a-minute commentary. The food was very unusual and very good. With every swallow I took, there were "ahs" and "oohs" and nods of approval. Then there would be a quick consultation, some scurrying around, and another dish was presented.

Language barriers were quickly overcome by smiles and gestures and alcohol. It was, for me, the beginning of a friendship that would greatly deepen with time, contrasting sharply with the view of the country I had first known in the jungles and base camps. And it was incredibly seductive. *Let the war go on without me, I think I'll stay here for a while.* But there were other, more sinister seductions as well, during our time at the Dragon House, as I felt my way into leadership and fatherhood and war. I cared about the men around me with a power I had never known before. The fact that I was also at least partly responsible for their lives was both moving and terrifying. It was essential that I learn as much as I could both from them and for them. I had to lead them and yet be one of them. I had to bring the new men in, and make them a part of us. I had to take some of the pressure off some of the old guys. I wanted to learn more about walking point, as it was the most important thing I asked my men to do.

I went walking with Redfeather, despite his objections. It seemed to him like an invasion of privacy, I suppose, and at first he moved stiffly, distracted, annoyed. But then he gradually settled in, getting catlike again. Noonan came along. Millhouse came along. Dennis came along. We began to do these little patrols, just leaving the perimeter on our own. We would even try tracking each other, looking for the secret signs, trying to tune in to the right frequency. This is how it works. You really have to concentrate, clear your head of all other thoughts. You have to become part of the jungle. Part of the secret is how you move, but if your head is in the right place your body will follow, and you move as though doing Tai Chi, as though you are mist in the jungle. You move your body, then you freeze. You move your eyes. You move your head side to side. You listen. This is what hunters try to do, but it is very different when people are hunting you. If there is moisture; rain drops or dew, you look at every leaf to see how the droplets run down. If some droplets are running differently, somebody was just there. You listen for what the jungle sounds like, listen if the jungle's heart skips a beat. If a leaf is bent, you look at the crease and see if it is turning yellow and think about how long it has been since somebody else was there. Every leaf, every plant provides a record of people passing by if you know how to read it; but there is more, which is harder to describe, which goes beyond what you see and hear and sometimes even smell. It is the part about going outside your own body, and seeing with the third eye. This is the part that is most important, and the most frightening because it is the most powerful stuff on earth and if you use too much you go nuts. I understood this, but I never was all that good at it and found my position in the rear of the point squad vastly preferable.

Most of the time, it was pretty obvious no VC were around. Most of the time, the degree of alertness could be toned down. One day we were out on one such sweep, lifted into the ominously deserted suburbs of Saigon by helicopter, when Mike Division entered a field of tall plants. When they went in they were just Mike Division, wearing the usual fatigues and web gear. But when they came out on the other side they were all wearing camouflage, with foliage draped on them like a platoon of greenhouse commandoes. I was quite impressed with this sudden interest in the tactics of concealment and was about to congratulate them when I looked more closely at the foliage they had stuck in their helmets and suspenders. It was marijuana. We had walked through a marijuana farm. I made them throw it away and they did. They knew my rules, they knew that while I had nothing against it, I would not tolerate it in the field. I would not tolerate anything that interfered with the natural vibes which kept us alive. Anyway, there was plenty of marijuana available in the rear, from the REMFS and the laundry girls. They had just done it as a joke. We didn't need any drugs. We were high already. Our brains were awash in chemicals, the hormones and enzymes of war. The countryside scintillated through our jazzed-up cells. Just being is very exciting when not-being is so near.

My father, already incredulous that I had gone to war in the first place, once asked me if I had ever thought I was going crazy. I answered "no" and he was even more incredulous, but now I think I would have been more honest if I had said "sort-of." We were all "sort-of" crazy, but we were in it together. Ours was a social psychosis, whereas real craziness is the stuff of isolation and maybe indulgence as well. I would never understand his craziness, which seemed to come on like the monsoon, come up with the thunderous temper that was his father's as well. Some of us were more crazy than others. Some of us would not survive. Our days at the Dragon House were coming to an end, and when I looked through the battalion log to see what else had happened I found an incident I had forgotten. One of the medics in another company committed suicide. Before he went to sleep the night before, he took enough pills to certainly kill himself, and I remember how angry I was with him at the time. How could he do this to us? How could he desert us when we needed him, how could he be so self-centered, so wrapped up in his own agony that he would leave the rest of us behind? Now I know that it was not so much his fault as that demons had carried him away.

We went back to the Rome Plow Shitpile again, doing security on the convoy route which had grown twenty kilometers long by this time. It was pretty grim to be going back there, but things were changing. The local VC were losing their punch. The intense fighting that had been going on earlier in the summer had taken its toll on them even more than us. The mining of the road had greatly diminished. Instead, small teams of VC had taken to ambushing the convoys, firing antitank rockets from the unplowed tree lines nearby. They did this several times a day, and it was rare for a convoy to run the whole route unscathed.

This time our tactic was to drop off three- or four-man observation posts every few hundred meters as we swept down the road looking for mines in the morning. These teams would hide in the bushes all day, watching and listening for any VC until the last convoy came through. Then the protective screen would be rolled up again. Of course it took a lot of men to do this; several battalions of infantry were now tied up this way, along with the engineer battalion and their Rome plows. We had gone over the map with dividers and figured out how far apart the teams should be spaced. Then we set out on our first day of the new mission. Although all the old fears, the brassy taste in the mouth and the light-headedness were back again, it also felt good to be back in the wilderness and away from the disturbing conflicts of Di An. And on the way out there I had a chance to speak privately with Defiant Six for the first time since the night I had offered to resign my commission. I didn't know quite what to say, but wanted to say something, to thank him at least for having tolerated my moment of collapse. He just looked at me quizzically; it was such ancient history by now. Then we took the point again, as was usual now when things looked touchy.

I was to establish the farthest outpost, and link up with another battalion sweeping south toward us. First Delta Company melted away into the bushes as we swept the road northward. Then Charlie Company disappeared in groups of three or four. Finally it was just Mike Division alone on the road. One by one, my teams melted into the woods until nobody was left but me, my romeo and three riflemen. Bravo Six had taken Wakefield to be his romeo by this time, now Bob Spahn was carrying the radio. Sgt. Noonan was leading the team of riflemen. It felt rather lonely, just the five of us, as we walked down the road in the hot midmorning sun, but it also felt good and we didn't have far to go. When we reached the point where we were supposed to link up, there was no sign of the other unit. So we ducked off into the woods ourselves to wait for them.

We waited and waited, swatting mosquitoes and picking at leeches, adjusting our gear and trying to remain as silent as possible. It was just like being one of the VC ourselves, this business of hiding beside a convoy route, and it was clear how well they held the advantage. It was impossible to see more than a few feet in the thick understory. A few men with rocket launchers could run up and down the roadside with impunity, out of sight, firing on convoys and disappearing before a single shot could be fired back in return. More and more, it was seeming to me, all we were really doing was providing targets.

Then we had movement, sort of. It was really just a matter of the gentle morning breeze blowing all the leaves north, except one, which went south, about two hundred meters beyond us in the roadside wood line. Then we saw nothing more. The movement was right where the last outpost of the other battalion was supposed to be. Could it be them, being super-sneaky, going through the woods instead of down the road? I radioed back to Bravo Six. He said the other unit had problems. They'd run out of men before they finished their sector. They were almost a kilometer away, waiting for another company of infantry to be brought up. I didn't tell him about the VC yet. We weren't even sure of what we had seen.

So we kept waiting, peering through the foliage, shifting back and forth very slowly and silently when a leg got cramped or a bug bit hard. We didn't see anything more, but the sense of the VC presence was overwhelming. We had grown to know them, because they wanted to kill us. Of course they had been shadowing the units on the road. Of course they had found the breach in our line of men, and filled it with an outpost of their own. Now they were there, two hundred meters away, waiting, slapping mosquitoes, picking at leeches too. I didn't like the situation at all. As with the forward observer running toward us, I didn't want to get into a fight, didn't like having to decide what to do. If we went after them, it would require all five of us sneaking through the woods behind them, a risky proposition which would leave our original outpost unmanned. And what if there were ten of them? Or what if there were none at all?

I radioed Bravo Six again and told him I was pretty sure we had company. He was skeptical. But at least they were in the other unit's area of operations; I was off the hook as far as going after them. Anyway, almost an hour had elapsed since the wayward leaf. Yet still, the sense of their presence, that sixth sense which had grown so very strong, seemed more solid than ever. What was certain now was that we had to keep our own position a secret. Otherwise they might try to sneak up behind us. Otherwise, we would lose the advantage we had learned to cherish, the advantage of knowing about them before they knew about us.

There is plenty of time, in this kind of situation, to evaluate all sorts of possible actions. We considered two man cloverleafs to our rear, scouting for a footpath and doing a hasty ambush. Recon by fire or mortars would have been ideal, but they were out of our AO. Then Bravo Six called again. Things were not going smoothly, and there was a lot more concern on this first day about smooth coordination than about still hypothetical Viet Cong. We didn't have the other unit's radio frequency, and the only way for things to get straightened out was for me to walk up the road to where the other unit was held up, show them my position on the map, show them the VC position on the map, and get the road secured. I pointed out that walking up the road in front of the VC might have its drawbacks. But convoys were backed up, waiting impatiently for the road to be opened. It was almost noontime. Anyway, if they fired on us, then we would really know where they were and those of us who survived could fire back and everyone else would know that I wasn't just paranoid.

But I knew I wasn't just paranoid. We could almost smell the fish sauce on their breath. We knew we hadn't seen any sign of them again because they were waiting in the woods, just as we were. So I left Noonan and another man at our position, back to back, super alert. I took Spahn and another man with me south, through the woods and as silently as possible, just a hundred meters, so we wouldn't walk into our next closest position, or disclose our last one. Then we just walked out to the road and began walking north again as nonchalantly as possible. First we walked past our own position. Then we walked past the VC position, as though strolling down the sidewalk back home. It was, literally, the gamble of a lifetime. I was counting on our judgement of the enemy character, our knowledge of his habits, and trusting instincts again. I was fairly certain they wouldn't fire on us, maybe seventy percent certain. It was just the three of us, not a prime target, and anyway infantrymen can respond a lot faster and more accurately than a moving convoy. No, they would not give themselves away by firing on us. They would wait. They did.

So we strolled up to the other unit and met an affable captain in the middle of the road. Along with his infantrymen, there was a long line of trucks waiting for the road to be declared secure. I showed the captain our position on the map, and showed him the VC position. He looked at me strangely, but said he'd send a unit in there. Then it was time for us to head back.

Meanwhile, a couple of engineers had been listening in, edging their way closer to our group. They were driving a three-quarter-ton truck, and they were headed for Saigon on a weekend R&R. They were anxious to get going. They didn't want to wait for security teams, and anyway, hadn't we just walked up the road unmolested? I repeated that there was an ambush down there, but now that I was with such a nice bunch of guys and away from the jungle, I was even beginning to doubt myself a little. Then, once again, the two guys with me began to bitch in characteristic Mike Division style. It was too fucking hot to walk. Wouldn't it be nice to ride back to our position in a truck, instead of walking down that nasty road again? "C'mon, Sir," they pleaded, eyes glittering. The engineers chimed in, too. Finally I gave in and we climbed aboard.

Then we were off, the driver clashing through the gears and getting up as much speed as he could. That was the plan, give them a hard target to hit. As soon as we reached The Spot, there was the unmistakable "thump" of an antitank rocket being fired. Charlie simply couldn't resist any longer, but he missed, and the round exploded in the roadside just short of us. Now, of course, the truck was really careening and we fired back at the puff of smoke in the tree line, but it was wild shooting because we mainly had to hang on to the truck to keep from falling out. They fired back with some AK-47s and a second rocket, but their shooting was as wild as ours. It was like riding on a stagecoach, trying to outrun bandits. Our adrenaline and momentum were such that we just kept on going, the driver wouldn't stop, and we went well past our own positions and practically ran over Bravo Six and his CP group coming up the road toward us.

When the truck stopped, we jumped off and were talking nonstop and chain-smoking cigarettes, jumping like marionettes. The sky was this brilliant blue and the roadside jungle seemed to be shimmering electric green and pulsating. And the best part, the most exciting part, was the personal honor thing again. As with the forward observer, they had disclosed themselves to me first and nobody got killed.

❖ X ❖

SOMETIMES THE EUPHORIA would return a decade later when I was running in Vermont, as though I had divined the enemy and outrun their ambush. On some days it would feel as though my legs were made of spring steel and I could keep running forever, or as though my feet were not actually touching the ground at all, and I was floating above the road. The trees would be shimmering with this electric green color, even vibrating. I would sometimes run through clouds of butterflies and they would gently brush my skin with their wings as they rose before me. At these times I would fully know the joy of survival again, remembering Mike Division and the Rome Plow Shitpile and the Ho Bo Woods. I could feel their presence even though I was so utterly alone most of the time.

I could endure the assaults of others as long as Mike Division was with me. My ex-wife would lob grenades, but they were mostly duds, and when my father suggested that I quit, surrender, and try carpentry or house painting for a living instead of standing up and assaulting publishers and television stations, I could endure that, too, knowing that I was so much stronger than either of them. Strong and loyal is what a father and a leader should be, and the loyalty must flow downward, not upward. This is the hardest part. How do you explain your loyalty to your children when they have been taken two thousand miles away by divorce, and they are as scared and lonely as you are? My euphoria would dissolve into grief, as it had in Vietnam.

At night I had the moonlight, shining on the bare floors of the farmhouse, which was nearly devoid of furniture. Not much to bump into as

I wandered the empty house at night in the moonlight, and later the dreams would come, returning me to the dark places along Highway Thirteen and Bad Vibes Hill, where the VC beckoned to me on the radio. There were VC everywhere on the farm in these dreams, in the pantry and the hayloft. Visiting friends and family remained unaware of this, ignoring my warnings while they idled about. Sometimes they would turn out to be VC themselves, having infiltrated my farm by posing as distant cousins or UPS men and refusing to leave. VC would show up at the dinner table, expecting to be served. Ultimately I would end up having to defend myself and my family alone, sometimes having to endure derisive remarks while I scoured the closets and cupboards for elusive weapons. Then bullets would suddenly swell to three or four times their normal size just when you needed them, or gun barrels would go limp and I would awaken to moonlight again.

This farm which I have been defending for so long lies at the end of the road in a little valley of its own, surrounded on all sides by deep woods with secret footpaths. The moment I saw it I realized that it would be perfect for a base camp, for starting a platoon of my own. The land drops steeply away on two sides, and when I stand on the highest part the farm seems to float above the rest of the world, especially when the fog rolls in like the sea itself at my feet. But I never envisioned how difficult the defense would become ten years later, with my two boys just three and seven years old and gone for two-thirds of the year, and my father telling me to surrender.

The trail that the settlers used in this part of Vermont and Canada comes up through here, right past the dooryard and the vegetable garden, and before that it was an Indian trail. I often find artifacts when I plow in the spring and half expect to find pieces of my own great-to-the-sixth power grandfather here too, someday. He was carried off his own Massachusetts farm by raiding Indians who had come down out of Canada and he may have been taken north along this trail, past my dooryard, if they allowed him to live that along; although I suspect that even the vertebrae are rotted away by now.

What did he know as a man? What was his struggle like, or the struggle of those who took him? And what did they visit upon their sons? When I was surrounded by enemies and in danger of being carried off, I would ask myself these things while standing on the Indian trail where it crosses the garden. A small spring rises from the earth just a little higher and runs alongside the trail through our place, running cold and clear over mossy boulders and shoulders of ledge. Down below it joins a larger stream, which soon tumbles into a river that caroms off valley walls for just a few more miles before joining the great Connecticut in a magical place that is accessible only by canoe. I would take women there, young and silky-haired, Nordic blondes with histories of abduction and dark, brooding French Canadian girls, some part Indian themselves. We would make love on the riverbank, sharing our loneliness; but mainly it is a place for fathers and sons to find each other. We begin in the spring, just as the Indians did, when the fish are running up to spawn. We return through the summer, wading the shallows, feeling the endless tug toward the sea, then again in the autumn, before the water turns black with mystery.

Twelve years ago, when my oldest boy was the same age as my youngest boy is now, we camped there overnight for the first time. It had not been an easy summer, with the divorce still fresh and raw. I was barely able to hang on as a father at times, even with the running and the moonlight on my side, as when I had offered to resign my commission. It was also a hauntingly beautiful summer, with evenings like the evenings at An Loc. I put aside nearly everything else I was doing so that I could be with my boys, and we began the summer with short day-excursions learning balance and control. Noontime we would stop and I would make sandwiches, stroking the bread with mayonnaise, making the sandwiches as lovingly as I would make their beds, while they played with their GI Joe action figures in the sand, and we had learned to like sandwiches that occasionally had sand in them just as the beds did; but soon it was time for a greater adventure, so we packed up supplies and put into the river which flows past the farm. First came the lazy midsummer drift, and I spoke in hushed tones of the rapids up ahead. Then the river began to quicken, almost imperceptibly at first, but growing steadily faster toward a narrow cleft in Devonian schists and the three of us hunkered down, feeling the tightening in the groin, hearing the rush of water up ahead.

This course, through a chute and S turn, is a rite of passage of sorts, which leads to an Amazonian place of estuaries and islands, blind creeks and sloughs. They were a little scared, but we made it through and then, giddy with excitement, wet with spray, the foliage scintillating green all around us, we then went on to explore, working our way toward the Connecticut just as the Indians had, dragging the canoe at times through the shallows of a dozen little waterways. Even the light was the same as the late afternoon light at An Loc, looking north toward Cambodia. The Connecticut roars through a field of boulders at this place; we could hear it well before we reached it and when we got there we just watched for a while, stunned by the beauty of so much fast water. Then we turned and wove our way back to the islands to make camp, picking berries along the way. We cleared a circle amid sweet smelling ferns, and I unpacked all the things I had provided for them.

We had food, we had stories, we had a campfire that cast a glow upon their faces and the silver maples arching overhead, and later that night, as on ambush, I stood watch far into the night while my boys slept. I listened to the rush of the water, and I listened to the rasp of mucus in my oldest son's lungs. We had timed our trip to coincide with the full moon, but the comfort the moon had given me before seemed suddenly to fail me. I felt as though I had been mortally wounded and now my blood had drained away leaving my flesh as pale as moonlight itself. All this time, I had been leading, cooking, telling stories and nobody had noticed the blood dripping from my body.

Mist began to gather in places, floating in the moonlight. In other places the moonlight glittered on fast-moving water. The huge ferns were limned in moonlight. The silver maples made a cathedral for moonlight, yet I was miserable. I thought my son was dying, and the other one was so stricken by loss already that he spent a lot of time hiding under tables, saying nothing. It was like the plume of smoke, rising like an exclamation point from Bad Vibes Hill, this dark, terrifying reality shattering a beautiful sight. Once again, I commiserated with our ancestors. Perhaps it was here, this spot, that the first of our kin to visit Vermont was killed. Perhaps he was looking at moonlight on water when the tomahawk came down on the back of his head, and his knees went limp as he thought of his own sons for the last time. Perhaps our Nordic ancestor was staring at the moon when a cosmic ray zapped his gonads and forever altered our DNA in a way that kills our children. I carry this, this is my inheritance along with war and anger and insanity all woven together in tangled spirals.

I had not told my sons that we might have to give up the farm. I had not told my sons that when I went to my father for help he got angry, and I had seen him for the first time the way he must have been at

Saipan, crazy with anger and his vision of God. He was so angry that he didn't even care when I told him the news about my son having cystic fibrosis, and referred instead to our ancestors who lost children all the time and carried on nonetheless, as though it was a weakness on my part to be so devastated. I did not yet know that my father himself was stricken, that he was the one who would not live much longer, that he had in a sense taken the grenade his own father had thrown at him and cradled it to his own chest and fallen down upon it, absorbing the blast. I did not know, as I stared at the moon on that night, that scientists were working their way down that strand of DNA, and would soon begin to unravel the secrets of this one curse of the many we carry. I did not know that I would survive, farm intact, remarry and bring a third son to camp on this very spot with the other two for many more glorious nights. All I knew was that I was surrounded and had no mortars to call upon; yet when I got up and stretched and urinated the next morning it was as though the river and ancestors had worked on me during the night. There were my two blond-haired sons warming themselves by the fire, there was the sunshine burning through mist, there was the water running fast, and there was the bold musculature of the earth rising through it, shaping the flow. This was manhood, this was the present, this was everything. Soon we were on the river again, shouting and swerving, and the sky was incredibly blue and again the woods alongside seemed to be shimmering, even pulsating green like at the Rome Plow Shitpile the day we divined the ambush and outran it.

Once we got coordinated at the Rome Plow Shitpile our outposts along the road proved effective and the convoys weren't hit anymore. We spent the rest of an uneventful week there while Firestone Freddy and Michelin Mike regrouped. I continued to find more pieces of the lieutenant from Delta Company, just as I find pieces of my father now in his letters, in conversations with others who knew him. I find vertebrae, the debris of his father's intolerance, the bleached and mossy reminders of a dissolute command. Then, one afternoon, as we returned to our NDP, we were told that our company was going to An Loc to replace a company from the Second Brigade. It was almost as good as suddenly hearing that we were all going home. We couldn't believe our luck. All the old-timers, Dennis and Renzel and Animal and Overton, the guys who were soon going home, had been telling us stories about An Loc for months, how great it was and especially about the short-time girls. They were right, too. It really was great there until the plume of smoke rose from Bad Vibes Hill, breaking the truce I liked to imagine we had forged, and we had to run up Highway Thirteen on our tanks to look for survivors.

Now I was left alone with the dead while the rest of my CP group went back for fire extinguishers. I was in a sort of gray-green chamber that had been carved into the thick bamboo by burning fuel, preoccupied by the grotesque sight and the sense of déjà vu until I realized it reminded me of the burning Buddhist monk. Then I pulled the two men who had been thrown from the wreckage a little farther back from the flames. They were both scorched hairless and naked. I tried not to look at them but there was nothing else to look at besides burned bamboo and the pile of flaming wreckage. Where were the fire extinguishers? It was not good for me to spend so much time alone surrounded and unnerved by the dead like this. I knew the Viet Cong had already been here because by now I had developed the ability to know these things. I knew they had been here and looked at the bodies and then run away again when they heard our tanks coming. We had not been first after all. If any weapons or radios had been thrown clear they had taken them; all I found later was the charred frame of a .45 pistol. Now they were circling us, while the helicopter fire team circled above. These were the Viet Cong who knew me, knew my name, and now whatever tenuous peace I thought we had agreed upon was in serious jeopardy. It was like the night when they surrounded our ambush. They would not wait much longer. They would not allow me much more time to get my four bodies and leave before they took the hill back again.

There should have been eight fire extinguishers, four on each tank, but when the guys finally got back they only had two, and one was just half-full. It was another sign of the falling apart; I suppose the tank crews had long ago resigned themselves to letting their vehicles burn, overwhelmed by hopelessness. At any rate, these extinguishers were just enough to knock the flames down, not enough to extinguish them. Meantime, the fire team of gunships overhead was low on fuel. I requested a second team from Quan Loi and got them, but I also got a slick carrying a couple of colonels who wanted to see the wreck. Their friends had been in it.

This complicated things. I tried to talk the colonels out if it: this was a dangerous situation and not a pretty sight, either, but they insisted even though it was twilight now. Their slick came out with the fire team and set down back at the road on the edge of the rubber plantation. I sent one tank back to pick them up. I guess all these guys were from an aviation outfit, and whatever low regard we may have had for both colonels and aviators was dissolved now. They may live in air-conditioned hooches and wear starched, ironed fatigues, but when they come down they come down hard. There wasn't much I could do to make things more presentable, and almost as soon as the two colonels came walking into our clearing one of them began sobbing and had to be led right back out and back to the helicopter by the other one.

Just after the slick had lifted the colonels out, the fire team saw some movement a few hundred yards down the slope from us and began firing rockets in there. We used the unburned ends of the helicopter rotor blades as shovels, or more like spatulas really, and began digging the pilot and copilot out, but there still was a lot of fire, even on the corpses, and the corpses themselves tended to fall apart at the joints. Then one of the tankers called in and said he had movement in the bamboo, just as I had expected. I double-checked with the security squad in that sector, and pretty soon he confirmed it, so I told the tanker he could open up with his fifty. The occasional whoosh and thud of the rockets, and the heavy-metal base tattoo of the fifty-caliber machine gun spurred us to work even harder.

Wakefield was back with me that day as my romeo, filling in for Bob Spahn, who had recently replaced him but got detailed to Quan Loi. Wakefield and I worked together side-by-side when I wasn't talking on the radio. It was so dark by now that I had to call in illumination from the 105 howitzer battery, and that meant the gunships had to clear out. Soon that swaying yellow light was filtering down on us, making the shadows sway too, making everything seem so much more ominous and weird in this ominous and weird bamboo thicket on Bad Vibes Hill. We had to get out of there, but I remembered how Defiant Six had roared at me about leaving the dead behind, and I remembered the crying colonel. I had two canteens of orange flavored "Kool-Aid" on my hips. My mother had sent Mike Division a whole case of Kool-Aid from home. I poured mine on top of the corpses and got more canteens of Kool-Aid from the other guys. Gradually, with the help of Kool-Aid and rotor blades we were able to work the corpses out of the wreckage and onto ponchos.

I knew we didn't have much time. I knew that Bad Vibes Hill was practically hollow inside, filled with VC like a hornet's nest. I knew they were trying to find a way around my infantry security so they could hit the tanks with rockets. They loved doing that. Then they would hit us. It looked like they had already hit the helicopter with a rocket. The tail boom had dozens of small holes in it, and one of the colonels had a hole in his abdomen. Finally we had all the corpses except one loaded on the tanks. But when we tried to lift that last one by grabbing the corners of the poncho, it was still so hot that it melted right through immediately and thumped to the ground again.

Meanwhile, the tank crews were really doing a good job, especially given the fact that one of them had never driven a tank before. They were showing great fire discipline for once, just shooting bursts of six or eight rounds at a time, skipping big fat red tracers through the bamboo, and I was thinking maybe I could really do something with these guys if I had them for a while. But the swaying yellow light made it look like everything was moving, and things could not hold together much longer. In desperation, I ended up urinating on that last corpse to extinguish a particular hot spot. I had hoped that nobody was looking when I did this, but Wakefield turned and saw me. He just said, "Oh sir," and then turned away and puked.

I felt really bad that I had to do that. I felt really bad that the goddamn armor outfit didn't have enough fire extinguishers, and that I had been put into such a position of having to piss on this corpse. But it helped. We were able to roll it onto a new poncho, and we ran back to the tanks with it and mounted up. I was surprised, when I got there, to find that Overton had already brought his squad in from security. It was uncharacteristic of him, and I got weird vibes when our eyes met, but I was too sick and scared and preoccupied to say anything. We just got cranked up and wove our way back out of the rubber and down the road. I was still so worried about ambush on this road, this road which belonged to the Viet Cong even in the daytime, that I kept calling in our coordinates to Oscar Five as we roared south, and he put a rolling umbrella of illumination up overhead.

It was real late by the time we crossed the runway and came in through the wire. The mess sergeant had saved dinner for us. I remember seeing the whites of his eyes as the last of the illumination rounds faded away, and feeling the touch of his hand on my shoulder. But almost as soon as he told me about dinner he knew there was no point. The smell of that clearing on Bad Vibes Hill had permeated our clothing, clung to our skin and hair. Nobody could eat. We all felt sick, felt as though our own skin had been scorched and peeled away, felt as raw as hamburger.

I was in a bad mood for days afterward, pissed off about everything, cruising about the firebase like one of those evening thunderstorms that sometimes cruised above us, looking for trouble. The war always pissed me off anyway, but now it was different. I had clung to my illusion of a separate peace at An Loc, and now the essence of those corpses was clinging to me no matter how much I bathed. I got mad at Overton for bringing his squad in early. He was getting too short. Overton, who was such a fine squad leader, who had been decorated for his courage in getting the wounded out while under fire, who was both personable and honorable, and who also had only ten days left in his tour. But sometimes the last ten days are as dangerous to short-timers as the first ten days are to FNG's. Short-timers sometimes get giddy, feeling immortal, and I had gotten those funny vibes when our eyes had met; and I was depending almost entirely on vibes, less and less on logic at this point.

When I sent him back to Quan Loi to decompress, when I separated him from the men he loved ten days earlier than he had anticipated, he was terribly hurt and couldn't understand that I was doing it out of love and respect for him, that I was afraid he might zig when he should have zagged. Then I got mad at Slider, a new guy. I had gotten Slider in a trade; the other lieutenants and I would trade men like baseball cards. Slider had gotten off to a bad start in Lima's platoon. He could hardly even turn around without stepping on his own dick, and we had adopted him. He just needed time and a new setting and he had begun to become quite popular. But then he borrowed my helmet for a trip into Quan Loi because he had lost his, and then he lost mine, too. I couldn't believe he had done that to me. I had worn that helmet for five months, and it had become a part of me which I cherished and I still miss to this day. As long as I had been wearing that helmet we had seen the enemy before they saw us. As long as I had been wearing that helmet nobody in the platoon had been killed. Now I really got mad at Slider, because by losing my helmet he was putting the whole platoon at risk just as Overton had, and he didn't understand my temper any better than Overton had, either.

Finally Niner Two was able to break my gloom by referring to the men who had died in the crash as "crispy critters," and that made me laugh in the kind of bitter, ironic way that we usually did, and that brought everybody even closer together than before. Doc Murphy helped, too. He was coming along as our platoon medic now, which was great because he was a very popular guy, hailed from Kearney, Nebraska, and hated the war profoundly but would stop at nothing to help another guy out. We kept sweeping the road for mines every day and not finding any, and we kept up our special Mike Division project in the Montagnard village at the south end of our sweep. That helped, too; it helped me particularly to see the children and feel that we were doing something good, something to restore life rather than take it away in this war which made no sense, but it also made me angry that the war had brought such suffering. I loved children long before I was to be a father myself.

This Montagnard village and the people in it had broken my heart when I had first seen them. It was not like the Montagnards villages north of An Loc, the villages on stilts where the people lived in the stone age, or maybe early bronze. In this village, in a dark hollow straddling busy Highway Thirteen, awash in the dust and diesel fumes of convoys, the people seemed to be displaced, refugee Montagnards who lived by making charcoal. They gathered wood in the forest and brought it to the village on their backs. They would cook it in long clay kilns, then bag it and put it on the bus to Saigon. They were the scorn of the Vietnamese, the Viet Cong, and even their fellow tribesmen. Co Dep, the smart and beautiful vendor who always walked with us and seemed so compassionate, even Co Dep did not want to have anything to do with them.

The first few times we walked through the village everybody hid from us. You would think it was deserted but for the smoldering charcoal kilns and the occasional chicken wandering about, a chicken nearly devoid of feathers. So this, too, was what the war had done, and I was angry again when I saw this and imagined the kind of atrocities which accumulate in a village like this next to a convoy route. Day after day I had stood in the empty village and called out, held up handfuls of cigarettes and candy to no avail, trying to find some kind of salvation in this war for both them and us. Finally after three or four days of doing this, when I had almost given up, a couple of children emerged and very shyly approached. These kids looked as bad as the chickens; they were covered with black charcoal dust and had sores all over their bodies. Their scalps were crusted with scabs.

The next time we came, Doc Murphy brought along some extra soap and medications and we got Co Dep reluctantly to translate for us. We got a half-dozen kids and one filthy emaciated *mamasan*. They backed away when we tried to give them things, the very opposite of the Vietnamese villagers we had seen before. But by the time of the crispy critter incident we were taking along a couple of extra medics along with Doc Murphy just to handle the load. We were spending at least an hour there, treating up to twenty or thirty villagers at a time, mostly for scabies, while dozens more villagers looked on. The supply sergeants back at Quan Loi were helping out, scrounging medical supplies and food for our project. Even Co Dep became enthusiastic, forgetting the old animosities and translating nonstop, even laughing at times.

Still, I was angry. Now that I was stronger myself, now that I knew how to find my way as a platoon leader, the war was eating away at me in a hundred different and more subtle ways in this exceptionally beautiful place, where the illusion of peace was so important, where the days ran on, one after another, under spectacular skies.

Our duties changed through a three-day rotation with the other platoons. On the day after we walked south twelve kilometers to the Montagnard village, we would walk westward about six kilometers on the access road toward Quan Loi. After we passed through the west gate of An Loc the road led down into the Vietnamese shantytown that had grown up around the rubber processing plant. It was a very grim place. The plant itself gave off a strong, somewhat rancid, rectal odor. Workers labored over steaming vats. Boilers hissed and farted, venting into the already steamy tropical air. Sheets of latex were fed through rollers and hung on lines to cure. In the hills all around, other workers cut spiraling grooves in the bark of endless rows of rubber trees. The gooey sap was collected in little ceramic bowls at the bottom of each cut, not unlike the way we collect maple sap here in Vermont. A filthy and profoundly putrid-smelling tank truck periodically drove through the rows, and buckets of collected sap were dumped in. This happened every day, day after day, no matter what the war was doing; it was more important.

This was the heart of the Michelin Rubber Plantation, a place infamous for its slave-like working conditions, a place, some said, where the war began. Here, down in the hollow on the road to Quan Loi, and out of sight of the gay streets of An Loc, the people were as dirty and poor as the Montagnards, but we were always being watched and were forbidden to have anything to do with them. Their clothing was, for men, just a filthy pair of shorts. Their eyes always avoided our stare. Their houses were thatch and cardboard boxes and sheets of beer-can tin that had been misprinted. They, in turn, had been forbidden to have anything to do with us. We figured it was because of the French.

The lovely Co Dep, who was almost certainly a communist as well as being a most skillful capitalist with her pushcart of Coke and french bread, the seductive but aloof Co Dep told us that the working conditions had always been hard, that a long time ago the workers had gone on strike, and the plantation owners had captured the strike leaders and killed them.Then after the war with the French, the communists reached an agreement with them and so that was why we were the enemy. Years later, I read that what Co Dep said was true. Most of the rubber workers had come from the north. They were either brought down by the French, who thought that the northerners were good workers and the southerners were lazy, or they were driven south by a great famine which many say the French caused. All this happened in the twenties and thirties, before the Japanese came, when the automobile had suddenly made rubber wildly profitable, and when the idea of a communist revolution and Vietnamese nationalism was becoming popular, especially in the north, where Ho Chi Minh returned after many years as an activist in France.

The efforts of the communist movement quickly focused upon the terrible conditions faced by rubber workers in the south. In the thirties, the workers began to unite and go on strike, threatening the feudal kingdom the French had built. After a particularly long strike, the plantation manager at Quan Loi finally agreed to negotiate, and invited the strike leaders up to his mansion to negotiate. There the leaders were captured, bound, and led back to the beautiful cobblestoned town square of An Loc. There, in front of everyone, they were first disemboweled and then beheaded.

Although we didn't know the details at the time, we trusted Co Dep more than almost anyone else outside Mike Division and the gist of her story was absorbed by us and became a part of our own discussions as we walked through the solemn, stinking shantytown of the rubber workers, and the hissing, flatulent rubber factory. Of course we were always talking to each other, sharing opinions, sharing anger. And the animosity toward the French was nothing new to Mike Division. The old-timers boasted to me of one of their accomplishments a month or so before I joined them. They were out on a sweep in the rubber one day when they got into a harmless exchange of gunfire with some withdrawing VC. It was little more than one of those times when both sides get to use up some old ammunition and make sure their weapons are functioning. A plantation road separated the two parties, and down the road came a Citroen sedan. This was one of the fancy ones, too, not just another of the little hunchbacked Citroens that were so common. Upon seeing the shooting, the car stopped and out stepped a Frenchman.

"Stop shooting," he yelled, waving his arms, "you are hurting zee rubber trees."

Mike Division didn't like being yelled at by this Frenchman. They yelled obscenities back at him, and fired over his head. He turned and ran back up the road. As soon as he had gone a safe distance, an unnamed member of Mike Division unlimbered his M-72 Light Antitank Weapon, took aim on the abandoned Citroen, and fired a rocket right into its nose. The most popular part of this story was the description of the hood fluttering upward through the rubber trees, and the front wheels flying off left and right. Tribal justice had been served, or so we thought, but the anger and resentment lingered, always there. And there should be no mystery as to why the French should equally hate us.

Co Dep would disappear now and then, her place of honor taken by second- and third-rate vendors. On one of those days, when she was off on one of her mysterious missions and not present to supervise us, we stepped off into the rubber to cool off for a while during a southward sweep. It was always a lot cooler in the rubber. We could see the vendors waiting patiently for us back on the road, unable to navigate their carts crosscountry. There we were, hot and tired and angry. There were the little ceramic bowls as always, row after endless row of them collecting sap while the war went on. Then one of the ceramic bowls suddenly exploded in a burst of automatic weapon fire. Looks of amusement were exchanged. Another burst of gunfire, and another bowl disappeared in a shower of pottery and latex. It was fun, everyone agreed. I tried it myself, firing my CAR-15 from the hip. It was the first time I had fired it in weeks. We were getting a bit rusty, so I got the whole platoon on line, and organized a rubber tree assault. We were over thirty strong by then, and we lined up and walked through the plantation rows, shattering bowl after bowl. At one point I looked back toward the road. The vendors were quickly leaving, pushing their carts back toward An Loc.

Thus began one of the other quirky things that Mike Division did, when nobody was watching, along with the doctoring of Montagnard children and hanging out in Vietnamese cafés. I pretended it was a training exercise, that we needed to break the new men in and make sure our ammunition was clean. But really it was the way we expressed our anger and frustration and contempt for the war. Now and then, on my signal, when nobody else was nearby, we would assault something and destroy it. I would just wave my hand, or give a verbal command, and all of a sudden Mike Division would be on line and assaulting just as General Ware had suggested. It was not as much fun as the Citroen, but it was still very satisfying with M-16s, machine guns, and grenade launchers all firing. Once we attacked a wrecked truck, left over from the days when the road was mined. Another time we attacked an abandoned building. Most of the time, we just attacked rubber trees, even though we knew that the U.S. was obligated to pay the French for each one we destroyed.

Our assaults became a cherished secret, a thrill we all looked forward to. We would walk until we were well out of earshot. Then I would give the signal, and whatever vendors may have been with us would exchange a few brief phrases and frightened glances, then quickly disappear, knowing some sort of atrocity was about to take place. We launched grenades into the tops of rubber trees, and white sap would rain down for days afterwards. Machine gunners would take out whole rows of ceramic bowls in one sweep. Antitank rockets would send trees toppling. And when we got back to the firebase at An Loc, nobody asked why we would spend the next hour cleaning our weapons, while Mike Five, ever faithful, kept us well supplied with fresh ammunition.

Once, when I miscalculated the distance a south wind would carry the noise, Bravo Six went ballistic hearing the distant drumrolls and thumps of a firefight, thinking we had been ambushed and were getting wiped out. He couldn't get us on the radio because we were out of range, so he started organizing a reaction force with his remaining tanks and platoon. It wasn't until a supply sergeant wisely pulled him aside and told him it was OK that he could calm down. But not even Bravo Six's anxiety was enough to get us to stop. Nor did we see any

irony in the fact that we could turn so quickly, turn on a dime and resume our project with the Montagnard village just an hour later. What
a lark it was for me, for all of us in the platoon, to play at war with real
guns, avoiding the reality of what this war, of what Devil Six had asked
of us. In the end, it was Co Dep who stopped us from assaulting the
rubber trees. She showed up one morning, back from whatever mysterious journey she had been on, and she gave us hell from the minute we
climbed off our tanks. She told us we were stupid. She told us we were
like children, so nice one minute, and so violent the next. She told us we
were scaring people on the road. She told us there were workers in the
rubber, beyond our vision, who were in danger, women and children lying on the ground afraid for their lives. We were more careful after that,
but we didn't entirely stop. Now and then, I would give the signal and
Mike Division would destroy something.

The country was nibbling me to death with its horror and beauty, its
crispy critters and naked children, and nowhere was it more visible
than from our red clay knob at the north end of An Loc. This knob,
called "Camp Alpha," or "Thunder Five," had already been a First Division firebase for more than two years when we got there. For more
than two years they had been digging positions, filling sandbags with
red clay, moving positions, emptying the sandbags again, digging
garbage pits, filling them, covering them, digging new pits, and mixing
excrement with diesel fuel and burning it. The coils of concertina wire
had been accumulating little bits of windblown trash for two years, just
the little bits that frequent police calls couldn't reach, but by now there
were zillions. Beyond the scabrous concertina wire lay myriad footpaths, an encircling complex of footpaths so intricate that from the air
it looked like the iris of an eye. Some of these were the footpaths our
own listening posts and observation posts used. Some were the footpaths that the vendors and beggars used to approach the perimeter and
hang out day after day, or the short-time girls used night after night,
and always there was the trash, although it had been heavily picked
over by the Vietnamese, who would salvage almost anything. The trash
left was the soda cans and cigarette butts, occasional condoms, fragments of garments or poncho liners too small to use, small pieces of the
two wrecked Caribou supply aircraft, very small scraps of plastic sheeting, candy wrappers, shell casings, cartridge cases from both sides,
feces and toilet paper, all in a great circle around us along with the footpaths, the trash and the footpaths getting increasingly sparse the farther

out you got, until just a few hundred meters out the footpaths were used by the Viet Cong as much as anyone else.

This really was, for the moment, the American frontier, as far as we got, as much as we accomplished. It really was as though a line had been drawn across the countryside, right through the town of An Loc. The footpaths that began at our firebase gradually fanned out and merged and spread like a river's estuaries farther into the hills to merge with the Ho Chi Minh Trail itself. Below An Loc, the margins of Highway Thirteen had been bulldozed back to lessen the chances of ambush. Above An Loc, the highway continued north as it always had been, mysterious and pretty much forbidden, across the border into Cambodia and beyond. Every third day, instead of sweeping the roads, we would go out on a short security patrol to the north, following footpaths beyond the circle of trash. We would skirt around Bad Vibes Hill. We would pass through the other Montagnard villages on stilts. There were no bomb craters, shattered forests, or vertebrae. There were a lot of well-worn paths. It was also really unspoiled, intensely beautiful, and profoundly communist. We never went too far, or looked too closely. There were some villages we dared not enter. In a few of the closer ones, the villagers would not hide or flee when they saw us coming. They would simply pay us no attention at all, seeing right through us, knowing that on this side of An Loc they held the advantage.

There were no vendors north of An Loc, but our firebase drew the drifting Vietnamese like flies. They would show up soon after dawn, looking for work, looking for a handout or a sale, looking for garbage, looking for anything, following the footpaths through the trash to our knoll. Vendors of the lowest caste, those who had not gained the right to work the highways, would hawk sodas, bread and third-rate watery popsicles, passing them to us through the coils of wire. Kids, dozens of kids, kids who should have been in school, should have been almost anyplace else, would beg, with their beautiful big brown eyes, bronze skin and filthy shorts. *Mamasans* offered a variety of services, depending upon their age.

The vendors, beggars, merchants and whores were always there, like the clouds and sky and jungle itself, wearing on nerves already frayed, breaking hearts already wrenched. In some other units, it was customary to hate the Vietnamese, calling them dinks or slopes or gooks, and while we too used those phrases, our hatred was mostly reserved for the French, for there was none among us who really knew the history of why and how we were there. In general, we liked the Vietnamese, though they could get to you, and we knew the soldiers were useless. We liked to hire boys from the crowd outside the wire and bring them in to help us fill sandbags. We were always filling sandbags; first to fix up the filthy mess we had found when we arrived, and later to prepare for the next great offensive that everybody expected.

These boys, who would work hard all day for fifty cents, were usually eight or ten years old, and most spoke no English. But there was one among them who was particularly memorable, and during our time at An Loc he practically became a member of Mike Division. He was twelve and spoke English well, so we put him in charge of the labor crew. He took to the responsibility well, and often became a participant in our ongoing discussions. He confided that he had five brothers who were Viet Cong, and that he himself had joined them too for a few months, but he didn't care for the harsh living conditions. To demonstrate his familiarity with military equipment, he once stripped and reassembled an M-60 machine gun in front of us in just a few minutes, rivaling our own gunners' times. It could really confuse you, this blending and mixing that took place on both sides of the concertina wire at An Loc.

Reminiscent of the pleasant social hours Mike Division had enjoyed at Dragon House, with our homemade meals cooked in army helmets, and again following my lead as a man who enjoys both cooking and eating, we began to commission some of the older *mamasans* by the wire to prepare us special midday feasts. These women, always willing to work, teeth stained black from chewing betel nut, became better and better at this every day. Generally we would order our meal a day in advance from a limited menu they provided. The menu was limited to what they could steal from the advisor compound inside An Loc. They would concoct their own delightfully loose interpretation of American food, fried chicken or steak, more protein than most Vietnamese would see in a week. Occasionally we would daringly request a native dish. Then we would all meet at the appointed hour, down at the foot of the airstrip amid the footpaths and garbage and airplane wreckage. The meals would be waiting, *mamasans* in the background, and often the meals were served on a paper tablecloth they had stolen, with "Happy Birthday" and colorful balloons all over it.

I think of my father at Saipan, waiting endlessly beneath the parade of Pacific clouds and sun, so like our clouds and sun at An Loc. He and his men were not allowed off the ship, not allowed to go ashore and mingle with the few natives who had survived the weeks of bombardment and the mass suicides, but his addition of balconies and turrets to the ship, fighting the boredom and weather, was not unlike the constructions we undertook, using ponchos and ammo crates, and not unlike the excursions outside military decorum I was so often undertaking. It almost was a great thing he did, it always was almost a great thing he did, almost succeeding in deriding the horror of the war and the huge bomb that had ended it, almost completing a perfect satire on navy life, almost giving his men a fun thing to do when there was nothing else to do, and maybe I was almost going crazy at An Loc too, almost nibbled to death by the clouds and the woods and the people. But while my father saw many truths where other men saw none, he didn't see other men very well, and "almost" was as far as he ever got before succumbing to the war within, while my war remained real and I continued to cling to whatever shreds of sanity I could, just to keep myself and my men alive. It wasn't easy, but sometimes it was fun, too.

A certain seduction was taking place at An Loc, as day after day the crowd of civilians around the base grew. There was the seduction of the people, of the decadent but beautiful French colonial town. There was the seduction of the landscape, and day after day without fighting. But it was in the evening, those wonderful An Loc evenings, that things got really interesting as well as hauntingly beautiful. As always, the frantic pace of the day would perceptibly slow; less and less aircraft overhead, less and less traffic on the roads. One by one, as the shadows lengthened, the vendors and solicitors and beggars would go home. The White Mice would close the village gates, and we could savor the setting sun without having to go out on ambush, or really even worry about the Viet Cong at all. Then, as soon as the sun sank into the rubber trees to the west, the short-time girls would start to call from the bushes, Butch and Nancy and Ann and the others, short hair, short shorts and T-shirts, calling softly like little evening birds.

"Hey, GI," they would sing, "you want souvenir?"

Or, more directly, "Ficky-ficky three dollah."

Lucky were the men assigned to listening posts at night. There was always a long list of volunteers. Other men would try to sneak out after dark, crawling through gaps in the wire. Farther beyond, just a few hundred meters out on the trails the girls would use later, at midnight, to find their own ways back home, the VC waited to collect a nightly tribute from them. This was all part of the fabric of arrangements at An Loc, the local VC protected the prostitutes in return for a cut; they all knew each other well. The North Vietnamese army was more difficult to deal with. They were not local and took a harder line, and we always knew when they were around. On the nights when the North Vietnamese army was surging past us, headed for impending battles to the south, the short-time girls begged to be allowed inside our perimeter. They were afraid of being robbed and raped. We opened the wire for them and let them stay all night. Another time we allowed the twelve-year-old boy to stay with us for a week, because, he said, his brothers were looking for him.

Were we taking the enemy in, or being taken in ourselves? It really didn't make much of a difference, because the enemy could be anyone, anybody who gave us a hard time. The desire to break free, to make our own rules, to start walking north up the highway instead of south, kept getting stronger. Cambodia sounded wonderful, like the Emerald City, a place of peace. We could run with the Montagnards, those mountain men who fascinated us so. Buddy Ebsen could play a Montagnard. Some of the guys began to wear the copper bracelets given to us by the Montagnards, and Millhouse bought himself a crossbow from them. He spent hours practicing with it, and wanted to carry it whenever he walked point, counting on the stealth and silence. With Co Dep, and the short-time girls, and the Montagnards as guides, we could probably walk all the way up Highway Thirteen to Cambodia and beyond.

Yet rehearsals were taking place in the darkest shadows of the jungle, not far from Highway Thirteen. We knew this; I had seen the intelligence reports at the advisor's compound. Just to the east of Bad Vibes Hill there was telephone wire strung for miles through the jungle. Special Forces Recon teams had followed the wire until they came to where it had been cut and rolled up by people who saw that they were following it. A few days later the wire was back again. More ominous yet, they had also found tank tracks. These were the tracks of Russian tanks. At this time no Russian tanks had yet been seen in South Vietnam, but North Vietnamese soldiers were practicing, rehearsing the inevitable within ten kilometers of An Loc while the rubber trees kept dripping.

Still, the sunsets were beautiful and the air was sweet and clean. It was nice to pretend that we had forged a separate peace of our own, that the VC had figured out that we were a good bunch of guys, that we would be granted safe passage, if only I had my helmet back. I could do anything with Mike Division, not just destroy rubber trees. They were mine, and I was theirs. I had grown to love them in a way which I would not know again until I had children of my own, and I would silently watch them as they slept. I liked looking at the men in Mike Division the way I like looking at my children. I liked to watch Mike Division working, stripped to the waist, stacking sandbags, strong and healthy and deeply tanned. I recognized them as kin, as family, and all that mattered was each other.

They cared for me, too.

"You take this war too seriously," they would say when I was angry and distraught, especially after the crispy critter incident, "You need to get laid, sir."

I replied that officers don't do that, and I watched more with admiration than envy with the starlight scope as elements of Mike Division sneaked out through the wire at night, now and then pausing to free a bit of clothing that had snagged on a barb, obeying nature's most powerful call. Niner Two and I would often stay up late together, sharing a beer or two we had smuggled in, and passing the starlight scope back and forth. It was a wondrous sight, like watching salmon on a spawning run. Over there, near the runway, a GI emerges from the bushes pulling his pants on in the eerie glow of the scope. Elsewhere, the flash of a white, untanned ass bobbing up and down amid the trash and footpaths draws hoots and gales of laughter.

One night Niner Two disappeared early and I was left to finish the beer by myself at the end of a disgruntling day. It was about eleven at night when I finally crawled back into my bunker, and I was pretty tired. I cupped the lens of my flashlight so that only a narrow, dim ray of light would show, and crept past the sleeping forms of Mike Five, who was back with us at the time, Doc Murphy and Bob Spahn. Then I saw to my utter disgust that somebody else had crawled onto MY sacred air mattress and was curled up asleep under MY sacred poncho liner. All I could see was this shining black hair, and the only person in my platoon with hair like that was Slider. I figured that he must have gotten drunk somehow and crawled into my bunk by mistake.

"Slider, you asshole," I yelled, "get out of my bunk."

But instead of Slider, there was this lilting female voice from under the poncho liner.

"Ah, Mike Six, you numbah one."

Sweet surrender. It turned out the guys were right, it was just exactly what I needed. Within moments I was a goner, totally lost in a darkness and warmth I had all but forgotten after almost half a year, while the other guys in the bunker pretended to be asleep and tried not to laugh. And then, just when the moment was becoming almost unbearably exquisite, I heard somebody playing the guitar on the roof of the bunker directly overhead. After a few opening strums, the singing started, loud singing as a company of infantry, an artillery battery, and an armored platoon were treated to a very spirited rendition of that Bobby Vinton classic, "Young Love."

I was in an excellent mood the next morning, for the first time in weeks. I still am whenever I think about it. Thanks, guys.

· XI ·

WHEN GOING DOWN THE RIVER, as when walking up Highway Thirteen, the moment is everything. We walk, in a column of twos, or we drift, letting the river take us. It is always a special time, even secretive. My boys and I have grown together on the river as my father and I never could on the sea. We go down the river again and again: it is like reading a book that is at once familiar and yet keeps changing. Sands shift, trees topple into the river as the bank erodes beneath them, debris marches haltingly toward the sea. In the quick places the river runs straight over rounded stones and humps of ledge. These are always followed by shoals of ever smaller stones where the channel often changes, and the best places to camp are the islands that part the water with a prow of driftwood, a long sandy bar in their wake. Here there are rainbow trout which rise like jewels and dance toward the frying pan on their tails.

In the slow places the river swerves back and forth, drunkenly working its way through sand and mud, repeating itself for miles with undercut banks on the outside of turns, and broad sandy beaches on the inside, so that it can seem like you are going in circles, especially in the late afternoon when you are tired and a strong south wind is swelling the silver maples along the bank. There are places between the turns where a long shallow suddenly gives way to a deep dark hole where big brown trout sulk, and black bass patrol the edge like gangs of thugs. You can watch the river changing, watch grains of sand or bits of leaf or stick roll past. You can feel the river changing while standing knee-deep on a shoal, as the river tries to suck you in with the steadily shifting sand.

Cycles of summer freshets and droughts leave their marks on the mud banks like the rings of trees, but higher up you can see how the real changes are made. Sometimes the bank-side trees have deep wounds in their bark ten or twenty feet above where the water is in summer. This is where huge cakes of ice have come thundering down during spring break-up, on a tide so powerful it seems incomprehensible on a summer evening. This is how the real changes are made, in a great scouring and cleansing and sweeping away. Sometimes trees and ice will form a dam upstream, sometimes water and more ice and more trees will gather behind this dam for days. The serenity downstream is deceptive. Sooner or later the dam will burst, and the wall of ice and water and debris will carry everything away, not only trees but houses and railroad bridges and cattle as well.

It was, during those days at An Loc, as though such a dam lay somewhere across the upper reaches of Highway Thirteen. Everyone knew the flood was coming, and that it would sweep everything away. The telephone wire and the tank tracks foretold of it. The ragged rubber workers and endlessly dripping trees foretold of it. Co Dep and the charcoal makers foretold of it. But for the moment, the serenity, or the illusion of serenity, was something to be savored. We would banter in baby talk with the Vietnamese kids filling our sandbags. We would watch the air force Caribous land and chase the White Mice.

August melted away into September, and the enemy unearthed two ancient 75mm pack howitzers. These had been left behind by the Japanese army twenty-five years before. The guns were hidden inside tunnels not far from An Loc, and enough ammunition had been scavenged for them to be trundled out at night and fired after decades of silence. They began to shell Quan Loi, just four or five shells every night, not enough to get a fix on their positions and deliver an effective counterfire. These shells had much greater penetrating power than mortars, and were more accurate than the 122mm rockets the enemy used. So we went back to work on our firebase, building walls for our sleeping positions out of wooden 105mm shell boxes filled with dirt, plus three more layers of sandbags all around. But they never shelled us at An Loc, though we could see the flashes and hear the muffled whumps, perhaps because our base was too small a target for the bores of those old howitzers, which must have been worn nearly smooth by now; or perhaps it was another agreement, perhaps with the vendors.

Yet the war was drawing me in deeper, spinning me like a pebble or twig, moving me in uncontrollable and inexplicable ways. It had me, like the river, even though I hated it. I kept trying to make sense of it and find virtue, while my father continued to write about progress on the pram. I was beginning to realize that there was a good chance I would survive the war after all, having made it through five-sixths of my tour as a platoon leader, and my father recommended some time at sea when I got back. He said that nothing clarified thinking better than being off-shore. It would bring the rest of the world into perspective. But already the river had pulled us farther apart. Shore was what I longed for.

The sea, and the pram, and the fishing had been a compromise for both of us from the start. It had not been by accident that every season at Camp Keewaydin began with a showing of the movie classic *Captains Courageous*. The film's theme of finding a surrogate father at sea was worth repeating, and the film remains a favorite of mine today. My own father had not fished until I showed him how, and talked him into using his boats for it. While our dory rocked in the swells outside Stonington harbor, my father and I succeeded in imagining that we had found each other. This pretending worked for both of us, with the hand-lines and the wonderful tugs, and he would rhapsodize the simple life. Later, his wife Mary or sister-in-law Rose would cook us a fish dinner as only a Portuguese woman can, further indulging our fantasies, and we would feast on our spoils. Then out would come the sketchpad again, and the pram would begin to take shape. Of course we both knew that really, fishing for a living is brutal work. Our expeditions in the pram were designed for those days when the economy had collapsed, and it was once again possible for a man to make a living in simple and medieval ways, when the spigots of growth and gasoline had gone dry and goats grazed upon the White House lawn.

I enjoyed the fantasies, but I had remained uncomfortable with the sea and, unfortunately, him. I remained secretly angry with him for his collapse in the harbor of Saipan, and remained secretly cold and uncomfortable in small boats at sea. While his married life in Stonington was wonderful in many ways, I was still suspicious of his long bache-lorhood in Brooklyn, even though he painted beautiful portraits of the working-class neighborhoods and backwaters there. If he really wanted fatherhood and a family life, why did he isolate himself there for so long? It was not until many year later when, during a moment of extreme drunkennes, he told me that he was a homosexual, that some of his behavior began to make more sense, but I was angry with him all along for not going somewhere, doing something with his amazing talents as an artist and storyteller. I had always declined his frequent invitations to join him on longer sea journeys, not daring until I was a man myself, and of course that was the night we got lost and ended up anchoring beside a bombing target. Not all that much ever changed since those primordial days of the toy tugboat, with both of us fishing for something, giving and taking away. I always needed the adventure that the river promised, and that neither the sea nor my father could deliver. I always needed the love that had eluded me until I met Mike Division. Now the charcoal makers were calling to me again. I had not been able to pass through that village without trying to do something. At first it was the children that broke my heart. Perhaps I had been so drawn to them in the first place because I saw in them myself as a child. In the weeks that followed they had in turn been drawn to us, gathering around Mike Division, clamoring for attention, and two weeks of antiseptic soap alone had worked miracles on them. This was an experience closer to my previous plans for going into medicine, closer to my present as a father. But then the river took another turn and presented an even deeper hole to me.

One day, while Co Dep was with us and we were distributing soap and medicine and candy, and what we thought was the entire village was gathered around us, the menfolk who had up until then been so mysteriously absent suddenly materialized. About a dozen of them emerged from hidden tunnels in the village, gawking nervously and blinking in the harsh morning light. Furthermore, they were wearing black pajamas and carrying weapons. Any less of a platoon than us would have shot them, but clearly they were friends with everybody in the village and also they were too old to be Viet Cong. It had taken them a long time to get up the courage to come out of hiding, and as they timidly approached I was transfixed not only by them, and their age, but by their weapons as well, which were even older and more unusual. They were members of the village's own Popular Defense Force, part of a little-known government effort to defend against communist insurgents at the grassroots level.

With Co Dep's help, they explained that the VC came to this village every night. They would hide in their tunnels while the VC recruited help and delivered lectures. The only time they ever came out was when the VC showed a movie. Then they hid from the Americans during the day, because they looked so much like VC themselves.

"Why don't you keep the VC out of the village?"

"Not enough ammunition," was the reply, and their spokesman reached down into the deep pocket of his baggy black gown and produced a handful of bullets, the brass casings all turned dull brown with time. I recognized a .45 caliber. Thompson carried by one of the men, the rest seemed to be vintage bolt-action models.

Naive as I still was, isolated from the totality of Vietnam as I still was, these men had tremendous appeal. They told me they thought they could defend the village if they had more ammunition, so off I went, down another stretch of river. I could hardly wait to get back to An Loc, and we all loaded up into hired *lambrettas* and headed north again. Then I left my men in one of the cafés and headed over to the advisor's compound to look for ammunition. I was fascinated by the place, always looking for an excuse to enter and poke around. I envied the officers assigned there. Instead of sacrificing the lives of fellow Americans, they were working with the people themselves, lending military assistance, doing civic action projects, gathering intelligence. But they couldn't help me out with the ammunition, so the next time we went to the village we brought along a case of hand grenades along with our medicine and soap. Of course the old men were delighted. In retrospect I'm sure the Viet Cong were, too.

On it went; days were ticked off on the short-timer calendars the men had drawn on their helmets. The guys who had already been in Mike Division for six months before I came along, the guys who had been through the Ho Bo Woods the first time, and Song Be Mountain and the Tet Offensive were going home now, with their bronze stars and silver stars and Purple Hearts. They carried the names of a platoon of dead with them. They'd seen a dozen platoon leaders and company commanders come and go. It seemed almost incomprehensible to me that they had endured so much for so long, seeing their friends killed, sometimes holding them as they died, and yet not being afraid to make new ones. Dennis went home. Overton went home. "Red" Renzel and Animal and Doc Murphy went home. What once had seemed too remote even to think about was about to become real. For a while, the freedom bird was theirs, and I would wonder often how they fared in the cruel battles to come.

Bravo Six, Lieutenant Erwin, who had done his allotted six months as a platoon leader, and then got stuck with six more as company commander, went home. He was one of us and knew his stuff, with the irreverent attitude of a grunt as well as the skill of leadership. We got a new Bravo Six, a captain on his second tour of Vietnam, and an old man of thirty or so with a wife and kids back home. Bob Spahn went home, and I got Millhouse to be my romeo. I really liked Millhouse; he was bright and fun, with a burning thirst for adventure. He reminded me of Bill Moss from high school, the first man I knew to be killed in Vietnam.

While I knew that I still had more than half a year in Vietnam ahead of me, I also knew that my time with Mike Division would end soon. Six months were all we were allowed and it made sense. I could feel myself burning out. It was more than the voices, the muttering trees and soothsaying butterflies. It was more than the fact that I had long ago reversed the priorities assigned to me with my commission; the welfare of my men had become far more important than the mission. It was more than the loss of distinction between myself and my men, the unquenchable desire to walk away from the war together. It was the love that had developed, that I would not know again until I was a father, that my father never quite knew. I was constantly fretting about perils, real and imagined, going over maps again and again, dreading the possibility of combat and loss, loss for which I might be held accountable. Yet I had to keep exploring. As much as I hated this war, I also knew I still had more than half a year to go, and I wanted to make the best of it.

The advisors at An Loc had told me about a new and exciting program that had just developed. Five-man teams of advisors were being deployed across the country like Special Forces teams; some of them even wore black berets. Called Mobile Advisor Teams, they worked with the local Vietnamese forces, worked with villages, worked with groups like the old men in black pajamas in the Montagnard village. I submitted an application.

My father wrote that he had broken a few ribs while tightening a keel bolt on the pram. It was painful but healing. He described the late summer weather, the village shrouded in mist, the foghorns and bells sounding. He had become like one of the Viet Cong himself, or so he would like to think, starting a newsletter to fight the proposed construction of a jetport in northeastern Connecticut. He included some savagely funny cartoons, one of a combination jet liner/ eagle/politician looming over the state. Shells continued to fall on Quan Loi. We were reinforced with antitank weapons at An Loc in anticipation of the flood. We increased our patrolling to the north; there was a big ARVN unit at An Loc, but they never seemed to stray from the well-worn path between their base and the local cafés. Yet still we saw nothing; nothing but Montagnard villages on stilts hidden among tall trees, steeped in darkness, where people greeted us; nothing but bright and well-tended Vietnamese villages where we seemed to be invisible, nothing but whispering bamboo hedges and long, brooding rows of rubber trees.

Often, on the footpaths approaching one of the Montagnard villages, we would see little trees deliberately placed and decorated like Christmas trees, with bright baubles and pendants of colored paper, tinfoil and glass. Each village had its own recipe, its own formulation of totems, charms and curses designed to keep some spirits out and invite others in. In their animistic beliefs, everything was alive and anything was possible, good and evil swirled through the jungle and one had to navigate with care. This made more sense to us than anything else; we really admired the Montagnards, felt a commonality with them, Red-feather especially so, and Millhouse too, carrying his crossbow, while others sported copper amulets, and our tribalism deepened more the farther we went up Thunder Road.

As a newcomer, Bravo Six wanted to familiarize himself with the area as quickly as possible, so during his first week of command he often went up in a light observation helicopter to scout around. He was several kilometers north of An Loc one day when the helicopter went down with engine failure. Luckily he and the pilot were able to jump clear and run before the ship beat itself to pieces with its own rotors and burst into flames. So there they were, in the middle of never-never land with only a .45 pistol and a chicken salad sandwich between them. They knew the VC would soon come looking for them, so they immediately set off, having discovered the maze of footpaths that had lain hidden beneath the jungle canopy. They began following one of the paths cautiously back south, in the general direction of An Loc.

They had not gone far when a tall dark man wearing a loin cloth and carrying a bow and arrows stepped into their path, intercepting them. Imagine hillbilly Buddy Ebsen in a loincloth, dark-skinned, his body covered with tattoos. Speaking no English but gesturing, he encouraged them to follow quickly and took off at a run. It was difficult for them to keep up with him as he ran, barefoot and utterly silent, through the network of trails, some VC, some Montagnard. He may have been twice their age, but he was sinuously agile. He would allow them only a few short pauses to catch their breath, then he would take off again. He led them directly to the foot of our hilltop base at An Loc, to where the trail became littered with condoms and cigarette butts. But when they tried to thank him, tried to persuade him to come inside our perimeter and be rewarded in some way, he just turned and ran back into the jungle again.

This would be one of the stories I would come to tell my father later, as we sat at the kitchen table drinking beer after eating fish. Then he would praise the noble savage, and go on to reach conclusions about society in general, and then describe his own gradual disenchantment with Catholicism. It was a safe story to tell. There were others I could never tell him, stories too open to his own misinterpretations, or too close to me, or that might widen the distance between us. The river continued to pull. The sun would rise yellow in the sky, and tendrils of mist would feather upward through the rubber trees. Midday the white sun would burn above traffic on Highway Thirteen; the two-and-a-half-ton army trucks, the gaily painted and grossly overloaded buses, the *lambrettas* and jeeps and bicycles. The sun would turn red and set. Now, as autumn's first chill was descending upon Stonington, the Special Forces camp at Loc Ninh was being hit. Loc Ninh, a colonial town like An Loc, lay on Highway Thirteen right where it crossed into Cambodia. It, too, had a cobblestoned square and a fountain. But it was off-limits, in the heart of never-never land, the domain of the Green Berets and their Khmer mercenaries who knew no borders.

Two great armies were maneuvering toward each other, maneuvering toward each other in the inexplicable and inevitable way that armies do, drawn together by the pheromone of war. Now, while the old Japanese howitzers were being trundled out almost nightly to shell Quan Loi, the Special Forces camp was being used for target practice with a new sort of weapon. The North Vietnamese had taken conventional Russian 122mm rockets and put on an oversize warhead. You could see them flying through the air; they looked like flying garbage cans and they made a crater twenty feet wide. No bunker could withstand their blast. Fortunately they were also very inaccurate. But the Special Forces camp was besieged, and the surrounding jungle had become a black hole. Patrols that dared venture forth would not re-emerge.

One September morning a resupply helicopter flying over Loc Ninh noticed hundreds of soldiers lounging around the fountain in the town square below. They were doing the sort of things soldiers do, washing their feet in the fountain, hanging out in cafés, listening to transistor radios and bartering for goods, but they were wearing tan uniforms instead of the camouflage "tiger suits" of the Khmer. The helicopter pilot circled lower for a closer look, then hightailed it back to Quan Loi. They were North Vietnamese soldiers, and this is how the battle of Loc Ninh, the biggest battle the Black Lions faced in Vietnam, had its beginning. It was, as were other great battles such as Bu Dop and Khe Sanh, centered upon an airstrip as though by previous agreement, for one of the very first things we had done in Vietnam was build airstrips, build more of them than we could possibly use, but build them anyway as settings for battle. By that afternoon, Defiant Six and all of his companies except for us had been lifted in and began setting up a defensive perimeter alongside the airstrip at Loc Ninh, a sumptuously inviting asphalt airstrip two kilometers long, with a Special Forces camp at either end.

Within moments of their arrival, Defiant was being hit hard with mortar barrages, small arms fire from the wood line alongside the strip, and occasional flying garbage cans. We could see the flashes of light on the horizon that night. Another battalion was lifted in the next morning, but the pressure on them simply increased, and resupply by air was becoming dangerous. The North Vietnamese had moved in heavy weapons. They had 20mm antiaircraft guns set up alongside the runway, and were hitting the infantry emplacements with recoilless rifles. The 11th Armored Cavalry, the Black Horse Regiment, was sent to Loc Ninh, a few elements at a time. The only way to get there was up Highway Thirteen, and our outpost at An Loc was the last safe haven on the route.

Our evening serenity was broken by the arrival of Black Horse elements; tanks and tracks grinding across the runway and into our perimeter to laager up for the night. I recognized an officer I had known at Fort Polk when the first elements of tanks and self-propelled 155 howitzers pulled in. He was scared, knowing what lay ahead the next day. They would have to run a gauntlet of antitank rockets fired from the rubber trees and bamboo hedges while they drove full speed all the way to Loc Ninh, and only then would the real battle begin. We were unnerved, too. Just having so many vehicles parked at our NDP was enough to make us wary. It was a flagrant violation of decorum. But nothing happened that night, and they continued north the next morning, heavy metal drawn by war's magnet.

Loc Ninh continued to develop into a major battle, almost within earshot. Every day we figured that we would be next, that we were being held in reserve for some awful mission. Yet every day turned out to be just like the one before. We swept the road for mines. There never were any mines. We patrolled to the north and saw nothing but sensed a lot. But the war was drawing closer, there was no doubt about that, and with more Black Horse elements expected to use our perimeter at night it became clear that we had to do something about the by now embarrassing number of civilians hanging out along the concertina wire. And it was true, the situation had gotten out of control. Our listening posts at night, and observation posts during the day, were totally compromised, nothing more than picnics and debauchery. Our fields of fire were obscured by ragged throngs hawking wares and seeking employment. Many Vietnamese were inside the wire, perfectly able to pace off distances to CPs and ammo dumps, or jot down the frequencies of radios. All this while the rest of our own battalion was being chopped to pieces just eighteen kilometers to the north, and once again the corpses of young men wrapped in ponchos were accumulating by the wire, and even those of us who watched from a distance fretted and grieved.

Our laxity was shameful under these circumstances. Something had to be done. So mid-afternoon we made all the civilians inside the NDP leave. This part was easy. These were the ones who knew us best anyway. Then we walked down to the wire yelling "Di, di di mao," which was about the only Vietnamese everybody knew, meaning "Go away." Only they wouldn't go away. They just smiled and waved back at us. We yelled louder, waved our arms, felt helpless. They weren't getting the message, couldn't understand there had been a change in policy. We began to get angry, felt they might even be ridiculing us after this went on for about an hour, and still the throngs, not the trusted throngs but the garbage pickers and third-rate vendors remained in place, perhaps even amused by our antics and lousy Vietnamese. So then we gave tear gas canisters to all the men with grenade launchers, and fired tear gas into their midst. They left fast, and the quick glance back at us over the shoulder as they fled said everything. They didn't come back.

Again, the sun swelled red and sank into the rubber trees. Again, the horizon to the north flickered like heat lightning through the night. Again, the sun rose yellow above the rubber trees. We rode the tanks west, on the shorter sweep toward Quan Loi. As we passed through the thatched hut squalor of the rubber workers, one of my men accidentally hit the magazine release button on his M-16. The magazine, with eighteen rounds, dropped from the weapon and disappeared into the engine grates of the tank. I can't remember the name of the guy who did this, but I sure remember his silly grin. Another Mike Division magic moment. I grinned back. Word quickly spread among the ten or twelve of us on the tank; live ammo on the hot engine. Everybody grinned and remained silent, waiting. The tank commander, looking straight ahead, TC helmet pulled down over his ears, remained unaware, as did the other crew members inside.

We only had to wait a minute or so before all the rounds began to cook off pretty much at once. We knew there wasn't any danger: the shell casings just rupture when this happens. At least we thought there wasn't any danger, but when the rounds began to pop the tank crew flew apart. The driver swerved sharply to the right, leaving the road, and slammed on the brakes, nearly throwing us off. Then all the hatches burst open and the crew popped out like corks and ran away into the bushes. It took us a couple of minutes to persuade them to come back, and it was pretty funny but it was really pathetic, too.

Day after day, convoys of tanks, armored personnel carriers, and self-propelled 155 howitzers would go north. Night after night, the sky would flicker and the short-time girls would return, more cautious now, always staying outside the wire. They knew more details about the battle to the north than we did. "*Beaucoup* VC," they would say. Our lives still seemed charmed, even after we gassed the civilians, and still, on morning sweeps or afternoon patrols, now and then when nobody else was nearby I would give the signal and Mike Division would destroy something, but it was beginning to get a little scary. It was getting harder to get them to stop. I was afraid of losing control, afraid of what might happen under slightly different circumstances with this awesome power at my command, not so much the awesome power of the weapons as the awesome power of angry and frustrated young men. So we stopped.

Out of boredom, Niner Two and I began converting signal rockets into high explosive rockets one afternoon. We removed the flare and parachute from one of these handheld munitions, and replaced it with a blasting cap and some C-4 plastic explosive. The result was even better than we had expected: the rocket would take off with a whoosh. Then there would be a pause. Then a hundred feet or so in the air there would be a really loud explosion. Those around us tolerated it for a while, and were no longer startled after the first half-dozen launches. Again I think of my father's question: "Did I ever think I was going crazy?" Again I think of the reply I should have given, "Well, sort of." Niner Two and I kept putting more explosive in, and this tended to make the rockets top-heavy, even harder to control than the flying garbage cans. Some of them would nose over a few seconds after launch and begin to skip and slither around on the ground, chasing people. They were pretty hard to dodge, too, zigzagging unpredictably, under the laundry lines and past the latrines, then exploding with the force of a half-stick of dynamite. How crazy is this, in the midst of war, assaulting rubber trees and launching explosives into your own midst while the sun beats down and the clouds build to tremendous heights above, day after day, and why can't I stop, even now, especially when my boys are with me and it is the Fourth of July? Just what sort of leadership and fatherhood is this?

The North Vietnamese regiments began hitting the positions at Loc Ninh with human wave attacks, not unlike the banzai charges of Saipan. The artillery lowered their tubes and fired canister rounds of buckshot and "fleshettes." The aptly named fleshette is a finishing nail, about an inch long, with fins in the back to keep it going straight. Still, some NVA would manage to get through and inside the wire before they were brought down. Then the NVA fired tear gas into our positions at Loc Ninh, the only time I have heard of them doing this. They kept launching the flying garbage cans, too. And then Niner Two had to go to Loc Ninh to replace the artillery officers who had been hit, leaving me to play with my rockets alone. I couldn't do it any more.

While on an afternoon patrol just west of Bad Vibes Hill, we were called to assist a stalled armor column headed for Loc Ninh. There was a barricade in the road, we were just a few hundred meters away, and they wanted us to clear it for them. Some logs and brush had been piled in the road, and a crudely lettered sign made of scrap plywood had been placed in front of the pile. The armor could have run right over it, a jeep could have run right over it, but they were afraid it might be booby-trapped or conceal a mine. So the lead elements of the convoy waited about a hundred meters back while we checked the barricade out. Meanwhile, it turned out that this Black Horse cavalry outfit had a Vietnamese scout along with them, so I asked that he be brought forward to translate the sign for us. This he did, explaining that the sign said there was an ambush in the road ahead, and that civilian traffic should take the detour to the left, up past Bad Vibes Hill. And sure enough, as we stood there, a couple of civilian *lambrettas* came up past the convoy, stopped, read the sign, and turned left.

I told the captain commanding the convoy what the sign said, and recommended that he turn left himself, but he said he couldn't do that. So I figured that was his problem, not mine. Meanwhile we had examined the barricade and it looked safe, just a sign and some sticks, but my men began to pull it apart with ropes and a grappling hook nonetheless just to be safe. As they did so, a man in the turret of the lead track yelled "BOOM" as a joke and then laughed. Then the column started up again, and we went back to our patrol. The column had only gone a few hundred meters more when there was the unmistakable thump of a rocket being launched, followed almost immediately by the crash of its impact. It hit the turret of that lead track, killing the man who had yelled "Boom." We ran up the grassy hillside toward where the rocket had been launched, but all we could find was the place where the gunner had waited patiently and smoked two cigarettes.

For fifty years, starting before they even had any real weapons, the VC, and the Annamite rebels before them had been placing barricades in this road. I like to think that this was just one very elderly VC, perhaps in his seventies, who still doggedly clung to the traditional barricade while his younger brethren resorted to less gentle tactics. What was most impressive was that the sign warned civilians away. He knew the armor units as well as we did, and was concerned that the American column would overreact to his rocket and fire indiscriminantly left and right, as they so often did. This was a very conscientious Viet Cong, as well as a good shot. And once again, we were clumsy, inept, and suffering grievously.

During the brief lulls at Loc Ninh, while the enemy regrouped for their next attack, it was unsafe even to send out observation posts a few hundred meters from the perimeter. Observer teams and scout patrols would simply disappear. Of course Devil Six, General Ware, went to Loc Ninh. He was on the ground there or aloft in his helicopter every day. Stories about what was happening there, and what he did, came back to us either by radio or by way of Quan Loi, which was where the wounded and dead were taken. We heard that Recon had gone out for the first time in over a week, and had been badly mauled just a few kilometers from the airstrip. Several men were severely wounded, with sucking chest wounds and uncontrollable bleeding. They needed to be evacuated fast if they were to live, but each time the medevac ships tried to approach Recon's position, they drew such heavy ground fire they didn't dare land. So Devil Six took his own helicopter in and brought them out.

A few days later Devil Six's helicopter was hit and he and the three men with him perished in the flaming crash. I know now that he was suffering, too. I know now that when he told me to get my men on line and assault, he did it because of his own pain. And I know that when he landed among us in the Ho Bo Woods to hand out medals, it was because he had been suffering with us. I know things as a father that I could not then understand as a son. We were all suffering, we were all bleeding on the inside, if not the outside, and sometimes our own suffering blinded us to the suffering of others. We were all on the same ship. The ship was foundering. Out of fear, out of pain, some blame the crew, others the shipwrights or even the travel agents. Major General Keith Ware, commander of the First Infantry Division, was the only general to die in the Vietnam War.

The nights were chilly. By sunrise the poncho liners would be soaked with dew. Mist made our An Loc hilltop seem even more like an island. Highway Thirteen would be empty, vacant, waiting for us. Certainly, I would be called upon again. Certainly, the heart-stopping cracks and crashes would resound among us again. And certainly, I was still an imposter myself, still a coward posing as a platoon leader. Certainly I would be caught at it, even though my only witness was now dead himself. I kept dark secrets hidden inside, covered with bravado, camouflaged by sun-bleached fatigues. Even at Camp Keewaydin, I had shied away from the mandatory boxing matches, unable to ratchet my emotions into aggression for aggression's sake alone. While other boy athletes rehearsed for great battles on the football fields of high school, I sold hot dogs to the fans. Even in basic training and officer candidate school, I dragged my feet and found excuses not to participate in the pugil stick matches, where the objective is to beat the shit out of somebody who moments before was a friend. There are even those today whose idea of a good time is to go to a bar and get drunk and fight, who see aggression and violence as manly, and there was my grandfather, who as an All-American quarterback had won the equivalent of the Medal of Honor in battle at a very young age, and continued to nurture the aggression that had brought him fame for the rest of his life. I was, then, secretly not quite fully a man. I was, then, perhaps like my father all along. I was, then, attacking rubber trees to make up for it, dreading that the test of combat would be administered to me again, while the battle of Loc Ninh raged on.

Afternoon clouds would build up like towers. Men would be detailed to drag the metal drums out from under the latrines, mix diesel fuel with the excrement, ignite the mess and slowly stir it for hours with a steel engineer stake. We would listen on the radio for reports from Loc Ninh. We would play cards and eat hot meals every day. At one point a dentist came to see us. He had just gotten out of dental school a few weeks before, and thought our outpost was the end of the earth. If Niner Two had been there we certainly would have launched one of our special rockets for the occasion, but he was still at Loc Ninh. So, while the rest of the battalion faced mortar barrages and ground attacks, Bravo Company lined up for dental examinations. The guy's equipment was monstrous, probably dating back to the Second World War, but it looked like it could have been World War I. His drill, on a long, articulated arm like any dentist's drill, was powered by his dental assistant who sat on a little bicycle seat rapidly turning a hand crank. When the dentist bore down hard, and the drill whined lower, the assistant cranked harder, pouring sweat. Most men chose extractions instead.

This dentist told me that I had a mossy tongue, and threatened to take out my wisdom teeth. My response was unfriendly. I still have my wisdom teeth and mossy tongue. Gradually, the night sky flickered less. Niner Two came back. He looked like shit, he was so tired and worn out, and he was covered from head to toe with brownish-purple slime. I asked him if it was blood or clay, and he said it was both. It was also gun oil: during the more ferocious moments he had been firing the howitzers himself. There had been few opportunities for sleep in over a week. He also told me about Recon going out to get Devil Six after the helicopter went down, knowing that I would appreciate it. It had been like that time for me, with the helicopter in flames and VC all around, scared and disgusted and deeply moved at the same time. Recon came back with what they thought were the four bodies, but then graves registration called up the next day to say that what Recon had really brought back was the bodies of three men and the body of Devil Six's German shepherd mascot. So Recon had to go back out again.

Then the armor units began their long, slow and painful trip back down Highway Thirteen, dragging themselves like crippled dinosaurs across the runway and into our perimeter for the night. It seemed like almost every vehicle bore the star-burst pattern of an antitank rocket's hit somewhere on its flanks, and everything was the same greasy reddish-purple color as Niner Two. Some tracks were being towed, others were on flatbed trailers, and many had been left behind. The column moved so slowly, pausing for occasional breakdowns, and still enduring the occasional rocket attack, that it was well after dark before the last elements came limping in.

We just watched. The raw and glistening scars in armor plate, the mudflaps and handrails torn away, the ooze of fuel and gear oil spoke eloquently of what the men themselves had been through. I saw my friend from Fort Polk again, filthy and gaunt and silent. The men, the machines, had the look of an army in retreat, an army which had been defeated, although of course many times as many North Vietnamese had been killed, and the strategists would see this as a clear victory. But these men knew that there are no winners, that there are only survivors, forever scarred by the agony and humiliation of war.

The war was following the survivors back to our hilltop, harassing their withdrawal. The 105 light howitzers began to fire as soon as the sun had set, and soon they were joined by the 155 medium artillery of the armored cavalry. Our position was crowded, too, far too crowded, with four or five times the number of men and machines it was meant to enclose. It was hard just getting around, finding one's way to the mess tent and back. The nearly constant firing of the big guns was unnerving. The Viet Cong had warned us on the radio. The Viet Cong had even gone to the extreme of leaving a warning sign in the road. But we had teargassed the *mamasans,* and Slider had lost my helmet.

It was easy to sleep through the intermittent booms of the artillery; we had long ago learned to sleep through those booms, with the ammobox walls shaking, the dirt sifting down, the air heavy with the smell of gun grease and smoke. Booms were OK.

"CRASH."

Crashes were not OK and I woke up instantly. Everybody woke up instantly.

"Crash, crash, crash," and the shouts of "INCOMING" from all over the base, and flashes of light, like lightning. The four of us scrambled from our sleeping bunker to our fighting hole. Rounds of mortar fire were raining down steadily, impacting very close by, in November's sector just fifty meters away. Again and again, there was the blue-white light and the sound of the air being ripped apart, and the rattle and thud of debris. Now and then there would be a brief pause while the VC shifted their aim to another sector, a pause filled with the shouts of men.

"You OK, Lima Five?"

"Medic, we need a medic over here."

I looked at our medic's face, instantly lit as the crashes began again. Then he was up and gone, out of the bunker in another crash. It seemed to be going on forever; a pause filled with human cries, and then more rounds crashing, debris falling. It reminded me of the times when I was a small child, and a thunderstorm was raging outside, filling the night with light and a certain amount of fear. But this was something else, this was pungent scented badness and death. There was nothing for us to do but hunker down and wait, crammed together in our hole, but there were others who were out there in it, dashing back and forth in the flickering light of explosions as the mortar fire shifted. There were medics out in it, who could not resist the cries for help. And Oscar Five was out there in it with his mortar crews, directing counterfire with our own gun tubes, Oscar Five whom fate had played with so that his contempt for this war had gotten him two tours, Oscar Five and his men were out there in the open shooting back.

Could I go out there myself? Could I stand up and assault? I think that generals are driven by the memory of their own fear when they were young, and combat becomes a personal test more important than the war itself. Fortunately, I didn't have to leave the bunker. Eventually, the only sound was of Oscar Five's mortars shooting. Then he put up an illumination round, and the rest of us emerged.

I can see the silhouettes of men now, in the swaying yellow light. I can see them wandering about, kicking the wreckage aside. I can smell the air, like ozone. And I can hear the sounds of grief for the dead. Our bunkers were strong enough to withstand the barrage of eighty rounds, but first you had to get to a bunker. I can see the stricken face of Lima Six as he stood above a man in his platoon he had loved; gallons of blood came out of a hole so small it was almost unnoticed, and now it was too late to warn him about the place he had chosen to sleep; he looked as though he was still peacefully asleep now, except for the blood. Two more dead lay elsewhere, among the armor and artillery-men, and there were more wails of anguish as they were found.

The next day the brigade chaplain came out to our firebase to hold a memorial service. It was the first time anyone could recall having seen a chaplain in the field, and it was the first time any of our dead had been given an official service by anyone other than their fellow infantrymen. Usually, it was Defiant Six or Bravo Six who called us together to stand over those bundles wrapped in ponchos, and said a few words over the bundles before the helicopter came to begin the long journey home. "Wasted," was the term we used. These guys got wasted. Now they were dead meat. This chaplain was an interloper, an anomaly, like the dentist, one of them, not one of us, no matter how hard he tried. His assistant passed out government-issue hymnals. The chaplain himself spoke from behind a folding field table, with three pairs of muddy, worn-out jungle boots on the table in front of him. Perhaps this helped his own pain, but there was nothing he, nor the dentist, nor the USO show could do or say to make the war any better, or the deaths any more acceptable. He would have done better to attempt a rendition of "The Girl From Ipanema." He would have done better pulling teeth, and to this day I keep wondering where he got those old boots. He must have had a footlocker full of them.

The bitterness, the resentment toward outsiders was part of our closeness and grief, too, not something to be shared beyond our own close circle. That is why we were so silent when we got home. It was not just the Viet Cong or NVA who were the enemy lying outside our wicked coils of concertina wire. The enemy could be anybody out there: newscasters, bus drivers, "Up With People" singers, former friends and relations. Very few would be welcome inside. Certain Viet Cong would be more welcome than certain high-ranking officers, and anyone who tried to convey the impression that what we were doing was just, or purposeful, or heroic was the least welcome of all. Nobody voluntarily sported an American flag. That was for the beer-bellied construction workers back home, whipped into a barroom brawl frenzy by jingoistic conservatives. We sported peace symbols, and car-ried grief and betrayal in our hearts. And now, during our last days at An Loc, things were taking a turn for the worse. We got a new brigade commander whose first initiative was to harass those beneath him as though they were first-week recruits. We were ordered to disassemble and then rebuild our magnificent bunkers. Such are the actions of weak leadership engaged upon a self-serving mission.

All we had was each other and the short-time girls, who remained intensely loyal throughout. Butch and Nancy and Ann stayed at our sides, endured the mortar attack with us, listened to our complaints. Their short-cropped hair showed their separation from the rest of Vietnamese society, just as we had separated from ours. I can see them now, in the glow of the starlight scope, as they pull down their shorts, squat, and cleanse themselves before continuing on their rounds of the listening posts.

Meanwhile, things were really falling apart in the rear, where a strong and compassionate command could have made a difference. Morale was so bad among the REMFS that it was becoming harder and harder to get proper supplies. The career sergeants like Mike Five, like our first sergeant and the supply sergeant and mess sergeant, were openly disgusted. Most of them said they were getting out, canceling their careers even though it meant losing the retirement benefits they had been working toward for so long. Personnel records were a shambles. Vehicle maintenance was a shambles. Only the medical corps seemed immune, steeped in blood and bandages, fighting the loneliest war of all.

Drugs, booze, violence and racism had finally reached Quan Loi, spreading up from the south. In a foreshadowing of our city streets today, gunfights were breaking out. As is true now, these fights were usually over race or possessions. One man was killed during an argument at the Quan Loi post exchange while we were at An Loc, and several more were wounded. These deaths and injuries were not being honestly reported. Stories were concocted for the folks back home. How do you explain to grieving parents that their son was shot during an argument over an ounce of marijuana or a tape deck? A terrible plague was spreading farther and faster, making it all the more tempting for Mike Division to go it alone if we could, maybe just taking the short-time girls along, wandering up Highway Thirteen. We were the best that there was, and there were fewer of us every day. The army itself was losing gallons of blood through a multitude of nearly invisible holes. It would require decades of convalescence.

Then within a few days of the mortar attack, we were pulled out of An Loc and sent back to Quan Loi ourselves to rejoin what was left of the battalion. It was the first time the battalion had been in Quan Loi, its home base, since the Tet Offensive seven months before. For seven months the battalion's tents and bunks had remained empty. During the brief stays by individuals, sent back there for administrative reasons or smallish wounds, there had been time to stow a radio or tape deck or camera from the PX in a footlocker, but that was all. Almost everybody had been doing that, though, building a hoard of cheap goods to take back on the freedom bird, but as the battalion settled in an awful realization began to spread through the ranks. Nearly every footlocker had been broken into. Nearly everything of value had been stolen. All the radios that played our music, all the cameras that took our pictures, all these talismans of our American way of life, the pathetic perks of life in Vietnam, all we really had to show for months in the field, had been stolen by REMFS in Quan Loi. So much of what we see today, on our streets, in our society, had its beginnings in Vietnam.

So then Mike Division got drunk. I must have crashed around midnight myself, my mouth tasting like lighter fluid. I had barely fallen asleep when there was somebody shaking me, making the liquids in my head slosh back and forth. I sat up, nearly fell over, and tried to focus my eyes. It was a runner, a private from some headquarters sent to fetch me. I was needed in the brigade's Tactical Operations Center.

I'd never been to the TOC, but I knew where it was. It was the nerve center of Quan Loi, entirely underground, deep underground, its presence marked only by a sandbagged entrance and a forest of radio antennas. I wove my way over to it, past the stinking rubber trees, past the urinals, trying to sober up but not succeeding much; trying just to walk a straight line was hard enough. I assumed that Mike Division had done something really awful during their night of revelries, that they had committed some sort of atrocity, and I was going to have to explain to the brigade commander why I led a platoon of outlaws.

A guard swung the heavy door to the TOC open. They were expecting me. I descended a steep, narrow stairway lit with incandescent bulbs, turned a corner, and met another guard at another heavy door, which he swung open. Wow! It was like a movie set in there, a large room lit with dim red lights. Maps covered the walls, symbols covered the maps. A few men were silently moving symbols around. Radios took up as much space as the maps, all sorts of radios and scramblers and decoders and various monitoring devices. There were men working at chart tables, men making coffee, men talking on radios. I couldn't even stand still without weaving. I had to find a corner of a chart table to hold onto. Bravo Six was there. Defiant Six was there. Everybody seemed very busy and excited. They didn't seem to be concerned about any damage done by Mike Division. Bravo Six was speaking to me. I tried to concentrate on what he was saying because he was being very serious. But it was hard to hear his words through the roaring in my ears. Then I heard Loc Ninh. He said we were going to Loc Ninh. I almost puked.

Then there was an artillery captain showing me things on a map. I couldn't believe I was being briefed by an artillery captain. I couldn't understand a thing he was saying, but I nodded my head carefully. I could see Loc Ninh on the map in front of us, see the red line of Highway Thirteen reaching up to it, the Cambodian border looping down. Now Defiant Six wanted a few words with me. It was real serious, I could tell that, but I still just couldn't take it all in or make sense of it. Couldn't they tell I was drunk? Didn't they know that I was incompetent, a coward at heart? I just kept nodding my head like I understood, and tried not to puke or pass out each time I nodded my head. It was going to be a big deal, super surprise, an attempt to outwit the VC intelligence system. Mike Division would go in at first light to secure the LZ. Then there were handshakes, even a few slaps on the back which almost toppled me.

I staggered back out of the TOC and into the cool, latex- and urine-scented air. We were going to be killed. They had given us a month at An Loc, and now they were going to kill us. It was now about one or two in the morning, and Mike Division was still dispersed all over Quan Loi, drunk, stoned, passed out, sick, beating on REMFS, or fucking some *mamasan* in the laundry room. And in three hours we were going to Loc Ninh to secure an LZ and get killed. I went back to the platoon tent and woke up the few men there, told them to go out and search for the others. I couldn't tell them anything more. It was three-thirty by the time we finally got the platoon assembled. Then I told them what was up. They were just as drunk and pissed and scared as I was. Then we tried to get an hour of sleep.

⟡ XII ⟡

ONE HOUR LATER. It is difficult to describe the pain in my head as I shouldered my gear and walked out to the runway. The stars were out. Quan Loi was silent, nearly everyone was sleeping except us. We ate cold C rations beside the still slumbering Chinook helicopter. We were a miserable lot, barely able to speak or move. An Loc, the soft comfort of the short-time girls, seemed like it had been a dream. Bravo Six was talking to me. We would be alone for about two hours, out of radio contact and beyond the range of artillery. The flight crew arrived and began to awaken the beast. We would go in at tree-top level, as soon as there was enough light to see. We would follow Highway Thirteen, the road I had always wanted to explore. We would secure a landing zone in the midst of what I assumed would be a North Vietnamese regiment. No gunships or support, those would tip them off that a major assault was coming.

Slowly the Chinook came to life as we finished our rations, first with the gentle whirring and ticking sounds and lights coming on, then the turbines themselves began to wail louder and the huge limp rotor blades began to turn slowly. The sky to the east, above An Loc, was starting to brighten. You could see the silhouette of the tree line. Kerosene exhaust belched out of the engines, just sort of wafting at first, then coming harder and harder, louder and louder, faster and faster. The rotors were a blur now, and the ship vibrated with their swings.

We filed inside the helicopter through the rear loading ramp and strapped ourselves into the red nylon seats that faced the center aisle.

The two door-gunners up by the nose of the ship had unlimbered their M-60s and were checking them over, placing the ends of ammunition belts in the feed tray, closing the feed tray cover. Now it was getting really light out, light enough to see, dark grayish-purple, light enough to fly. Soon the old man would swing open the gate to An Loc. Soon Co Dep would show up with her pushcart. Soon another unit would sweep the highway south, looking for mines and finding none. Bravo Six gave me the high sign from beside the loading ramp. The noise was deafening now. My head throbbed to the beat of the rotors, and the stench of kerosene was nauseating.

Then the deck vibrated faster and faster and we began to lift. I watched Bravo Six drop away below, fatigues fluttering in the blast of wind. We rose up high coming out of Quan Loi, pretending to be another resupply ship. We passed above the French plantation manager's compound, with its red tile roofs, emerald lawns and turquoise pool. Then came the squalid line of bunkers, the barbed wire, the no-man's-land of shrapnel-riven tree stumps. We continued high over the road to An Loc, over the plantations, the putrid processing plant, the workers' settlement. Above An Loc itself, the ship banked sharply to the right. You could see the streets almost directly below, outside the starboard windows. You could see the wisps of smoke from cooking fires, vendors, *lambrettas* and the bus to Saigon lining up by the gate, and the village market filling with people.

Then, just beyond the runway, we suddenly dropped down to tree-top level, even below the trees where the road was still open, and began to follow the red clay highway. We went screaming past all the old landmarks, the fork to Bad Vibes Hill, the barricade with the sign, and plunged deeper into the dreamland of the Annamite Kingdom. I watched the road race away from me at eighty knots outside the open rear door. It was like watching a movie rewind at high speed. Now and then we would pass a startled *lambretta* driver or bicyclist. I would see them reeling, swerving in our wake. The helicopter moved with the contours of this beautiful, gently rising and falling and turning road. When the helicopter rose suddenly, I knew there were trees ahead, enclosing the road. Then we would drop down again, eight, ten, twelve feet above the surface. We rose and swept over half-hidden villages, shaded by trees and untouched by war. We dropped to the road again.

Some of the men across from me were trying to sleep. Some were craning their necks, trying to see outside. Most were just staring straight ahead, zombie-like, facing each other across the cargo aisle, sick, scared, half-drunk, unable to talk or even think much in all the noise. Nothing made you feel more like a piece of canned meat than a trip in a Chinook anyway. And there was this sense that we were being used as bait. All we knew of Loc Ninh was what we had heard about the fighting, none of the old-timers had been there. The vision in my mind was of a filthy mudpile strewn with broken sandbags, shell craters, unclaimed body parts, bits of clothing and equipment. My map showed a huge runway, a ridiculously huge runway just a few clicks from town, with a Special Forces camp at each end. We were to secure the middle of the runway, on the eastern side.

Just south of the village of Loc Ninh the helicopter banked to the right and we began to skim above dense, trackless jungle with mist rising through the trees; endless jungle, like the Ho Bo Woods, endless hangover and headache, endless hills, nothing, end of everything. Then a clearing appeared below in the rapid movie rewind view, an abandoned outpost, mud fort, then suddenly the land rising up abruptly and the runway, right there atop a ridge, the vast, paved runway streaming past our feet with dense jungle growing right up to the edge of it. The helicopter reared up and slowed down, preparing to land. The door-gunners were alert, but they weren't shooting. As soon as we felt the shudder of the wheels touching the ground we were out the back, scrambling over to the left side of the runway. Then the helicopter was gone, wheeling around and skimming the ground back to Quan Loi.

For a while we just lay prone in a circle beside the runway, listening to the beat of the helicopter fade farther and farther away. We were lying atop purple clay. It was the only purple clay I have ever seen, and it was tempting to think it had been stained that color by the blood that had been shed upon it, except that I couldn't see any of the signs of bloodshed that I had expected. There wasn't any litter of personal effects fluttering in the breeze. There wasn't any smell of putrefying flesh, no circling vultures. Gradually the sound of the helicopter receded to nothing, and the place was totally silent. This was so different from our usual air assaults, which were all noise, helicopters swarming overhead, people yelling on the radio.

I still thought this might be the end for us, that we would soon die on this vast asphalt desert. How ironic, after we had come so far, gone so long unscathed. Ahead of me were some abandoned buildings; an airplane hangar and an equipment shed. The equipment shed was huge, modern, framed with steel girder trusses twenty feet above a concrete pad. The sheet metal walls and most of the roof had been blown away. What remained of the roof was just a sieve of shrapnel holes. I gave the signal and we got up and ran as one a bit farther to the side, then lay down again in a circle beside the equipment shed, weapons ready, listening. I didn't like this place tactically: it would be hard to defend. I didn't like the buildings, and I didn't like the thick brush behind them. But this was where we were supposed to be, so we began to dig in, building our fighting holes. The clay was incredibly hard, the worst digging ever besides the Rome Plow Shitpile.

I kept trying to get a sense of the lay of the land, expecting an attack at any minute, as had happened here before. They would not come across the runway, they would use the buildings for cover. The equipment shed, at our twelve o'clock, no longer offered any cover or concealment. But there were some more buildings at nine o'clock that I could just barely discern through the brush. They were about two hundred meters away, and a regiment could easily sneak up behind them. Or maybe they would use a dense thicket at seven o'clock. I really wanted to get us dug in fast, but that was proving impossible. The clay was too hard. Of course the enemy knew this already. If they came now, we would have to withdraw, probably to the airplane hanger, perhaps farther if we could. Even then, we would be a lost platoon unless we managed to make our way to the Special Forces camp.

But still, they didn't come. Still, the silence was simply amazing. The sun was fully up, beating down through a sky that was even a brighter blue than the sky at An Loc, and the place seemed totally deserted. There were no sounds of human activity other than our own; no airplanes or trucks, nothing. It was the only time I recall complete silence during the daytime in Vietnam. The silence, the deserted buildings, and that huge, empty runway were also quite haunting, even hauntingly beautiful with the dense jungle across the way. It began to feel better and better to be there as we felt more secure. It was really good to be on our own again, even if just for a little while, and even though I was still expecting an attack. The hard physical labor of trying to scrape holes into that hard clay helped disperse the hangovers. This was Mike Division at our best, on our own and alone, away from the REMFS, nobody above us, working together. We had the sunshine, and we had each other.

We were all on our hands and knees, picking away at the clay and bitching in soft, muttering tones except for the guys on outposts. I would work at it myself for a while, then stand up, look around and listen. I would slowly walk the circle, on the watch for hordes of North Vietnamese rushing us, or a VC rocket team hidden in the bushes. As the day warmed, a gentle breeze sprang out of the south. That was when we first heard it; one of the guys on observation post heard it first and called me over. Then we all heard it, stopped working so that we could concentrate on the sound, rising and falling, coming from the southeast. It was a motor of some sort, a small motor, but not a *lambretta* or motorbike. On and on it droned, louder, then softer, laboring hard, then laboring easy. It seemed more like an outboard motor on a boat, but there was no water nearby. Tillage equipment? A pump? We all listened very intently. Then somebody identified it, said incredulously, "It's a fucking lawn mower!"

Of course it was. That was exactly what it was. The place wasn't deserted after all. Somewhere to the southeast, somebody was mowing the lawn. For the first time, we began to relax a little. The sunshine shimmered on brilliant trees. Heat waves rose from the runway and the abandoned, rubble-strewn buildings. And the lawn mower droned on and on, like on a Sunday morning in suburbia, the sound rising and falling with the breeze. You could almost smell the freshly cut grass.

Shortly after that, somebody discovered the first land mine, discovered it by digging it up, not by stepping on it. It was an American-made antipersonnel mine, and a very old one at that. The detonator was broken off, but it had been planted there, so there had to be more. Sure enough, as we looked closer, we began to find more. We were digging into an abandoned and unmarked minefield. It looked as though somebody had driven a bulldozer over the minefield in an attempt to clear it, shearing the detonators off most of the mines.

At eleven in the morning the Chinook came back, shuttling in the rest of Bravo Company. We kept digging in our sector, which faced those buildings I had seen partly hidden by brush, while the other platoons began digging the rest of our perimeter. Because we had a head start, we finished early and turned our attention back to the minefield. Mine detectors had been requested, and would come in with the evening supply ship. But that wasn't soon enough, so we all lined up on our hands and knees and crawled slowly forward, probing the ground with our bayonets. In all, we found about thirty mines. Some had been broken by the bulldozer. Some were rusted through. And some were perfect specimens, the size and shape of a coffee can, with the detonator on a pole sticking out the top. Although they were American, they must have been put there by the French. They must have been buried nearly twenty years for them to have rusted like that, and anyway the whole French campaign in Vietnam had largely been supplied and financed by the United States. Still, it was easier for us to get mad at the French again, blaming them for the war, blaming them for leaving this unmarked minefield behind. I would guess the bulldozer came along two or three years before us, in '66 or so, when we began frantically building these dumb runways, and it was still safe to do that at Loc Ninh.

As had become customary long ago in my love affair with explosives, I dug out and carried away most of the mines myself. This was something I felt confident about, while some men really hated it. They, in turn, would do things like walk point day after day, which to me was an unbearable risk. So as each mine was found, I would carefully remove it and carry it out to a place in the bushes just beyond our perimeter, toward those half-hidden buildings. I placed them side by side on the ground. Sometimes, I would then light a cigarette and stare at those buildings some more. The closest and largest one looked like a Hollywood mansion, or Greek temple or something. Definitely not Vietnamese. The more I saw, the more I wanted to explore.

At about two in the afternoon the rest of the battalion began to arrive. Bravo Six had warned me of this when he came in, but I was feeling angry about it anyway. Perhaps it was still the hangover. They arrived in giant C-130 transports, blasting away whatever was left of our tranquility with screaming turboprops and chaotic running back and forth and shouting. It also prompted a confrontation of sorts. I had laid out a company-size perimeter. We had worked hard on our hands and knees digging in that wretched purple clay. Now we were expected to move and dig in all over again elsewhere, in a greatly expanded circle.

I refused to move. I pointed out that we were there first, had dug decent holes and didn't want to hand them over. Then I suggested that there were probably a lot more mines that we hadn't dug out yet. We were the only ones who knew where they might be, the only ones with the experience to deal with them. Bravo Six and Defiant Six conferred, out of earshot. Then, astonishingly enough, they gave in. The rest of the battalion had to move. But Mike Division stayed right where we had been since early that morning, facing the sector where I most feared attack, facing the land and buildings beyond, which I so longed to explore. Four hundred other men grumbled and complained and filled the holes they had already started, and the whole perimeter spread, amoeba-like, away from Mike Division.

Meanwhile, the C-130s kept coming. Toward evening they lifted in an artillery battery. They were equipped with new, lightweight 105s and this was the first time I'd seen these guns. Obviously, we were settling in for a good long stay. Surely, we would begin the sweeps soon; but there was no talk of that and furthermore, we weren't going to be sending out any ambushes at night. As twilight descended and the last C-130 left, I walked out to my mine pile for one last look at the mansion. It was grayish-white stucco, with a flat roof and two-story columns in front. A white gravel driveway led to a covered entranceway. To one side there was a covered walkway leading to a smaller, one-story building. Of course it wasn't entirely unscathed; even in the twilight I could see that most of the glass was gone from the tall, almost floor to ceiling windows, and the walls bore the spatter-marks of bullets and shrapnel. Here, the lawns had gone long unmowed and there were some enormous craters from shells or bombs. But still, it seemed to be from another world.

We ate C rations, set up watches, sent the listening posts out. At last, with the airplanes gone, the quiet which had been so wonderful in the morning began to return. The stars that night were amazingly bright, a zillion galaxies spread overhead. I had heard that at night, when the wind was from the north, you could hear the North Vietnamese trucks on the Ho Chi Minh Trail, hauling in more men and supplies. What a place this was, with lawn mowers by day and trucks by night, here on the Cambodian border. But there was no wind that night, only stars. My orders were coming any day now. The most perilous part of my journey was nearly ended. I was not the same person, and I had come to dislike the country that had sent me to this place as intensely as I disliked the French colonialists. I was seriously considering emigrating to Australia when I got out. Meanwhile, I still had my men, and the stars, from whence we had all come, and where we would eventually return.

Again the dawn, again the sun wheeling upward, the light coming back, the colors coming back, the mist rising and the men rising and urinating. I dreaded the sweeps that would surely begin; it was easy for me to envision a bad time, a return to those traumatic early weeks, during these last days with my platoon. We were the only platoon which hadn't had any men killed since I had joined Bravo Company, and I desperately wanted to keep it that way. Nor had my own personal courage been tested for a long time. I desperately wanted to avoid that, too, and keep coasting on bravado, attacking rubber trees. So far, Loc Ninh was proving to be blessedly quiet. There was nothing on the agenda for us besides more digging and sandbagging. We had time on our hands. Itching to explore, I asked Bravo Six if I could take Mike Division out on a security patrol of our own. I wanted to check out those buildings.

He let us go. So a bunch of us assembled and filed out through the wire to where I had piled the mines. We crouched down in the bushes and looked at the palace ahead of us. We waited and watched for a long time, looking for any movement. It was totally still. The surrounding lawns, unmowed but still open, came almost to our feet. Shade trees were spotted all across the lawns. Then the first squad dashed across the lawns to the building. Backs against the white walls, they peered around the corners, ducked inside, then signaled that it was clear for the rest of us. We dashed across and joined them.

The building was huge. A couple of fire teams did a quick cloverleaf search around the outside, then we went in and gawked. It wasn't a mansion or a palatial residence as I had expected. It really was more like a temple. There was just one huge main room inside, with a ceiling two stories high, and a second-floor balcony going all around. In the middle of the floor of the big room was a long concrete trough. At first I thought it might have been a swimming pool, but it had raised concrete walls. It would have been awkward climbing in. Perhaps it was a reflecting pool, or indoor garden. Lots of light flooded in through the tall windows. Broken glass and cartridge cases covered the floor. The cartridge cases were all the copper-coated Russian ones, and there were thousands of them. I had been right about the enemy choosing this place.

But what was it? All the furniture had been removed, but obviously it wasn't a home. There were smaller rooms all around, downstairs and off the balcony as well, but they seemed more like foyers or changing rooms. Then we found a larger room with no windows which turned out to be a small movie theater. The two ancient silent-era thirty-five millimeter movie projectors were the only movable objects that had been left behind. So it was a good guess that this place dated back to the

1920s, when Michelin hit the big money. Any more modern projectors had been removed. Our conclusion was that this palace was just used for entertaining. While Ho Chi Minh himself was in Paris, studying revolution, the plantation managers had partied. While the striking rubber workers had been beheaded, the party just kept on going. They partied right through World War II. It must have been quite a life. They were probably partying someplace else now.

We went on to explore the one-story wing that was connected by a sort of breezeway. These seemed to be the kitchen and servant's quarters, confirming our suspicions. This was indeed the Emerald City, the heart of a kingdom built upon automobile tires. Now broken glass and cartridge cases littered the marble floors, and our footsteps echoed in the empty halls. We had seen from upstairs windows that there were lots more buildings ranged across the unmowed lawns, connected by gravel drives. These appeared to be smaller but no less enticing, for they looked like the family residences of an upper-class Los Angeles suburb, except for the shell craters and shrapnel wounds. There was no time left to explore on this patrol, however; we had to get back. We were careful not to talk about it with outsiders, too. We wanted to keep it to ourselves.

Meanwhile, things were really buzzing back at the NDP. At about midday, elements of the Eleventh Cavalry showed up again with their tanks and APCs and self-propelled howitzers. They had run up the road from An Loc without a single shot being fired at them, which seemed fantastic, as though the VC and NVA had simply vanished from the earth. But stranger still was the performance that elements of the air force began to stage. It started when one of the C-130s, which had been arriving pretty steadily, disgorged a crew of pale technicians in ironed fatigues carrying metal Haliburton cases. They looked like doctors or scientists of some sort. Next came a forklift, and pallet loads of stuff covered with heavy canvas tarps.

Watching them provided entertainment for the rest of the day. I suppose that we, in turn, were entertaining to them, grunting and filthy like pigs, squirming about in our mud holes. Now and then, one of our mortar crews would fire a round to settle a baseplate, and the air force guys would duck and look around nervously. But most of the time they were very businesslike, and they seemed to be enjoying their work. The work turned out to be a portable aircraft control tower, which began to rise in the middle of our NDP. Now at last I understood why I had been asked to secure an LZ in such a tactically unfavorable place. Of course we had to secure the middle of the airfield, because that was where the tower belonged. It was like watching a giant erector set being put together. When it was completed by nightfall, the tower was about thirty feet high, with a little glass room on top, and people in the room. Lots of radio antennas and stuff like generator sheds were ranged around the tower, and the airmen even had their own little portable dormitory.

Toward evening, we pulled security for the water truck for the first time. The only source of water was a spring down below the south end of the runway, and with so many men here the truck had to drive down the runway for a load of water several times a day. The truck had drawn sniper fire from the wood line on several of these trips, probably from another elderly VC like the one who had left the sign in the road, so all the platoons took turns providing security for the truck. We climbed on the footboards and held the handrails, and rode down the strip with a solid wall of jungle to our left. Like at the Rome Plow Shit-pile, it seemed to me that an enterprising VC could have done anything he wanted in this ominous setting, but for now, at least, he didn't seem to want to. Then the Special Forces camp came into view, on a knob to the right of where the runway ended. The land dropped away sharply on three sides, affording quite a view to the south, toward Quan Loi, across unbroken miles of jungle. The truck descended through steep turns a few hundred meters to the spring, where a couple of men set up their equipment and started pumping water.

There wasn't any sniper fire, but there was a deserted "strategic hamlet" below the foot of the runway, near the spring. I had noticed it briefly as we came in on the Chinook. I had never actually seen one outside of army training films, since the idea of strategic hamlets had been abandoned, as this one was, several years before. It was readily recognizable by the moat and berm of *punji* stakes which surrounded it. *Punji* stakes, which are sharpened slivers of bamboo and a poor substitute for barbed wire, were a relic of an earlier era, too. They're in every Vietnam War movie, but this was the first time I'd ever seen them myself. This whole little fortified village was surrounded by a bristling twenty-foot-wide circle of them. The point of this futile exercise had been to depopulate the countryside and bring all the natives in under government control at night. The wall of *punji* stakes would either: *(a)* keep the Viet Cong out, or *(b)* keep the Viet Cong in; but in fact it did neither and simply alienated the peasantry even further. Now, as a relic of yet another failure, the village invited exploration. We went in.

The *punji* stakes were rotten where they entered the earth, and were beginning to topple over. A square of mud walls, with strong points at each corner, enclosed the "hamlet" itself. There were just a couple of dilapidated buildings; it didn't look to me as though the place had ever been used much. In the center there was a tall watchtower made of jungle trees, rising fifty feet or so. This whole pathetic little ruin of a compound lay in the shadow of the Special Forces camp on the hilltop above, which was also built of mud but had the far more durable concertina wire around it.

We hadn't been in the strategic hamlet for long before some Khmer mercenaries up at the compound saw us and drifted down for a visit. They were not at all like the Vietnamese soldiers we had met before. After several years with the Special Forces many of them spoke English quite well. They had no interest in the politics of the war; they had been hired in their native Cambodia. They were professionals, more professional than we were. They wore nifty camouflage fatigues, and carried M-16 rifles, but they were still tribesmen as primitive as the Montagnards. They were, historically, a tribe of warriors. They had extensive body tattoos and wore jewelry with the initials "K.K.K." engraved upon it, "K.K.K." being their tribal initials as well as, coincidently, the initials of my boy's camp. They also carried large knives, and boasted to us that they preferred to kill with the knives, slipping into North Vietnamese units at night, and silently slitting throats. This made a big impression on my collection of nineteen-year-olds, who listened with rapt attention.

Surely this place was the very edge of the earth, the outermost fringe of the war. Passing his knife around, flashing a gold front tooth, our most verbal visitor went on even further, went on to explain that he liked to eat the heart and liver of a man he had killed if time and circumstance permitted. This served two purposes. First, it would cripple the spirit of the dead man, and prevent the spirit from haunting the Khmer. Second, it would give the Khmer some of the dead man's powers, powers that reside in the heart and liver. Hearing these things, as the twilight gathered in this strange land, was an affirmation of sorts.

We were very far from home. Whatever goals we had brought to Vietnam had been lost or forgotten long ago, along with the rules and regulations. There was no guidance beyond that which we could divine for ourselves, and each man had his own formulation, like the animist offerings outside Montagnard villages. Then the men by the water truck shouted that they were finished, and we headed back.

That night the stars were just as bright as before, and we still couldn't hear the trucks, but they must have been there, because near midnight another C-130 showed up, droning on in big, slow circles about ten thousand feet overhead. This was called a "night owl," for the way it slowly turned in the sky on its huge black wings, just a shape, blacking out the stars as it moved across them. On board were devices comparable to the NOD we had used back at Dragon House. Some amplified the night light. Some amplified infrared, the heat from engines or groups of men. Now and then the plane would bank and a hot orange stream would pour from its side with a ghostly moan. Thousands of rounds of 20mm cannon fire were impacting just four or five kilometers from us; you could clearly hear the rippling thuds of explosions and see the flashes. According to my map, it was shooting just over the border. Still the NVA didn't come, and the night owl stayed overhead for hours, droning through our dreams.

Of course we were looking forward to continuing our explorations the next morning, and again there were no sweeps scheduled. So I asked Bravo Six if I could take out another patrol, and he agreed. He, too, knew that these were my last days with Mike Division, and I was being given a lot of liberty. Once again, I said "Saddle up," and although these patrols were voluntary, most of the guys went along. What a contrast with my first days as a platoon leader, the agonizing fear and numbing fatigue. Now, as we filed out through the wire, it was like stepping into sunshine and freedom. There was hardly any need for cloverleafs this time, our instincts told us that we had the place to ourselves and that was enough. The sky was bright blue, the air was dry, and even though the lawns hadn't been mowed for years, there was still a very pleasant park-like atmosphere.

We wasted little time at the party house, just a quick check to see if anyone else had been there during the night. Then we began to wander the gravel paths towards the southeast, where those other houses stood. There were about half a dozen of them, spaced widely apart, 1920s modern architecture of wealthy Europeans. Some had been hit by stray artillery rounds, but most were in pretty good shape. They were a lot like the houses we had grown up in, except for the shell craters and the odd lack of a garage. Each house was two stories, with a kitchen, living room and dining room downstairs, and two bedrooms upstairs. The master bedroom had a balcony with an iron railing. I suppose they were guest houses. Again, everything movable was gone, even the appliances, but you could see where the kitchen range and the refrigerator had been, and as we explored we began to hear the lawn mowers again, much closer now.

This was such a strange place. Ozzie and Harriet could have lived in one of these houses. I can imagine them sitting at the kitchen table as the NVA swarm through. "Would you like some cookies?" says Harriet, always hospitable. "Have fun, boys," says Ozzie as they depart. Then the first shell slams into the lawn. "What was that, Ozzie?"

"Sounds like a 155 to me."

And just two kilometers away, there were six hundred Khmer under contract with the U.S. government, practicing cannibalism. Five kilometers to the north lay Cambodia, with the border marked by a red and white striped pole across Highway Thirteen. I wanted to take Mike Division there next; it was easy to do, and others told me that there was just a guard shack there, and a girl selling chrysanthemums. The border would be opened for a pack of cigarettes, and anything was possible beyond that. I wanted to take Mike Division into the town of Loc Ninh, too, just a little farther to the south, but beyond this last guest house we had reached, the lawns were still being mowed.

This last house had taken a hit; one corner had been blasted away, but we entered and poked around as usual. We were always looking for souvenirs, but there were none; a spoon here, a broken chair there. We went up to the second-floor balcony and looked out across the mowed lawns.

WOW! There was the main house, across a paved road, partly hidden by formal gardens and neatly trimmed hedges. It was three stories high and built of stone, with a red tile mansard roof. Tall, narrow windows had green wooden shutters. Not a pane of glass was broken. Gardeners were at work here and there, pushing lawn mowers, trimming hedges, weeding flower beds. It seemed like a hallucination, lifted out of Europe and deposited here, far more grand than the French compound at Quan Loi, more grand than anything any of us had ever seen, anywhere.

We just stood there on the balcony and gawked at this zillionaire's estate, an estate that was not only untouched by war, but was quite probably profiting by it as well. What I also remember now of that moment was the anger, an anger that was so great that it took years and years to dissipate. It had not been so long since the Ho Bo Woods, the grief and suffering and loss of the Iron Triangle, and for years afterward I could not even stand the sound of the French language. We had, after all, grown up amid the glorifying mythology of the Second World War, and had naively expected the French to welcome us again, showering us with champagne and kisses from beautiful girls as we marched toward Loc Ninh, driving the evil communists before us. It had been disillusioning to find that the French in Vietnam disliked us more than they seemed to dislike the Viet Cong themselves. We could not understand that the French had been goaded, cajoled, even bribed into going to war in Vietnam by the United States in the first place. Nor did we understand that Dien Bien Phu had been a defeat of the spirit, not a military defeat, and that they had reached terms of peace in 1954, hoping the war was over. But we would not leave the war alone, kept prodding and pushing and finally returned in force, prolonging the war in what had been French Indochina for what would turn out to be another tragic twenty years. These things we did not understand at all. All we knew was our own anger, and at the moment it was a lot easier to blame the French than ourselves. So we threatened to shoot a Frenchman, and blew up his Citroen. So we attacked rubber trees.

Now a couple of gardeners had spotted us on the balcony, and came walking over. Seeing that I was the leader, they came upstairs and joined me.

"French number ten," one of us said in the popular jargon of ranking, ten being the lowest, and they smiled politely and nodded. Then one of them said to me, quite clearly, that we had to go away, that we were not welcome here.

None of us had ever been told that we were not welcome anyplace in Vietnam before. We had been shot at, yes, but not told to go away. And these guys clearly meant it, too. They were shorter than we were, and unarmed, but they were firm.

"No Americans allowed here," they repeated.

So we left, trespassers that we were, feeling strange and hurt, like we had seen something we really shouldn't have seen. It was so beautiful, surrounded by flowers, while we had been so filthy and scared, with our friends dying, and our innocence dying as well. We took a slightly different course back towards the NDP, drifting in zigzags, checking out some hedges that were interspersed with unmowed lawn. Then, in a small clearing about halfway back, we made another discovery. It was an artesian well, an incredible artesian well. There was an eight-inch iron pipe wellhead standing about a foot above the ground, and even though the well had been capped, the pressure of the water below was so great that water was spraying out for several feet all around the seam of the cap. It was wonderful water, too, very cold and clear and sweet tasting.

What a discovery! I could hardly wait to tell Defiant Six. No more filling the tank truck at what was hardly more than a swamp. No more sniper fire. Here was enough water for a regiment, within easy walking distance. We began to fiddle with the cap, just to see if we could remove it, but what we really needed was a crescent wrench. And for once, our guard was down. For once, we had not watched our rear. Or perhaps it was just that while we had developed a good nose for Viet Cong, we were unprepared for this fresh scent. At any rate, we were taken by surprise by a Frenchman, who had been shadowing us and who now leaped out of the bushes and came rapidly striding toward us as we fiddled with the well cap.

"You cannot have zat water. Zat is not your water," he was yelling. He was very angry. In my memory I also see him as cadaverous, with long bony fingers and yellow teeth. He was waving his arms, as though shooing away flies. "You cannot have zees water. Go away."

We froze and looked hard at this thing, this personification of our own disillusionment. I could feel what Mike Division was thinking, what I was thinking with them. All you had to do was look down, and see how the hands were tightening on the grips of the M-16s. We were thinking, and feeling, the same thing that the black REMFS in Di An were thinking and feeling when I had stumbled upon them smoking dope. We could take this guy. We could take him and waste him and the world would be a better place.

But we didn't. We just gave him a long, hard stare and then wordlessly got up and left. Everybody was pretty silent as we continued back to the NDP, feeling that all too familiar feeling of being screwed again. Then somebody finally said: "Hey, wasn't that the same guy that had the Citroen?" and everybody had a good laugh.

As soon as we got back to the NDP I went to Defiant Six's tent and told him about the well we had found. I felt that perhaps some sort of agreement could be worked out; after all, it was such a great source of water and it would be a lot more secure should a siege develop. He listened patiently; he had this way of listening patiently with his head turned slightly aside, looking preoccupied; he could be preoccupied by what you are saying, or by something else. This way, he maintained a certain distance and kept you in suspense, as fathers often do, especially when they are unsure of the answers, and in doubt themselves. He gave the impression of concern, but you could never really be sure. Therefore, as his lieutenant, I would go to ever greater lengths to gain his approval.

Defiant Six had taken the battalion to Loc Ninh before, and had lost about a hundred men on this ridge of purple clay. He must have asked himself the same questions that I was asking. He knew that the French would keep their well, and that we would drink from the swamp, but still he wouldn't say anything, wouldn't even look directly at me.

But then he did. He looked right at me, and changed the subject completely. He said that I could have the Recon platoon if I wanted it. He said that Recon six was getting short. He knew my orders were coming, but he could get them changed.

I was completely taken by surprise, still feeling like an imposter in the first place. Five months before, he had listened with his head turned while I told him that I wanted to resign my commission. I was, for a moment, even insulted. Didn't he know how much I hated this job, how much I longed to be relieved of the burden of leadership in this lousy war?

I said I'd think about it. He told me he'd give me a day. It was our turn with the water truck again that evening. We climbed aboard and headed down the runway, past the Special Forces camp, down the slope to the strategic hamlet. I told the guys that Defiant Six had offered me Recon. They were all very enthusiastic. They said that they had been talking about it, and that most of them were planning on transferring to Recon anyway as soon as I left. It put them in a very upbeat mood to think that maybe we would still be together and doing nothing but Recon, which was what we did best.

Pretty soon some of the Khmer saw us and came down to chat and barter, but Millhouse and Noonan and Redfeather and I decided to go explore the strategic hamlet a little. We went in through a broken-down gate and poked around the ramshackle buildings. We wanted to climb the big, central observation tower. It must have been quite a job to build it, using four big jungle trees, stripped of limbs and bark, and stood on end like giant telephone poles. The lower rungs of the ladder going up were all rotted away, but Millhouse in particular remained determined to climb the tower. Scouring the buildings, he managed to come up with a two-by-four-inch piece of lumber which could reach over to some good rungs on the ladder from the roof of an adjacent building. I said he was crazy. The two-by-four was too flimsy, and probably rotten as well.

"Come on," he said, taunting me as he stepped out upon it, like a man on a tightrope, "Don't be a chickenshit."

We watched him gingerly step out across the board. He made it to the ladder and began to climb up, calling for the rest of us to follow. I told him he was nuts, and began to look around for a stronger board. Eventually I found one, slid it across on top of his board, and then inched across on my hands and knees, calling him an asshole several times for enticing me into this. The rest of the rungs on the ladder were very rotten, too. Several gave way as I climbed, with Redfeather and Noonan close behind, but enough remained sound for us to make it to the top, a giddy fifty feet up. The trick was to put your feet on the outside edges of the rungs, and hope that there were enough sound ones left by the time we were all up for us to get down again.

There was a poured concrete platform on top, to keep people from shooting up through the floor, and rotten sandbag walls.

"It's really great up here, isn't it," said Millhouse, and it was. We just stood there for a while, looking out over the countryside. There was no rubber, just wild jungle which stretched to the horizon and was already beginning to reclaim the clearing of the strategic hamlet as well. The day was overcast and gray, but dry, and the jungle seemed to glow with a light of its own. Each species of tree had its own particular shade of green, like its own voice, some yellow and some almost black, with their own unique textures. If you stared long enough, it began to seem as though the jungle was gently moving, undulating, or the tower was swaying back and forth.

The river had all four of us now, pulling us farther and farther along. It was pulling them toward Recon and they wanted me to come with them, climb more towers. I could feel myself being swirled, in the current's grip. For the first time in my life, I was really good at something, good at something in a widely recognizable way, and it may have been the same for these other guys, too. We had come a long way together. But now I felt myself being pulled in another direction, even farther out than Recon. We talked about it while the jungle pulsated and the tower swayed. I wanted to explore without a battalion to answer to. I wanted to know more of the Khmer, the Montagnard, follow every little estuary deeper into the jungle, and of course they understood perfectly and wished they could come along. Millhouse asked me if he could have my CAR-15 weapon, and I said he could.

I also felt a great sadness at that moment, certain that some of us would not survive the next six months. That, perhaps, was the best reason of all for me to go. The four of us would pay dearly for our view from the top of the tower later. I wanted to keep the memory of it unspoiled for now, and go on without them, go on without responsibility for them. The light was beginning to fade again. Soon night would reclaim the land. The guys below were calling for us to come back. More rungs broke on the way down, and the last man had to jump.

Later that night the skies cleared again and the night owl came back. Perhaps the air force tower was somehow related; perhaps they were providing calibration or reference data. At any rate, there still wasn't much for us to do the next day, so we decided to get rid of those old mines. Defiant Six told the Special Forces camps that we were going to blow some old ordnance, and they showed up about an hour later with some stuff they wanted to get rid of, too, a whole jeep trailer full. There were dud artillery rounds, ancient oozing blocks of TNT, broken claymores, all sorts of good stuff. As Defiant Six and I looked the collection over, I told him I didn't want Recon and he did his usual listening while looking away bit. I wondered if, once again, this was the sort of decision I would spend the rest of my life trying to reconcile. But I think he noticed my eyes following the jeep as it drove back to the camp, the two Green Berets and their Khmer, and understood.

It took us most of the day to shuttle all the old ordnance out to the party house. There had been some debate as to whether we should actually put all the explosives inside the house or not. The place was already a mess, and it would make a political statement. But what stopped me was simply that I was afraid pieces of the house would come down inside our perimeter. I decided to put everything in a shell crater on the other side of the house, and let the house itself shield us from the blast.

Boy, was that a fortunate decision, because there we were, midafter-noon, actually setting the charges, when this voice hailed us from the servants' quarters. It was a lilting, female voice. It said; "Hey, Mike Di-vision, you want beaucoup fuck-fuck?"

There they were, waving from the shattered windows, Butch and Nancy and Ann. We dropped what we were doing and ran to them, amazed. I had about eight men with me, and the girls were all over us as soon as we got inside, fondling our cocks and whispering in our ears.

"See, they really love us," said one guy.

"They risked their lives to be with us," said another, melting in a swoon.

Word had reached them, probably through the gardeners, that Mike Division, 1/28 Infantry was at Loc Ninh, so they had hired a *lambretta* to take them up from An Loc. This was a tremendous boost to our egos; we had always treated them well and now they promised to do the same for us. I wandered back to the NDP alone, but very amused. Behind me, the party house which had been deserted for so long was coming to life again. In the foyers with the shattered plaster walls, on the marble floors littered with broken glass and bullet shells, a great party was once again underway.

I kept dragging my feet on blowing the ordnance, drawing it out as long as possible, soliciting dud shells from the artillery, even searching for more mines so that I could send another detail from Mike Division out to the party house over the next few days. Often, it would require as many as six or eight men just to carry a hand grenade with a worn pin out to the crater behind the house. Only a few men from the other pla-toons were ever let in on this, and they, too, were sworn to secrecy. I don't think any of my fellow officers knew.

Meanwhile, the air force came up with something of their own, and it was definitely revenge of the nerds. On about the third day of their presence with the tower, the excitement among the technicians sud-denly intensified. They told us there was going to be an "Arc Light" mission. I didn't know, until I asked, that "Arc Light" was the code name for a B-52 strike. We hadn't even seen a B-52 strike from a dis-tance since our days down south, and this was going to be a close one. I quickly dispatched a detail out to warn the girls. We only had about fifteen minutes. Everyone was to get by their bunker and wait. The ex-citement over by the tower built higher. The air force guys were getting out cameras and focusing toward the jungle on the other side of the runway. Four minutes to go. The detail came back from the party house, breathless. The girls were ready. One minute. It was like the guys in the tower were actually flying the bombers. They were going to strike less than a kilometer beyond the other side of the runway. They were going to blow the long, gentle downward slope of the jungle on the other side of the runway to pieces. This was a little strange, because there was nobody out there I knew of, besides the sniper who had shot at the water truck a few days before.

As usual, the sky was deep, clear blue. If we hadn't been warned, there would have been no way we would have suspected what was coming. Then there was this sound, like the gentle rushing of a rising wind. But there was no wind. The rushing sound kept getting louder, coming from everywhere, or nowhere, rising in pitch, getting more intense, like God's vacuum cleaner, about to suck us all up, then like a jet engine, a turbine scream. Then shock waves came rushing out of the jungle and across the runway, the jungle itself was bulging, the runway heaving, and the ground shook as though standing beside a fast and heavy freight train. We couldn't see the flash of the explosions because of the way the land sloped, but the continuous roll of detonations beat on our heads and chests. It was difficult to stand up because of the ground shaking and the shock waves.

Great clouds of black and brown and gray and white smoke lofted upward in the wake of the shock waves as the bombs marched in a line exactly parallel to the runway. Long after the last of the bombs had exploded, the clouds were still rising and rising, billowing outward and upward. This was what we had so often seen from a distance, this ominous, almost convective, volcanic rising of hot smoke. The clouds were still growing minutes later, blocking out the sun, casting us in darkness. The air force guys were all whooping and cheering, and just before the clouds obscured them, we got a glimpse of the bombers themselves, six silver chevrons glistening in the serene cool of the upper atmosphere.

After the bomb clouds had drifted away from over the target area, a pair of camouflage painted F-100 fighter-bombers came diving out of nowhere and began to unload more ordnance on the same area, bravely attacking any trees left standing by the B-52s. This took them about ten minutes, swooping down, bombing, swooping up again. When they were finished they made a spectacular pass down the runway, just ten or twenty feet above it, doing a little better than Mach One. It scared the shit out of anyone who didn't see them coming, because the boom was louder than anything the B-52s had done. Then they climbed straight up, came around for another higher pass with a victory roll, and left.

To this day, I have no idea what it was all about. No bad guys were around that I knew of, and no patrols were sent out afterward to count vertebrae. It was definitely a photo opportunity that the air force had planned well in advance, and I guess it was designed to demonstrate what we could do should the North Vietnamese attempt to attack Loc Ninh as they had once before. It certainly had something to do with the tower. B-52s never dared bomb that close to friendly troops normally, and they certainly weren't going to be allowed any room for errors with their fellow air force personnel on the ground. Those guys in the tower must have been measuring every puff of wind and cranking the data aloft to the bomber's computers. They must have been measuring flea farts.

Late in the afternoon, when the short-time girls had gone back to where they were staying in the village of Loc Ninh, but there was still enough light to see clearly, we finally made our explosion. I cut what I figured to be about ten minutes of fuse, lit it, and walked back to the NDP. As we had with the B-52s, everyone put on their helmets and waited. Ten minutes came. Ten minutes went. For a moment, I was crestfallen. Then it came, my best explosion yet, with tree stumps and clods of earth climbing high above the party house, followed by a giant white mushroom cloud from some white phosphorus rounds. Then a couple of us ran back out there to see if we had maybe blown out the back wall, but the party house was pretty much unscathed, just some more shrapnel holes. It was very strongly built.

I'm not sure just how many days we were at Loc Ninh, with the Khmer and the B-52s and the short-time girls; four or five or six. Still, there were no sweeps, still, Mike Division came and went as it pleased. Still the sun shone in the daytime, limning the leaves of the shade trees over the unmowed lawns, and the stars shone at night, wheeling silently above us. Then I got my orders. It was very simple: just after the morning resupply ship left, Bravo Six said that I had been reassigned to the Military Assistance Command, and was to board a C-123 in three hours.

I wandered back to our position and told the platoon. We just stood there, all gathered together. Noonan, speaking for the rest, confirmed that most of Mike Division was going to transfer over to Recon. I told them they were a bunch of assholes, that for six months I'd been trying to keep them alive. Now they wanted to go to Recon. But I didn't mean it. I knew it was better in Recon. You were with the best people there, people you could count on. Anyway, these guys didn't have many options. The war was changing. There were too many new guys coming in, too many fuck-ups. The war still had a certain purity to it in Recon.

I went back to my own hole in a daze, and began packing my gear together. I was certainly leaving Mike Division in better condition than when I had arrived. From our lowest point, when we had spent our night of terror, just twelve of us, lost and surrounded, the platoon had grown to about thirty-five men. We had a great reputation in the battalion, and got treated with respect. Now we even had our own women, too. Loc Ninh was a great place to leave Mike Division. And with my departure, Mike Division would essentially cease to exist.

A couple of the old-timers came over to be with me during those last hours. Noonan and Redfeather were there; Millhouse had gone back to Quan Loi for a day or two with an infected foot, and I wouldn't get a chance to say good-bye to him. I told Noonan he could have my CAR-15 until Millhouse got back. Then somebody suggested that we take one last patrol together. Not all of us, just the hard core, half the platoon. So we got up and silently filed out through the wire toward the party house again. The rest of the guys in the NDP gaped at us, wondering what the hell it was that we kept doing out there.

Third squad took the point, and even though we were accustomed to walking back and forth to the party house with nonchalance, we moved with stealth and care now, spaced well apart, staying behind cover where possible, and rushing across the openings. We were a perfect team, in harmony and communicating without words. We didn't even go inside the party house, turned south instead, toward the guest houses. The point man raised his arm, and we all crouched and froze, looking ahead at the houses. There was no movement. Not even an insect was moving. I signaled the second squad to circle around to the left of the first house. As soon as they were in place the rest of us moved closer, one at a time, running from tree to tree until we reached the house. We checked it out; I made a circle in the air over my head with my right hand to bring the second squad back in.

Concealed inside the house, we peered over the window sills toward the next one, the last one before the lawns were kept mowed. Still, no movement. No lawn mowers. Just silent sunshine. We decided to take the house. We went outside and lay down in the tall grass. The squad leaders crawled over to my side. This time the first squad would circle to the left and lay down a base of fire. Then the second and third would stand up and assault. It was a good plan.

As soon as the first squad was in place, they began to yell, "Bang bang, ratatatatatat!" The rest of us stood up and aggressively assaulted, yelling "Bang, bang, bang," and throwing imaginary hand grenades. I watched, somewhat removed but still participating, in a state of amazement as the line of seasoned, war-weary infantrymen played army. In reality, I had been unwilling to make them get on line and assault. But this was not reality. They were moving forward nicely, taking cover from imaginary hostile fire, returning it, then moving forward again and making gun noises, like the children we had all been not so many years before. When the lead man reached the front door, he threw an imaginary grenade inside and then flattened himself against the outside wall. He waited four and a half seconds, then yelled "BOOM!" We charged inside, kicking open doors, hurling more imaginary grenades, checking every room for die-hard holdout resistance. Then we went up to the balcony for a smoke and a last look at the mansion.

Pretty soon it was time to head back to the NDP, so we just began to amble back, unmilitary style again. Then we got hailed from the servants' quarters of the party house. The girls were back. We went inside. Soft light was filtering in across the glass-strewn floors. Nancy started putting the make on me. "Mike Six, you numbah one," she was saying, whispering in my ear and fondling me. My cock felt like a freshly minted 155 howitzer. But I declined, amid howls of protest. There was just half an hour to plane time; it was already on the runway when we got back.

I brought everybody together for the farewell. It was more difficult than I had expected. I told them to be careful, that nobody needs dead heros, that the only thing that mattered here was their safety, and that I loved them, stuff like that; and I cried, and I saluted them, and they cried, and saluted me. It was like the end of the movie *Casablanca,* with the old radial engines of the C-123 coming to life, spewing oil smoke, backfiring and sputtering, everybody crying and saluting.

❖ XIII ❖

IT WAS A GOOD TIME FOR ME to take the five-day R&R allotted to every serviceman in Vietnam, and I chose Bangkok. I went there in a daze, unsure of who I was or where I had been. I met another officer on the airplane, a lieutenant like myself but one who had never been close to combat. He was intelligent and personable, but intensely focused upon his mission in Bangkok, which he had planned well in advance. He ignored the flood of suggestions from the cabbie who drove us to our hotels. He was unable to accompany me to the recommended brothel, where within an hour I was gawking through a two-way mirror at about fifty young girls in a sort of amphitheater, reading comic books and doing their nails, watching *I Love Lucy* reruns dubbed in Thai. While I sampled the wares, pigging out on teenage opium addicts and abductees and exiles from the remote uplands, he activated the bank account he had previously established, and began buying emeralds and tiger skins for a syndicate of investors he had lined up back in the States.

I stopped by his hotel suite a few times with one of my girls. He seldom left it himself; instead, he ordered from room service while a steady parade of dark-suited Oriental businessmen displayed their wares. Emeralds were spread on velvet, glowing brighter than the jungle itself. Tiger skins were unrolled on the floor, skins ranging from flaming orange to pale yellow, but always with the black stripes dark as eternity, big skins and small skins, dead like the one I had seen in the bomb crater, but so many of them all bundled together after death that it seemed like a holocaust of tigers.

Meanwhile there were these girls who spoke English pretty well and who knew which restaurants to suggest and had a lot more class than Butch or Nancy or Ann. They would pretend to be your friend, carrying on conversation and pointing out highlights of Thai culture for the six or twelve or twenty-four hours they were contracted for. We would do the tourist scene together, visiting temples and nightclubs, and they were candid about their own aspirations: an air-conditioned apartment, a refrigerator, more opium; and one of them robbed me while I slept, but I kept going back for more, feeling layer upon layer of grime, dead skin, crusty filth slough away from me with the steam baths and massages and sex. For a while, I didn't think about Mike Division at all. But by the fifth day it was getting to me, with the anger welling up inside again like the summer thunderstorm. Even the prostitutes began to lose their allure, what with all the hustling, the profiteering. How could this be going on, the emeralds glowing green, and the skins of tigers pulsating, and the sweet golden bodies of adolescent girls all spread before us, while Mike Division huddled together out on ambush in the rain. It was too much like the party house at Loc Ninh must have once been, and I began to feel the first pangs of emptiness and longing. It was actually good to get back on the plane to Saigon.

Next came two weeks of advisor school, which was back in Di An of all places. The classes were fun, a smattering of Vietnamese culture and language, more on weapons and tactics, a lot about how to survive in isolation, often amid treachery, which I wish I had listened to more closely. Then, while my mind remained upbeat, focused upon a future I had once doubted I would survive to see, my body began to react as though emerging too fast from a great depth. First I came down with a racking cold, and sat through the classes in an antihistamine daze. Then toward the end of the course my cold transformed into unrelenting stomach cramps and dysentery. Already the deal I had made was beginning to sour. I soon recognized that not all the men had come to this place with the same idealistic goals that I had. There were some, such as our team leader, but others were there because it promised an easy escape from responsibility, and more were there because their former units were desperate to get rid of them. The four other men on my team were all career men, three sergeants and a captain, but only one of them came close to being like Mike Five or the mess sergeant.

Now the great and mysterious river carried me down to the delta, to a place at once both strange and familiar, where sea and land and river all melded together. It should have been a place for compromise, for giving and taking as estuaries are, and a place of rebirth and growth, for these were the places where my father and I so often met, me of the river and he of the sea. It was among the broad fertile beds of silt, the meandering waterways, the pungent salt marches that we had found each other exploring. There were lessons to be found for both of us in the abandoned coal barges of the Arthur Kill behind Staten Island, or the rotting and mud-bound hulks of schooners at Noank. He would have loved the delta for its boats and the nearness of the sea, while I would have chosen the fertile land and vegetation. He could have been the eleven-year-old with the scow his mother gave him, poking about the harbor, and I could have been the eleven-year-old at my boys' camp, with the river and the army, but instead the delta became a place of death and loss.

It was a place which I could hardly even see for the first two weeks because it was raining so hard. It seemed miasmic and unfathomable and shrouded in misery. As before, it seemed impossible that I would survive, but this time our enemy was each other. For two weeks the five of us lived in one small room of a bombed-out schoolhouse beside a river, a river subject to enormous tides. We lived like rats, penned up with a huge stack of twenty cases of C rations. We had neither orders nor mission, we had just been deposited there. The Vietnamese soldiers were as indifferent to our presence as our supervisors were, twenty-three kilometers away over bad roads, and we had neither jeep nor radio. There was a Ninth Infantry Division firebase with a battery of 155s at Rach Kien, just nine kilometers away, but the only way to get a fire mission to them would be to borrow a bicycle and deliver it by hand. Sick, unable to eat, I watched this river in the rain while the others played cards and ate all the canned fruit. The tides rose and fell, eight or ten feet. Mud banks would appear, then sink again. I wrote a desperate letter to my grandmother asking her to send me books, any books at all, by the fastest means possible. There was nothing to do. Now and then a pair of helicopter gunships would strafe the other side of the river with rockets and machine guns in the rain. The roof leaked, and when it rained hard the water would slowly spread across the red and white tile floor. If this happened when the river was rising as well, it seemed as though we would all surely drown. Watching this great turbid river rise and fall so rhythmically, so slowly, watching the water creep across the tile floor, was like watching my father die.

We were waiting. We were waiting for the rain to stop, but mostly we were waiting for our jeep and CONEX to arrive. It was becoming clear to me, hearing the conversation of the others on the team, that the CONEX and its contents were a major incentive for being here in the first place. The CONEX was a steel shipping container which contained, among other things, six army cots with mattresses and bedding, a full-size white enamel propane stove, a matching full-size propane refrigerator, eight chairs, four tables, two AN/PRC-25 radios, and an M-60 machine gun. The plan was to live like kings once the CONEX arrived, while the jeep promised mobility. Beyond that, there was hardly any plan at all.

We were supposed to have a sixth member of the team, a Vietnamese interpreter, but he, like the CONEX, seemed to have been delayed in transit. Because we knew we were supposed to get an interpreter, none of us had paid sufficient attention during our language classes and the local Vietnamese soldiers showed no signs of speaking English at all. Right across the river from us and a little west, near where a highway bridge crossed, there was a regular ARVN fort built up out of mud, built up shovelful by shovelful much as the villages were and surrounded by a dozen concentric rings of half-submerged concertina wire. Inside was a whole battalion of soldiers, and another team of five American advisors. But we didn't see them. It would be months before we saw them; apparently the Vietnamese officers had been forbidden to speak with the Americans, and the soldiers themselves refused to leave the fort or let the Americans leave, all this the result of some dispute which had been going on for months already. I remembered my starry-eyed days at Loc Ninh, my envy of the Special Forces there. Niner Two had spent some time with them, and told me that they too, were fort-bound and isolated, and spent evenings watching John Wayne's sappy propaganda epic, *The Green Berets* again and again, drinking beer and marking off the days.

Once a day, the commander of the local unit we had been assigned to would poke his head into our sodden room and see if we were still alive. He was a short, heavyset Chinese captain named Tu, and his initial distrust of us was as palpable as our distrust of him. After about a week our interpreter did show up; he was very friendly and intelligent, spoke English quite well, getting our hopes up, took one good look around, spent one sodden night, and disappeared forever. And still, it would rain. Still, the helicopters would come and strafe the other side of the river. Still, the river would rise and fall, flowing both ways. I did not yet know the village we had fallen into, like aliens from outer space, did not yet know the people. All I knew was that I was sick and miserable. The village latrine was next to our room, perched on stilts above the river. I tried to time my visits there with the secluded hours of dawn and dusk, but this was not always possible. I began to know the village, and they began to know me, through my frequent trips to the latrine. They had never seen an American shit before, were uncertain if they even did, and sometimes the river bank would be lined with an audience of dozens, all babbling enthusiastically.

Our team leader, an artillery captain, began a series of familiarization meetings with Tu and the village chief, a Mr. Thanh, between deluges. We wanted to know what we could do to help them, in terms of both civil and military assistance, but these meetings were very difficult without an interpreter and there was little we could do anyway without a jeep and radios. I remained isolated, withdrawn from the others by my stomach cramps. Now and then, a Ninth Division convoy would roar through the village at thirty miles an hour. If I heard them coming in time, I would go out to the street and watch them pass. I would look at the filthy, sad-eyed infantrymen sprawled atop the vehicles, slumped over the machine guns, and feel a great sadness and longing. I would look for the platoon leader or company commander, look for the one with the grease pencils and maps, try to meet his eyes with mine so that I could wish him godspeed. If our eyes met, his would quickly dart away again, like a wild animal. And when, now and then, a line of slicks would come fluttering over our village, infantrymen dangling their legs from the doors, my heart would bob up and down with them.

I had to escape by any means possible. I couldn't stand the constant drumming of the rain, the constant drumming of a poker game, the ebb and flow of water through our room any longer. And, secretly, I couldn't stand being second in command. As soon as I felt well enough I began to explore the village between downpours, doing recon on my own again. Our little room was next to a much larger schoolhouse which had taken a direct hit and no longer had a roof. Apparently, sometimes the helicopters strafed this side of the riverbank as well. The main road, which was an alternate route between Saigon and the vast reaches of the delta farther south, came into the village from the west, turned south at the central market square, and vaulted over the river on a triple-span Bailey bridge next to the schoolhouse. This bridge was guarded by a platoon of Popular Forces, a separate outfit from Tu's, and they had erected little sandbag bunkers and watchtowers along the span.

There were no cobblestones; all the roads were dirt, but the buildings in this central part of the village were quite handsome, stucco, either French colonial or Oriental in design. But this village was not untouched by war, as An Loc had been. Craters, bullet spatters and fragment damage was everywhere. Many buildings had been abandoned, left unpainted and unmaintained. Yet commerce still endured, with three or four cafés and a thriving market in the morning, drawing buyers and sellers from all the smaller surrounding hamlets, even though half the covered marketplace had been destroyed when a Vietnamese A1E Skyraider crashed into it a few months before, after the pilot had bailed out for no explicable reason, as they often did.

Wherever I went on these early reconnoiters I was followed by a couple of Vietnamese soldiers. I don't know whether this was their assignment, or they were just curious. Among them almost always was "Baby-San," a fourteen-year-old orphaned soldier who had tuberculosis. He was a very good-natured boy, the illegitimate product of a French-Vietnamese coupling, not much taller than the M-1 rifle he carried. Like the rest of Tu's company of about ninety irregulars, he was somebody they had gathered up along the way and made a part of the "family." The rest of Tu's soldiers were of similarly diverse backgrounds. The leadership cadre were mostly Tonkin Chinese, like Tu, who had lived in the Cholon district south of Saigon for many generations. There were also some Khmer and Montagnard that Tu had brought with him from his days as a major working with the Special Forces in the Central Highlands. Only about half his company were ethnic Vietnamese, and of those there were many who had been assigned to the company, and whom Tu did not trust.

One of the more prominent buildings in the village, besides the marketplace, was the Cao Dai temple. This sect, derived from Confucianism, was the dominant one here, but there were also many Hoa Hao, a rival sect, among Tu's soldiers as well as Taoists, Buddhists, Animists and Roman Catholics. There was a small Catholic cemetery just outside the western gate to the village which spoke of close ties to the colonial empire, and before the war had swept through, the village had been a popular retreat for wealthy Saigon businessmen. Their opulent homes, each enclosed by a high wall, were empty and shell pocked. It was the hope of a few, such as Mr. Thanh, who spoke French fluently and offered cognac lavishly, that an American victory, or just our presence, would bring a return of affluence. I was advised not to venture into the eastern part of the village alone. Here, the villas of the wealthy abruptly gave way to the thatch and tin shacks of the poor who farmed and fished in the strange interlacing of land and sea that surrounded us. The eastern part of the village belonged to the Viet Cong, and every evening Mr. Thanh would find a different place to sleep in the western part of the village, in case the Viet Cong came looking for him.

How my father would have loved this place, with the sea so nearby, with the fleet of fishing boats and canoes, each carved by hand, planks riven from huge jungle trees. He would have started sketching immediately, the glaring eyes painted on high prows, the nets drying in festoons, the buildings that in ways almost seemed Carpenter's Gothic cast in stucco, and of course always the sky above and the magnificent clouds. He would have drawn comparisons between the society here and medieval Europe which were as charming as they were mistaken, and he would have found vestiges of the feudal system, which he so admired.

Inevitably he would have sided with the Viet Cong, for he was always thinking of himself as a revolutionary and a populist if not a communist, but I never gave him that opportunity. I never talked about this part at all when I got back. This village, the people, the war, were all a secret I carried inside of me for a decade, as so many of us did, never speaking although it was always there, too important and indescribable to share. Instead, my father and I talked about the pram and how with a summer of effort we could have it in the water by that autumn, me indulging him and goading him at the same time, giving and taking away, with love and anger like the tides. Anyway, he would not have understood it if I had tried to articulate what began to happen to me in the village. I could not understand it myself, and was ashamed enough already without his inevitable criticism.

I made a token effort on the pram, but the vision of us together as fishermen was losing its luster for both of us. He accepted my ambition to make films in New York, as long as I claimed these would be revolutionary documentaries. He fumbled along on the pram alone for a few more years while I tried to forget but couldn't.

Our jeep and CONEX finally arrived, and we moved into the finest vacant building in town. This had also once been a school, a lycée run by the French, right by the western gate with the Catholic cemetery close by. In the backyard was our own private little stucco outhouse, artfully spattered by a machine gun burst. Beyond that was some paddy land, a small square brick blockhouse built on an artificial island where, we were told, eight French soldiers had been killed, and then another tendril of the river with the shacks of the poor, an extension of the eastern part of the village. My biggest immediate concern was that the bullet-spattered outhouse was all that stood between us and the enemy, while the others busied themselves with comfortably settling in.

We were assured of safety by Tu, whose command of English seemed to be improving with time. He agreed to keep a few guards posted in the backyard at night. We took over the middle of the three downstairs rooms. Tu, his wife and young children, and his most trusted bodyguards took over the rooms beside us, stringing up hammocks and using the big cardboard crates our stove and refrigerator had come in to construct little apartments. The rest of the soldiers lived in a single, vast open room upstairs. A trip to Saigon in the new jeep was an immediate priority, fetching a battery-powered television. Almost nobody in the village had ever seen television, and for weeks people would crowd around our main street storefront type window, craning their necks for a fleeting glimpse at this, the only real magic we seemed to possess.

Then, once we were settled in and the rain had stopped, we slowly began to get to work. Our commander focused mainly upon the civic action aspects of our job. The career sergeants put their expertise as scroungers to work, and made scrounging forays in the jeep almost every day. They obtained cases of pastel blue paint, which we gave to the Cao Dai temple. They got mortar for patching bullet holes, and our captain got the Ninth Division to lend us a bulldozer for a day. We used it to bulldoze the wreckage of the airplane and marketplace away. The villagers watched stoically, occasionally feigning enthusiasm as the huge caterpillar scraped wreckage and laterite and the building stones the villagers had hoped to save into the river. A basketball hoop was put up outside our headquarters. Volleyball teams were organized. The place began to look spiffy and fun.

One of the first concerns the village chief had expressed to us was that the American convoys drove too fast through the village, and he was right. The dusty, or muddy, main street was by tradition a place where people strolled and socialized and children played, watched over by nobody in particular. The rare civilian vehicles proceeded very slowly, constantly honking their horn. But the U.S. convoys were still in their ambush avoidance mode, and came thundering through, shaking the ground and covering everything nearby with mud or dust. People would yell warnings as they approached, and shout back and forth in the aftermath to reassure each other they were still alive. So we put up a sign by the village gate: "U.S. Drivers: Keep this hamlet friendly, SLOW DOWN!"

The sign worked. For one thing, the U.S. drivers had no idea this hamlet was friendly in the first place. And it gave me more time to stare at the infantrymen, my sense of loss and mourning growing constantly. I didn't understand these feelings, tried to ignore them. It was not until fifteen years later, when that same ache came back, that I could finally name it as love and loss. By then it had become love for my own children, whom divorce had taken away for so much of the year. Being a father was so important to me, the most important thing on earth. I would feel fine, pulling myself up by the bootstraps most of the time, but then I would drive by a schoolyard and see tow-headed boys and the lump in my throat would rise again, so painful and yet strangely familiar, like moonlight and mortars.

As I was the only team member with combat experience, I was put in charge of the military aspects of our mission. With the one sergeant I liked, I began by getting sandbags and ammunition crates and barbed wire for our backyard. I got concrete and used it to build a sort of baffle between our front door and the main street. I would work into the evening while the others watched television, mixing sand and stone and cement one bucket at a time until it got dark or my hands got too sore. We scrounged perforated steel planks and railroad ties, and built a helipad out by the village gate. I mixed up napalm and put cans of it around the helipad so that we could bring in helicopters at night if we had to. I tried to lose myself and find myself in the military aspects of our mission.

Saigon was just an hour's drive away, going west, then north through government-controlled areas. Once a week, two members of the team would drive to Saigon to obtain food, military equipment, and other items. We had a liberal cash allowance for purchasing food locally, and we bartered for equipment using food, liquor, and later captured VC equipment and phony North Vietnamese flags, which were made by a local seamstress and which we shot holes in and sprinkled with chicken blood. The air force, in particular, loved the flags and would give us all sorts of stuff in return. I got a complete set of arctic gear this way, with my eyes already on Vermont. I wore it in 1981, when my marriage was breaking up and I was working for a PBS station in Boston, and returning to Vermont on weekends. That was the winter it snowed so much you could climb on snowbanks all the way to the peak of the farmhouse roof, then slide down, which I did wearing my air force arctic outfit and holding my two-year-old son in my lap. That was the winter when my father's relationship with his wife was sliding down hill as well, with him growing more critical of both of us, and me clinging to my boys and my air force arctic outfit, which the air force had inexplicably sent to Vietnam.

I hated Saigon, the bile rising inside of me. It was noisy and filthy, overflowing with REMFS and hucksters of all sorts. The population had increased tenfold because of the war, and the very foundations of the city were exploitation of one sort or another, East meeting West at its very worst. The air was heavy with exhaust fumes and the constant hustle of survival, the great open market of Mammon beside heart-breaking slums. Everything was for sale: drugs, weapons, people, principles, the past, the future. We had brought Walmart to Saigon, with blow jobs and televisions offered side by side, while beggars with their legs blown off, with puffy napalm scars and white, unseeing eyes, fought for scraps. At the famous Saigon dump, thousands of families lived in the crates that refrigerators and air conditioners had arrived in and picked through the garbage. Worse yet was the Military Assistance Command headquarters, where there were lawns between the concrete block buildings, lawns and fucking lawn mowers again as at Loc Ninh, cutting the grass at what resembled a great corporate headquarters. I dreaded the times I had to go there. It was almost all officers, and they were clean and smelled good. I ate in the cafeteria once. It was like a stateside corporate cafeteria. A captain sat down beside me and within moments he was extolling the virtues of the local smoke, said it was almost like LSD and tried to persuade me to try some. He couldn't understand why I declined, why I didn't dare, how the war had me. I had smoked before, and would again, but in Vietnam I didn't dare tip the precarious balance of reality, afraid to end up like my father.

Up through the chain of command in the Military Assistance Command, Vietnam, from the District Headquarters in Can Giuoc, through the Province Headquarters in Tan An, to the Corps Headquarters in Saigon, I tended to be contemptuous of the officers I met. A lot of this was as much my fault as theirs: the Iron Triangle had left me bristling. There were too many REMFS, too many merchandisers of emeralds and tiger skins. I remember a breathless lieutenant showing me the shrapnel holes in his air-conditioned trailer. The Viet Cong had the audacity, just once during his tour, to mortar the District Headquarters, and some shrapnel had gone right through the side of the trailer and through the drawer of his dresser and through the underwear neatly folded within. This would be his war story.

I am reminded now that I forgot myself for a while when I got back to the States, forgot how the war had changed me and tried to forget the war itself. New York reminded me of Saigon, and I began to feel my way through it as I had before, pretending that this was a time of peace. It was so easy to outmaneuver almost everyone, not just my father, like dodging traffic on Tu Do Street. The machine guns became movie cameras. The revolutionary documentaries I had promised my father became public service spots for the environment and against the war. All this was good but I still carried the war inside me, like malaria.

Feeling weaker and weaker, I perceived a cure in getting married and settling down. It didn't help. When I was offered the position of producer at a big advertising agency, with the promise of lawns, I took it. It seemed safer at the moment to imagine myself wrapped in the balm of money than to remember who I was and what I had done before. So I began producing commercials for Gillette and Pillsbury and Lever Brothers, a huckster if ever there was one, even making "Ring-around-the-collar" commercials. My father was so furious he could hardly say the name of the agency, sputtering "Batten Barton Farting Bombs Bursting in Air." I did this for a while, pretending to be somebody else, trying to explain that I was just doing it so I could buy a place in Vermont, but I was surrounded by assholes and couldn't resist being subversive and doing recon again. I returned to the antiwar and environmental movements, using the company WATS line, using company time. I got so depressed at times, so worn out and almost rent asunder by the beckoning emerald lawns pulling one way, and the war I had seen pulling the other, that I would fall asleep at my desk. They fired me, and they rehired me, and then they fired me again in less than a year, something my first wife never forgave me for. So there I was, caught between my wife and my father, while these dreams began in which the war had come to New York, and the sky turned brown like the sky over Saigon, filled with the acrid smog of *lambrettas* and motorbikes, jet turbine exhausts and cooking fires.

When I went to Saigon, I went scrounging at the supply depots while the others on the team went whoring. I got an 81mm mortar, so we could fire illumination. I got more PRC-25 radios, for better communication with Tu and his men. I got five .50 caliber machine guns, put a light barrel on one of them, doubling its rate of fire for a while, until the barrel melted. I got tons of ammunition, which I gave to Tu. I got more sandbags and barbed wire and lumber and cement. I was probably the only American to spend a night in a Saigon hotel without a prostitute. People worried about me. But I remained faithful to Mike Division, and Butch and Nancy and Ann. That was how much I hated Saigon.

Meanwhile, our creature comforts increased. We got a generator, and had electric lights. We built a shower, punching nail holes in an ammo can and hefting buckets of water into it. We even got a movie projector once, and showed a movie to the whole village. The movie was *Too Many Girls* starring Elvis Presley, a surefire hit, only the movie was in cinemascope and the projector we had borrowed had the wrong kind of lens. So for hundreds of villagers, the impression of America was of a place where unusually tall, thin people obsessed with sex chased each other around in short, fat automobiles. And when we returned from Saigon once with a hundred pounds of hamburger, and attempted to put on a good old-fashioned American barbecue, the villagers we had invited went wild, stuffing raw hamburger inside the folds of their clothing and running off with it before we could even cook it for them.

And still the tides would rise and fall, still I found myself sinking deeper into the depths of the delta, slipping away from America, finding friends among the Vietnamese. At dawn, the street outside would fill with the melody of voices as women went to market, and someplace in the hills far to the north Mike Division would be rising and urinating and rolling up their claymores. I would walk through the market, slowly learning to recognize people. Vietnamese people did not all look the same anymore. Slowly, with time and familiarity, racial differences became less important than individual differences. My fellow Americans, who continued to speak of gooks and dinks and slopes, were all beginning to look the same to me.

With the sun fully up, the airplanes would come to bomb the swamp southeast of the village. They did this almost every morning, so that the rising and falling buzz of the engines, the whump of the bombs and the shaking of the sodden earth beneath our feet became unnoticed. I would go to a café by the market and have a bowl of soup and the strong, dark, European-style coffee, with lots of sugar and condensed milk. By the time I was finished the heat would already be stifling, and I would think of Mike Division again. They would have filed out through the wire by now, beginning their day of sweeps. We would go scrounging, or help train Tu's men with their new M-16 rifles, or go on short sweeps ourselves through the surrounding countryside. Mike Division would be spaced five meters apart, moving through the jungle in a column of two. In the late afternoon a gentle breeze would spring up. We would shower, and open the first cold beers of the evening while Mike Division prepared for ambush. Two more interpreters came, assessed the situation, and disappeared. We didn't bother to request them anymore. We were communicating at last. We got the local seamstress to make black silk pajamas for all of us, and strutted about the village wearing this, the uniform of the Viet Cong as well as the traditional peasant dress, impressing the occasional American convoys to no end with our black pajamas and black berets. We learned to eat with chopsticks, to squat instead of sit, in that seemingly uncomfortable way the Vietnamese have. We learned never to point the sole of our foot toward anyone else because that was an insult, but otherwise we could do almost anything we wanted to because nobody else was watching or cared.

For years I was silent about all this, unwilling to allow anyone else to comment, but it felt good to turn the soil of Vermont at last and be away from the REMFS and lawn mowers. I gained my father's approval again; the survival strategy was more up his alley, and he would bring bags of seed corn and jugs of cider when he visited, and for a while we both subscribed to *Mother Earth News*. This was the coming together which we repeated so many times in our lives; we both had our gardens and root cellars, we both shared dark visions of the future. This business of lawn mowers and corporate well-being and emeralds and tiger skins had taken a toll on both of us, and for a while I even sang with him the rhapsodies of the simple life of the peasant, although I was still secretly scheming for more. I never told him about the black pajamas, but I had adopted a uniform myself, just as he had. His was the "Dickies" khaki work clothes, it was almost the only thing he ever wore, while mine was blue jeans and a military style shirt, a part of me still playing army. People would say that I moved like him as I grew older, that we looked the same from a distance, but this was not always what I wanted to hear; and he admired what I was doing with the farm, buildings, fences and barns, but said several times that he was afraid some day I might have a driveway of crunchy gravel with white board fences alongside. This was the tidal pulling away.

Then, when the firefights with my first wife were becoming increasingly sharp, close in and dirty, his wife Mary began to die. She suffered a heart attack, recovered, then came down with cancer. And something more began to die with her, not just the nice life she had given all of us in Stonington, but the hopes I still held for a better relationship with my father. She had alluded to "bad times" with him while I was in Vietnam, and I could see back then from some of his letters what she had meant, with the handwriting getting bigger and bigger, going off the page, making less sense. Now, whatever it was that had afflicted my father off and on throughout his life was coming back again. What could in the past be dismissed as eccentricities were becoming obnoxious. His glorification of the simple life became mixed with cruel tirades against Mary's "middle class values," and in his efforts at self-sufficiency he began to go to the extreme of composting his own feces in the basement as garden fertilizer. He was also making his own cider down there, and would spend hours in the basement surrounded by cider and feces. At the dinner table, his manners declined as well. He would take all the food before him, and more off the plates of others if he still wasn't satisfied. His anger and self-centeredness grew malignantly beside my two tow-headed sons, as though he could not stand not being the baby himself.

For my father, a trip to Vermont meant an escape from Mary's illness. We drove up together once, and along with the usual six-pack of beer, he also brought a bag of hash brownies he had concocted, and proceeded to eat, washing them down with beer. Although I was not entirely free of vices myself, I was unwilling to share that much with him and saw this as an unacceptable breach of father-son decorum.

I could hardly stand it, confined with him in the car for three hours. When at one point a helicopter passed by, he remarked on how he would like to shoot them down, and of course as always I remained silent, keeping my memory of the "crispy critters" to myself.

We were supposed to be working together on building a new equipment shed, but by then I had become so much more efficient at work than he was that his presence was more of a liability. He kept criticizing Mary and getting angry at helicopters, and it became harder and harder for me to hide my own anger at what he was saying and at his fumbling hands. I was, in a way, becoming what he had feared most all along, I was becoming his father, critical and threatening. I did not yet fully understand what his father had done to him, or that there was little I could do to remedy things other than stare at the mossy vertebrae. My own world was falling apart, and his, too; my son was very ill and nobody yet knew why, and his wife was dying, and neither of us had happy marriages anymore, and I could hardly wait until it was time to put him on the bus to Connecticut again. Then I would have the silence of the farm to myself again, pausing while putting up rafters as the sun went down to stare at the place that reminded me of Bad Vibes Hill.

Sometimes in the delta, if I had been up late on radio watch, I would awaken to the sounds of the planes bombing, my cot gently shaking. Sometimes I would go to the rooftop by the marketplace, the highest rooftop in town, where I had mounted one of my fifty-caliber machine guns, and I would watch the airplanes bomb, feel the building shake, watch the greasy bomb clouds rise against the sun while the river flowed past like molten silver. Sometimes I would go there in the evening, too. I would listen to the voices of families below, this universal music of families in evening, the most beautiful music of all. What I wanted, more than anything else, was a family of my own, and in this strange, imperfect way of divining things I saw this petite blonde woman and two daughters while standing on the rooftop, but of course had no idea how much lay ahead and between before the vision would be realized. Meanwhile, as I walked the village streets, the children began to follow me, and sometimes I would pick them up and carry them for a while, or swing them around and entertain them the way a Vietnamese father never would. And sometimes my eyes would meet those of a young Vietnamese woman, the bride of one of Tu's cadre, and we would both quickly look away again, or I would be standing alone on the rooftop, and see her alone on the street below, standing still, look-ing upward at me.

So much lay between me and home. From my rooftop, the clay tile roofs below gradually blended in among the tops of palms, then ended at the river bank, while the river itself continued its swing toward the sea, feeling its way with a thousand fingers, past more villages like this, through untracked palmetto swamps, then the mangrove swamps of the Rung Sat, with the salty sea breathing in and out, and the clouds building above. Then lay the sea itself, which I had traversed in a long night of flying, and my father had crossed in two weeks, but which in fact represented an almost unfathomable distance, light-years of heaving ocean and sky. I had already known this woman with two daughters for ten years when she lost her infant son. We suddenly found ourselves together, needing to share our loss, and of course we went to the river immediately to talk, watching the glistening, gliding water. The river drew us in, surrounded us; soon we were nearly drowning in the river and the warmth of each other. When, two years later, we were living together on this farm and our son had been born, and the evening voices of family, three sons and two daughters, were rising through the still air, when I felt the full reciprocity of love at last, my father asked incredulously, "You really like this?" Such was the ocean that lay between us by then. I was getting to love this place, this delta, too, this place on the margin of earth, awash in the stuff of life. While I was spending more and more time with the Vietnamese, less with my fellow Americans, I was even more obsessed with the notion that there was something I should be doing, some way to make things better. Early on, I had realized that Tu and his men were quite different from most of the Vietnamese military. Tu himself was sufficiently inde-pendent and strong-minded that it had gotten him in trouble in the past, demoted and exiled to this place. As a result he was more immune to the bureaucratic despair that held the regular ARVN forces in a death grip. He was also extremely intelligent and sophisticated, with a fully developed wartime mentality of personal survival.

Tu and I also began to recognize things in each other, almost as though we had known each other once before. We courted each other. I offered him guns and ammunition. Tu, in return, began by offering me women. I declined, which puzzled him. It was my newly evolved "This country is getting fucked enough as it is" reasoning. A bit later, he offered me drugs, and again I declined. In desperation one evening, he offered me boys, which I vehemently declined. He did discover, however, that I was very receptive to food, and this became a language we could always share, wherever we went. It was a passion the other team members didn't share, so food was one of the ways I got closer to Tu and his cadre than I was to my fellow Americans, and was eventually completely seduced. I began to prefer the *nuoc mam* fish sauce over catsup. Not only would I breakfast at the local cafés, I also began to shop at the local market, causing a great stir of hilarity among the vendors. Villagers who were amused in the early days by watching me shit were now delighted to watch me eat.

If we went out on sweeps during the day, Tu would gather food for a midday meal as we passed through isolated farmsteads and hamlets. He would confiscate a chicken here, a cabbage there, rationalizing that these people were all Viet Cong suspects anyway. If we happened by one of the fishponds that were often dug in backyards, the soldiers would toss in a grenade or two, then wade about and feel for the concussed fish with their feet. Any wild game was welcome; if a man shot a heron with his M-16, there was much excitement and it went in the pot. Wild rats, which lived in coconut palms, were savored and went in the pot. Dogs went in the pot when they were found, which was rare.

As the dinner hour approached, we would halt and lounge about while Tu's Chinese men went to work. One of them had actually been a chef at a hotel in Saigon. They would get a fire going, and set up an enormous wok over it. They would make rice. If banana plants were nearby, the stalk would be shredded like coleslaw. Then we would have a great meal, right there, in the field. If we had come up with a chicken, I would usually be presented with its boiled head. This was a great delicacy reserved for the guest of honor. With great flair, and in the accustomed manner, I would put one finger over the opposing eye socket, and suck the brains out through the nearest one with a great phlegmy sound which drew nods of approval. As host, Tu would eat the bony, cartilaginous feet.

As word spread, Tu's commander, a profoundly corrupt major, would sometimes show up with food, such as shrimp the size of lobsters. Occasionally, prominent villagers would invite me for dinner and attempt to speak to me in French. Often, Tu would put on a big evening dinner, especially as the celebration of Tet approached. Preparations for these would begin days in advance, with ingredients solicited far and wide, and once, as a special treat, Tu took me to Cholon with him. Just being in Cholon in the first place was a special treat, because Americans were seldom allowed there. In this exclusively Chinese community, there was a remarkable degree of autonomy from the rest of the country. The law of the family reigned supreme, timeless and contemptuous of the laws of outsiders.

It was just Tu and me and two of his most trusted cadre. We wove through crowded back streets, crowded but clean, and with no soldiers in sight. There were no beggars or prostitutes, either, there was just the bustling Chinese street commerce he had grown up with. We went into an unmarked building and up to the second floor, where about half a dozen cooks and assistants were waiting for us. Then, for the next three hours or so, we were treated to the finest meal I have ever had. It was Tonkin cuisine, much of it exotic seafood, exquisitely prepared and presented by bustling relay teams. The aromas alone were enough to send me into a swoon.

We headed back later that afternoon in a daze, hardly speaking, letting every molecule suffuse through our bodies. A short way south of Saigon, there was a terrible traffic jam. This would often happen, but this time it was worse than usual, *lambrettas* and lorries and buses stopped dead, nothing moving at all. So after a while we got impatient, and I put our jeep into four-wheel drive and went crosscountry on the embankments for a while, passing the traffic stalled on the two-lane blacktop of Route Four.

We soon came abreast of the cause of the delay. A young man on a motorcycle had been struck and killed. He lay there in the road in the kind of impossible position that only the dead can assume, and what was causing the delay was not so much his death as the subsequent pillaging. A crowd had gathered and was stripping his corpse of everything, watch, ballpoint pens, shirt, while others stripped his mashed motorcycle. Tu was silent for a long time after we passed, and continued on down the long, straight, open highway into the delta. Then at last he said, "So now you see what your war has done to my country."

His remark was to haunt me for long afterward; I had not thought of it as my war before. As we continued south, the suburbs thinned out, and the dry scrub lands became lower and flatter. Tendrils of the great Mekong began to wander closer to the road. We had to be home by twilight, before the land inverted on the delta's mirror surface, light becoming dark, us becoming them. We turned east, off the paved road, and began weaving our way toward the village. Now the road was hardly more than a widened, flattened dike, crossing the flooded paddy land which reflected the sky, so that sometimes it seemed as though we were crossing the sky itself. Then our village loomed ahead, an island of dark trees and rooflines. A squad of black-pajama-clad Popular Defense Forces, like those of the charcoal makers, greeted us at the village gate. Tu's soldiers greeted us in front of our headquarters. Soon, the security guards and ambush patrols would be dispersing into the night, and inside I could see the gray glow of the television.

In spite of what Tu had said, in spite of what I knew, both Tu and I continued to do what Redfeather would have done, what Millhouse and the others would have done, what Defiant Six would have done, which was to try to kill Viet Cong. With each of us, this effort had only a personal meaning, since political meaning had been lost long ago. Part of it was ambition, part fear of our own weakness and the desire for revenge. Some of Tu's soldiers practiced cannibalism, too, just as the Khmer of Loc Ninh did, and it made sense because we were all threatened by the spirits of the dead in one way or another, while the river rose and fell.

I would stand on my rooftop in the evening and I would gently swab my fifty-caliber machine gun with oily rags. I would tenderly examine the ammunition, looking for signs of corrosion on every round. This ammunition was a special blend, which I had painstakingly assembled by hand, just as my captain at Fort Polk had told me he did in Korea. There were the blue-tipped rounds of antiaircraft incendiary mixed with the black-tipped rounds of armor-piercing and the orange-tipped tracers and the plain ball, all put together in sequence link by link. Then I would open up the beast, expose its innards, take my gauges and check the head space and timing, swabbing with more oil. Sometimes I would fire my fifty-caliber from the rooftop. Tracers would soar out over the village, out over the river and the swamps and little settlements beyond, the glowing orange slowly growing smaller, then slowly sinking toward the ground, spent long before reaching the sea.

After a while, the villagers became accustomed to my firing the fifty-caliber over their heads, just as they had become accustomed to the airplanes bombing the swamp every morning, accustomed to the war itself. I would grip the silky-smooth wooden handles, push the butterfly trigger with my thumb, and the beast would shake and roar, spitting out ball and tracer and armor-piercing and incendiary. If my father were to get angry with me, he would have better chosen this playing with such deadly power. And if he were to puzzle over the ocean between us, this could have been an example. Before I went into the army, I had brought guns to Stonington, and we would sail the dory over to Napatree Point, where a World War I shore battery lay crumbling amid sand dunes and I could shoot safely. He would watch patiently while I embraced the power in my hands and destroyed beer cans. Even before that, long before that, great naval battles had been fought in my bathtub, with gray-hulled destroyers and cruisers and battleships dueling valiantly, only to go down in the end, rolling down through the soapsuds, carrying their imaginary crews with them.

Now my youngest son lines up his knights inside his fortresses, methodically assembles them for battle, but all this was never part of my father's persona. He was never meant for war. He should have been left alone, allowed to be the artist he really was. Yet still, I would goad him. He could have gotten angry with me for all this, but it was something else which made him get the chain saw, take it down to the workshop, and begin cutting the pram into pieces. It was because I had needed him, in the time after Mary had died, and before I had remarried, needed him emotionally and worse yet financially, that he used the chain saw to cut down through the timbers we had assembled together, sliced the plywood hull, loaded it all in a pickup truck and hauled it to the dump.

Vietnam was, more than anything else, a place of betrayal. Vietnam was where fathers betrayed sons, and sons betrayed fathers. I knew this, even then, just as I knew I had nothing invested at all in this mysterious land. I knew that I would soon go back across that vast ocean and try to resume my life where unusually tall, thin people obsessed with sex chased each other around in short, fat automobiles. Still I was drawn in deeper. I was drawn in by the innocence of the love I was developing for the place, drawn in by the guilt of fear. Tu became very much a part of this. We began to depend upon each other, even while betraying each other. This was something quite different from my time with Mike Division, much more sinister, a seduction of guilt and innocence.

The tide rolled in, the tide rolled out. The marketplace filled, the marketplace emptied. At five in the evening, Armed Forces Television began its broadcast day with a Vietnamese language lesson taught by My Lam, an aristocratic Vietnamese girl. This was followed by the news, and the first cold beers would pop open. The weather was presented by a sprightly nymph in short-shorts named Sherry. "Looks like a rainy day up in Two Corps," she would coo, placing a little frowning cloud on the map of Vietnam. She did the stateside weather, too. "For all you Georgia crackers, the high in Atlanta was 92 under sunny skies."

Next came the immensely popular reruns of the television series *Combat.* Then there were stateside shows like *Rowan and Martin's Laugh-In.* And lastly, every night, as a sort of wry joke, we were treated to old "Charlie Chan" movies. You could, for a while, almost imagine the ocean narrowing again. Sometimes, later, if I had radio watch, I would go up and down the military frequencies, listening to long, dry logistical reports, occasionally interspersed with desperate cries for medical evacuations and artillery support. Sometimes I would step outside to the street, where the air was now cooler.

The village was enveloped in darkness, quiet and still except for the reptilian songs in the swamp. Tu's men would be spread out, hiding in various places. Baby-San would be sitting in our jeep. We would engage in the usual dialogue.

"No VC *Trungoui,*" he would say to me, calling me by the Vietnamese word for "lieutenant."

"No VC tonight Baby-San," I would reply.

"*Beaucoup* VC Phouc Hau, *Trungoui,*" he would say, referring to one of the hamlets to the southeast, "VC numbah ten. Baby-San shoot VC."

"Baby-San number one," I would reply.

Sometimes Baby-San would stroke my forearm while talking to me. A lot of Vietnamese did this once they became familiar enough. They were fascinated by our body hair. And later, as I lay in my cot, I would hear Baby-San coughing all through the night, and know that he was loyally awake.

❖ XIV ❖

I DON'T REMEMBER HEARING the explosion; perhaps in my sleep I figured it was an eight-inch howitzer. But the sound of debris falling, the clank and clunk of metal dropping into the street and on the rooftops outside had me bolt upright and wide awake instantly. At first we had no idea what had happened. The village was ominously silent as we scrambled in the dark to get dressed and find our weapons. I ran to the backyard with one of the sergeants, opened an illumination round container, set the fuse, hung it, and dropped it. As the round fired, I realized that in my excitement I had neglected to remove the safety. We only had four or five precious illumination rounds left. Then a machine gun began to fire, slowly and methodically, from the other side of the river, sweeping back and forth through the village in bursts of eight or ten rounds.

We hung and fired a second round successfully. Then I left the sergeant at the mortar pit and ran back through our hooch to the street outside. More weapons began to fire, on both sides of the river. Baby-San was hiding under the jeep. He came crawling out when he saw me and Tu and a few of the others. Orange tracers were snapping overhead, spattering on the walls, but the fire was high and inaccurate. We were able to run down the street to the marketplace, to where the road turned right, but then we had to take shelter behind the pastel blue columns of the Cao Dai temple because bullets were sending up dust puffs and whining as they ricocheted off the laterite street. We had never been allowed in the Cao Dai temple; it had been explained to us by the village chief that the temple was a very special magical place, that in the past aerial rockets fired at it had simply gone in one door and out the other without exploding. In the swaying yellow light, I could also see that the temple was being used to warehouse all sorts of appropriated American aid such as brand new rototillers and irrigation pumps, tons of bagged fertilizer, and building supplies. It was also immediately clear that we didn't have a bridge any more. Twisted chunks of metal lay in the street in front of us, along with other ragged lumps which I took to be the remains of the platoon of soldiers that had been on the bridge, guarding it.

Our contingency plan in the event of an overwhelming attack was somehow to make our way to the ARVN fort on the other side of the river, but it seemed that we were unwelcome there. The intense firefight in progress was not with the Viet Cong, but between Tu's men in our village, and the ARVN battalion on the opposite shore. Gradually, with a lot of shouting back and forth, the firing dribbled to a halt and we were able to venture back out into the street to look for bodies, or parts of bodies.

There weren't any. The ragged lumps scattered amid twisted steel were all that was left of the sandbag gun emplacements on the bridge. Clearly, the guards had been warned and had left their posts before the explosion. Nobody had been injured in the explosion or the firefight that had followed. I never got a satisfactory explanation for this from the Vietnamese. Our own engineers later estimated that six hundred pounds of TNT had been floated on a raft beneath the bridge, then detonated. The central span was totally disintegrated. The southern span had been lifted, turned ninety degrees, and dropped high on the bank some twenty meters from the abutment. The northern span had dropped from its supports and lay in the water.

The blowing of the bridge was a wake-up call of sorts, jarring us from the complacency the village seemed to invite. Higher command, both Vietnamese and American, was not pleased. It would have been better if some guards had died. But it also left us more isolated than ever. American convoys would not pass through the village anymore. The district headquarters was now a full day's drive distant. In order to visit us, our higher command would have to hire canoes. Yet even by sunrise that very day, dozens of canoes appeared, as though they, too, had been warned, and the throngs of market-goers that gathered on the opposite bank were soon being ferried across for a modest fee. Tu and I were particularly embarrassed.

Those great tides, coming and going, were what made crossing the river particularly difficult. One could not set foot in the mudflats at low tide; the stinking black muck would suck you in and mire you hopelessly. Planks with crude supports were cobbled together leading out to the canoes, but these had to be removed before the tide came in again. Yet we had to go, now more than ever, drawn toward the swamps to the southeast, toward the sea. Tu and I hired canoes. While the ARVNs remained shamed and fort-bound, we went across the river, then east into the land of the Viet Cong, where the airplanes bombed and the helicopters strafed. We would glide across the river in the twilight and set up ambushes, or glide south with the flow in the morning, carried on the shoulders of the river deep into where thick palm swamps made it twilight midday, then sweep back to the village on foot.

This was my own form of madness, canoeing in estuaries, unable to stop playing army. This amazing place began to reveal its secrets when explored by canoe, as though the boats were a form of bronchoscope, taking us inside the body of Vietnam, and revealing things inside of me as well. I began to find fragments of Mike Division in Tu. We spoke the common language of men, the language of the lonely hunter, and I found myself closer to the hunted than I had ever been before. This place, this strange land, seen from above looks like a biopsy of lung tissue. There, to the south, you see the great trachea of the Mekong, rising and falling with the tides. Bronchi fan outward, from the mangrove swamps of the Rung Sat to the Plain of Reeds, branching into bronchioles which lead at last to the alveoli, the cul-de-sacs of palmetto swamp south and east of our village, where the Viet Cong virus lived and the airplanes would bomb every morning. We would move silently along paddy dikes, carefully stepping over the *punji* pits that surrounded each settlement, while on the adjacent paddy dikes women tending rice would convey our position and route of travel to the enemy by coded arrangements of sticks and stones. We would nose our canoes through leads of black water, parting fronds of vegetation, smelling the dinner the Viet Cong were cooking just a few dozen meters away.

I wish I had known my father when he was a boy with a scow, exploring places like this with such complete innocence, an innocence forever lost for both of us. I recapture some innocence now canoeing with my boys, but the guilt is always there too, guilt for playing army, guilt for being afraid, guilt passed down from father to son. I don't know what drove my father mad. Years later, I would try to dissect him as I would try to dissect my own actions, but I got nowhere. When Mary died my hopes for a renaissance, for reconciliation were rekindled, but within a year he had remarried again, this time to a woman only seven years older than me. They made quite a pair, canoeing together in mysterious waters of their own. My father's cancer of the esophagus was diagnosed within a month or so after the wedding, so I went back down to Stonington, which had become hostile ground, and we rowed about in the harbor for one evening, trying to be upbeat about it. It was one of those still evenings when village sounds carry across the harbor, and there was a pink tinge to the sky as the sun set. It brought back a lot of fond memories, but whatever it was that held my father in its grip was so strong, stronger even than the cancer itself, that I held little hope, and it was the last time we were on the water together. A surgeon removed much of the esophagus, there was the exorcism of radiation and chemotherapy, the roller coaster of euphoria and despair. Meanwhile, with the help of lawyers, a reserve of money was uncovered like an underground oil field, and it began to bubble forth. This, too, had been one of my father's secrets which had kept him shamed and humiliated. In his anger with me, in his determination to live life to its fullest, he took what had been promised as my inheritance and bought a fiberglass sloop. He then proceeded to operate upon it as ruthlessly as the surgeons had operated upon him, ripping out masts and fittings, and converting it into his interpretation of a Chinese junk.

Meanwhile Tu and I began to do what few other units were doing. We began to get a body count. The wet, limp corpses which had eluded me for so long were beginning to show up, brought back to the village in the morning slung under a pole. They would be dumped by the roadside near the village gate, for people to gawk at and relatives to identify secretly. Flies would gather in the tears of open eyes.

One reason for the bodies was that, lacking any air or artillery support to speak of, the firefights were up close and dirty, just dozens of meters apart, with a few quick bursts of gunfire and no awkward periods of disengagement and withdrawal while support was called in, periods which almost always allowed the enemy to withdraw, taking their casualties with them. But the main reason for such success was Tu's aggressive techniques of intelligence gathering. His confidence boosted by the Americans at his side, he would burst into every mud and thatch hut we encountered in the infected area. Old women, their mouths stained red, their teeth blackened by betel nut, would cower in a corner while Tu fired questions at them. Children, half-naked, would pee with fright.

Young men were seldom to be found, but old men were still fair game. Usually they were farmers, but sometimes they were priests in the rival sect of the Hoa Hao. They would be brought before Tu roughly, one arm held upward behind the back, their long, flowing white robes torn and muddied. Sometimes Tu's soldiers would casually stick a foot out and trip the prisoner as he passed. Then Tu himself would pull the man's garment up over his head and tie it, so that his head was covered with cloth. He would use a helmet to dip water from the nearest bronchiole and poured it over the man's head. This vividly conveyed the impression of drowning and suffocation.

Most soldiers had seen this done so often that they wouldn't bother to watch. Tu and his most trusted cadre would carry out their interrogation, now and then pausing to kick the man in his ribs while he gasped for breath. Other soldiers would wander about aimlessly. If there was a fishpond, a soldier would toss a grenade in. The fish would lie there on the pond embankment, rubber lipped and gasping for breath, just like the old man, while the great tide of innocence and guilt, love and anger flowed slowly in and out, like my father dying.

We assembled a list of suspects; I still have mine. Ut Lau, a twenty-four-year-old girl with a Colt revolver. Hugnh Van Nam, born in 1925, joined the Viet Cong in 1962. Nguyen Van Lam, who wore a false beard as a disguise, and many more. They would meet like the local board of selectmen, at the home of Mr. Nam Cuu and his son-in-law, Nguyen Thi Gio, coordinates XS764778, with a hidden tunnel connecting to the nearest alveolus. A similar list was kept at the Provincial Headquarters by the Phoenix advisor, who was an official of the CIA and with whom I frequently consulted. Tu, of course, carried a much longer list entirely in his head. More names were added, usually by interrogation. Other names were deleted, usually with a gunshot.

As trust was gained, there was an added financial incentive. We paid for names, paid much more for bodies. Our backyard became an interrogation center. Tu built some tiger cages; these were cages constructed of barbed wire and engineer stakes in such a way that there was not enough room to stand up, nor enough room to lie down. More often than not, we would find one of Tu's own soldiers in the cage, for many of them were Viet Cong, too, or had committed some other infraction. Hard-core Viet Cong suspects from the outlying countryside usually didn't survive as far as the tiger cages. But if they did, they would be hooked up to a field telephone. Bare wires leading from the telephone would be attached to various body parts, then the crank on the phone would be turned and the suspect would scream and convulse. Often, this would take place in the backyard while we were trying to watch television, and the laugh track of some old sitcom rerun would be interspersed with screams. We were attacking the lung virus relentlessly, while the river flowed back and forth.

My father got shock treatment when he was hospitalized for his psychosis, and I wonder in what ways it was different from hooking him up to a field telephone. Was this the same sort of treatment as we were administering in our own crude way? I always assumed that it had left him with something missing or permanently weakened, which is also the objective of torture. Of course the cancer returned, opportunistic as always, feeling its way through the alveoli like Ut Lau and Nam Cuu had with their AK-47s and satchel charges while my own life blossomed. I tried to keep my distance while remaining sympathetic; he had totally estranged his sisters as well by this time, failing to accept his illness gracefully, threatening neighbors with lawsuits and so on. I visited when I had to, when the news of his condition was particularly bad. I was very uncomfortable in the house I had once known and loved; what had once just been one of the many simple fishermen's row houses had become a sort of Danish Modern showplace, lots of glass and intimidating appliances. We managed to walk down to the point of land overlooking the harbor; it was cold, he would be leaving for his condominium in Florida soon, and I noticed that I could see through him. It was more than the fact that he had lost so much weight, and looked ten or twenty years older than he was, it was that I could see through his flesh to the breakwaters, to the gray glistening sea.

Later, when we were alone in the kitchen, he made codfish cakes. In his weakened condition he was trying, now, to be sympathetic with me, listening to me explain my various projects, yet his temper kept flaring up as though he had Tourette's syndrome. He would suddenly almost shake with anger at random things, like Ronald Reagan or modern potato peelers. So I asked him why he was so angry with me.

"Because you were telling me what to do," he replied, which was ironic, as he had so willingly abdicated so much by now. It took a few years for me to figure out what he meant, but now I see that he meant I had indeed become his father in his eyes, so now he was twice betrayed.

I slept that night in the downstairs room which had once been a guest room but was now his wife's office, with a fold-out bed. Before retiring, while looking for something to read, I discovered an assault rifle in the closet. It was a Ruger Mini-14, with a twenty-round magazine and two boxes of ammunition. This was the same magazine and ammunition we had used in Vietnam, and it was the first time I had handled them since then. I felt the bullets; they carry a sleek weight far beyond brass and copper and lead and powder. I was unnerved. Apparently, during a moment of euphoria and paranoia, they had bought this weapon to defend themselves against drug-smuggling pirates when they sailed the sloop-cum-junk to Florida. The idea of anyone wanting to hijack this boat, which drew numerous comments but no wind, was as ludicrous as the vision of him quickly learning to use it. I secretly decided that I wanted that gun more than anything else, partly because I was concerned about safety given his state of mind, and partly because somehow guns had given me what my father couldn't all along, and clearly now never would.

Such is the dreadful magic. During those bad times, when summer was over and I was alone again, I would begin the new season by picking up the toys my sons had left scattered about, and the toys were often guns. Or I would be tilling the soil, or mowing the lawn, and a gun would appear, or one of those little plastic soldiers which are everywhere. Such are the toys of boys with which to stave off loneliness and mortality. Such is the route toward loss of innocence. Down in the delta, it occurred to me that with all this great intelligence Tu was gathering, we were missing a vital tool, for often we knew exactly where the Viet Cong were; often, especially at night, we could get quite close to them, but not quite close enough. So I borrowed from my experience with the NOD, north of Di An, and decided that what Tu really needed was a starlight scope. The open terrain of rice paddies was perfect for it, but of course this was impossible: we could never allow such a sensitive device into the hands of the Vietnamese. But my discussions with Provincial Headquarters in Tan An led to the temporary attachment of two Ninth Division snipers to our team. They arrived by jeep one afternoon with their scopes and rifles packed in hard cases, like a scientist's or doctor's instruments, and we decided to shoot some suspects that very night at a meeting place Tu knew about.

I realized, as soon as I saw those guys, that I was making a mistake, that this was not the way to find Mike Division. I was repelled by them, and already repelled by myself and the mechanism I had devised and would soon put into action. Guided by Tu as though he was guiding sportsmen toward big game, we canoed across the bronchi to the southeastern land and crawled in total darkness to within a stone's throw of the meeting which was taking place in a hut. You could see two Viet Cong sitting across from each other at a table with a candle on it through the window, but then Tu and I got into an argument. He wanted to rush the hut with his men, which was his usual way, but night assaults were a tactic which was unfamiliar and uncomfortable for me and the snipers. We wanted to shoot them both instantly, and besides, command at both Ninth Division and MACV were awaiting the results. Our discussion actually became rather heated, with lots of whispering and crawling back and forth, and the Viet Cong apparently heard us, because next thing we knew they had doused the light and slipped away, leaving us empty-handed.

The snipers would only be with us for a few days, so we decided to try them in the daytime as well. Once again, Tu was quick to suggest a likely place, so back across the river we went, hiding in a hut ourselves this time. After a wait of a few hours, a single figure emerged from the nearest palmetto swamp alveolus and walked down a rice paddy dike toward us. He was carrying an AK-47 casually at his side, and he was wearing the black and white checked scarf of the Khmer Rouge. The Khmer Rouge were an army few would hear of until three years later, when two million Cambodians would die, but here was one right in front of us. When he was about two hundred meters away, he turned his back on us and sat down on the paddy dike.

He was waiting, and we waited with him. We watched while he smoked a cigarette. After a while, the snipers and I became impatient. We wanted to shoot him. But Tu insisted that we wait, that more Viet Cong were coming. It began to get dark. The snipers silently removed their telescopic sights and mounted the starlight scopes. We continued to wait as darkness descended, but surely the VC had been tipped off by now, almost certainly by Tu's own men. It was always just a matter of time before this happened, and too much time had gone by. We looked again. He was gone. Tu was strangely smug. He had been annoyed with me for balking the night before, and it seemed to me that this whole afternoon had been engineered as subtle revenge.

To me, the whole episode was a miserable failure and once again I was ashamed of myself, feeling guilty for being afraid again, for being unwilling to jump up and assault the hut at night, for giving legitimacy to two young American sociopathic killers, layer upon layer of guilt and shame accumulating like delta sediment; yet still I could not stop playing this deadly game. It did not matter that the war had lost its meaning. The river that was pulling me ran deeper than human politics. It did not matter that my country had become like my father, both malevolent and incompetent at once, or that I had been betrayed. Currents of guilt and innocence, anger and love had me swirling.

When seen from the air, the St. John's River could be the Mekong, with estuarine whorls and palmetto swamps as it winds past Jacksonville and my father's condo upstream. But there were no tides, no voices of children ringing like temple bells in the evening. In the aftermath of war, black men picked up the garbage outside this stucco imitation of the Alhambra where my father was spending his last winter, with security checkpoints and the equivalent of a concertina wire perimeter. The era of assassination, the era of my war and my father's war, was over. This was the time of dementia and denial. The lawns were exquisite, lush, and impeccably mowed. The stock market had never been higher. There were crunchy gravel driveways everywhere down here, while my own up north was still mud. The yacht club was right below my father's balcony. The yacht club! How he used to revile yacht clubs, the people and their boats, capitalist fools and their chicken noodle sloops. He had indoctrinated me more than he would ever know. I was more his son than he would ever know. Now he spent his days sitting there, looking out upon the club and the river beyond, breathing heavily, wheezily through a tube in his neck. His wife would shuck fresh oysters for him with a scraping, phlegmy sound. In the afternoon the wind would rise, coming in from the sea, and the yachts would begin to rock. A hundred halyards would slap against a hundred aluminum masts, the constant arrhythmic "ting ting ting" like a prayer offering, the chant of bond market Buddhas, the song of Charon who was waiting patiently in a black fiberglass sloop.

The VC began to call me on the radio again. They would call at odd hours, and yell epithets: "You fuck pig, *Trungoui* Tripp, eat shit," that sort of thing. They announced a price on my head, although a ridiculously low one: two hundred dollars. We were paying more than that for just any old head that could be made to fit a list. Reassured, even inspired, Tu went to ever greater lengths to please us and regain favor among the Vietnamese command that had exiled him to this isolated post. Flush with the excitement of a fresh kill, Tu burst in one morning to boast that he had just killed a major VC political figure. He had managed to arrange a meeting with this person at a café in one of the outlying hamlets. Of course, no weapons would be allowed at this meeting, but Tu had cleverly taped his .25 caliber automatic to the underside of the table well beforehand. Midway through the meeting, Tu began to shoot this man in the stomach, having deceived him much as the French had deceived the striking rubber workers of An Loc.

My attempts to find Mike Division, my attempts to regain honor and find the right path, were turning into a miserable failure. At some point, we had stopped being soldiers and become instead the gestapo. We worked from a list of names furnished by informants whose motives were as varied as the items hawked at the morning market. When we swept the outlying districts, it was impossible to tell whether we were interrogating VC suspects, seeking revenge, or collecting overdue rent. As the gestapo, however, we were a great success. Brothers began to turn against brothers in the eastern part of the village. We raided houses. I watched while AK-47s were discovered, and the rebellious teenagers who had hidden them were dragged out, kicked and beaten, then carried off to the tiger cages and telephone.

So this, then was the place to which my country had finally led me. These were the memories that would haunt me to this day, that I could not articulate, that made my time in the infantry seem like child's play. Here, in the village, the war's fundamental evil finally came unmasked, and whatever numbness I had previously developed as a soldier was no longer sufficient. I began to hate my fatherland, with the television laugh track and screams of torture blending together. I grew detached, aloof, unable to even feign friendship with Tu, dragging my feet on military operations, despising that part of me which had remained the loyal soldier. Instead of considering resigning my commission, as I once had in the infantry, I began to seriously consider resigning my citizenship entirely.

It has been said by some of the aged fathers of the Vietnam war, awash in their own bitterness, that we could have won, that we came so close to winning, only to be subverted by public opinion. Similar words are sometimes heard in the beer halls of Munich and Vienna, their speakers never asking why or to what end. We came that close, now accusations of betrayal fly back and forth. Yes, it is true, we came that close. Acting on tips, our little patrols would gravitate toward the center of a certain rice paddy. A clod of mud would be removed, revealing a small opening made with an American ammunition can, which was used to seal a fifty-five-gallon steel drum, which was filled with AK-47s and SKS carbines. A few pokes with a bayonet into a bamboo hedge would find metal. We would unearth literally tons of ammunition, thirty- and fifty-caliber, all sealed in tins like giant sardines. We found caches of land mines and fuse and rocket launchers, caches so huge that Chinook helicopters had to be brought in to lift the booty out as sling loads. With a small core of twenty men we were accomplishing more than the Black Lions of Cantigny. These accomplishments were based upon betrayal; the war was based upon betrayal; I was betraying Tu, and he was betraying me; we were all betraying and being betrayed in turn.

I still have one of the SKS carbines we found. It sits in my office beside the Mini-14 assault rifle my father eventually gave me without my ever asking. I was flying down to Jacksonville once a month or so for a while then. I would sit on the balcony and watch the broad, shining river roll past while his wife suctioned mucus from his lungs with a sound similar to that of shucking oysters, and the masts went "ting ting ting." I was feeling strong. My third son had just been born. I was running twenty miles every week. I would go out and run past the condos that lined the river's bank while my father slept.

During the daytime, if he was strong enough, we would go out on little sweeps of the surrounding countryside. Once, toward the end, amid the endless tract houses and palmetto swamps, we really did make a wonderful find, an arms cache for both of us. Beyond the naval air station, farther up the river to where it narrows, we came upon the ruins of what had once been an enormous military base built during World War II, and subsequently abandoned to the forces of nature and free enterprise. We ignored the sign that said "No Trespassing," on an open chainlink gate, drawn inward by the sight of slanting masts on the horizon. I could hardly hear him, he could hardly speak, but my father began to croak excitedly. Tracks had been laid upon an abandoned airfield, and were accumulating long lines of rusted boxcars. Lines of locomotives lay with weeds crawling up through the frames, cab windows shattered and birds nesting within. As we got closer to the waterfront, there were more and more abandoned boats hauled out, canted over, split open. Long concrete wharves lined the river, with larger vessels tied up alongside, and some of these had sunk at their moorings. There were rusting coastal freighters, confiscated from drug runners, and a steam-powered dredge. There were ships from the era of Rye in 1931, when my father had his scow, a steam tugboat with tall stacks and fine lines, like the toy he had built for me. It was the sort of thing we both had enjoyed so much when I was still a boy myself, innocent and relatively unbetrayed, meeting him on weekends, meeting more as playmates than as father and son.

My father became increasingly excited, tears of excitement in his eyes, croaks of excitement in his voice. He insisted upon getting out and walking for a while, even though he was so weak by then that he could hardly walk at all. But we got out and limped along for a hundred yards or so. There were even two minesweepers there, minesweepers like the ones my father had been on himself as a young officer, minesweepers built of wood and now split in half at the bow, with the superstructure slowly sinking into the decks. We stood together silently, looking at the minesweepers, for it was war that had come between us, instead of bringing us together as it does for so many men. It was war that had made me grow up, while he steadfastly remained an aged, dying Peter Pan. There were a few croaks about the feudal system, and the end of civilization. Then it was back to the condo, back to the fairy knell of halyards slapping against aluminum masts.

I flew home to Vermont with the gun, over the lung tissue of the Savannah, the Roanoke and the Delaware, back to where the waters ran fresh and clear. I loaded bullets into the magazine, went out into the yard, inserted the magazine into the gun, pulled back the bolt and fired away, destroying an old barbecue grill, just as when in the delta, as evening descended, I sometimes went up on the rooftop and fired the fifty-caliber toward the sea. Lost somewhere between sky and sea and endless verdure, we were foundering. There were outbursts of anger, as with my father, irrational assumptions, paranoia and self-deception. We were reaping the grim harvest of seeds sown in the fifties, frontier ballads of Davy Crockett anticommunist paranoia. Our country was crazy, senescent, staggering about and pissing in its pants. Yet I was still trying to be the good son, not yet the father myself.

Although I felt swaddled in failure, our operations with the snipers were judged to be a great success. The snipers themselves raved about how close we had brought them to a kill, and Americans with scopes were teamed up with Vietnamese intelligence squads all across the delta, and more names were eliminated from lists. Between me, with my military operations, and our captain, with his civic action projects, our success was such that we were able to remain in the village instead of moving on to other units and locations, the way Mobile Advisory Teams were supposed to. Some MAT teams had actually to live inside their CONEX. Some lived like rats. But we were able to refuse to move, refuse to give up the comfort of our classroom and stucco outhouse. Instead, people came to us. We were touted as an example of a program that really worked. Visiting congressmen were brought to us by the Military Assistance Command, alighting at our helipad. ABC News was brought to us. We put on a big medical clinic for the occasion, and were seen on the stateside evening news. And the CIA came to us. John Paul Vann himself came to us, alighting in the silver Air America ship. I wasn't sure just who this portly man in a safari suit was at the time, but was told in hushed tones that he was more powerful than General Abrams or Westmoreland. I did my presentation to him, like I was doing a presentation of an advertising campaign, but he seemed unimpressed, bored and thirsty.

Because our team refused to move, sometimes other Vietnamese units came to our village to spend time going out on operations with us in the hope that something would rub off. And sometimes we were attached to a Vietnamese Ranger unit for riverine operations far to the east, on the edge of the Rung Sat, the famous swamp sanctuary. We would hire motorized fishing boats, powered by the same "one-lunger" engines my father used to rhapsodize and imitate. He would have liked the boats, too, all built by hand according to timeless designs, with crooked masts and sails patched together of a dozen different shades of tan. The hull design of these vessels was not unlike that of the dory we used to fish from in Stonington, with a flat bottom and flaring sides, but they were much bigger, perhaps thirty feet long. A platoon would clamber into each one at the dock in Can Giuoc and off we would go, everybody chattering excitedly and trying to keep feet out of the bilges. Sometimes we would set sail, and ghost down the Song Vam Co on the morning breeze just as my father and I had, no sound but the swish of wind and sea. Sometimes we would use power, heaving across the broad choppy water of Cua Soai Rap, navigating the trachea, thumping past endless islands of echoing vegetation. Once, I watched with astonishment as we landed on a lonely white sand beach, and a hundred North Vietnamese regulars suddenly jumped up and fled before us, just out of rifle range. We had no artillery, no aircraft, just our thumping fishing boats. Such a strange game it was we were playing, moving back and forth like the tides.

Of course it was a mistake to credit our team with Tu's extraordinary success. The success was due to him, and he was exceptional. Most Vietnamese units were like the one that had fled during the firefight half a century ago, or the platoon that had been guarding the village bridge. Most Vietnamese units did not have the network or ambition of a Tu at the helm, and when, now and then, a more typical unit came to our village in need of training or inspiration, we were annoyed and depressed and cautious. Toward the end of my time in Vietnam, we were out on an operation with one such unit when the broader reality of Vietnam interceded in a particularly scary way. I was with the sergeant I liked, a platoon sergeant with about sixteen years of service, and about forty Vietnamese soldiers. We were in the desolate eastern paddy land, it was midafternoon, and we were headed back toward the boats. It was also one of those times when the river had breathed out, leaving a slough of black mud about fifty feet wide, which everybody began to cross. The Vietnamese didn't have much trouble with this; they were lighter than we were to begin with, and besides they weren't carrying much equipment, just rifles and a clip or two of ammunition. We, on the other hand, were carrying full combat loads plus a radio, and as we sank deeper, just knee-deep at first, we began to fall behind. In a sense, it was not unlike our involvement in Vietnam in the first place.

I began to tell, from the sidelong glances, that this could easily develop into a bad situation. This time there was no Tu along to hold the threat of tiger cages over these men, and the men themselves had no vested interest in us. By the time the sergeant and I had reached the middle of the slough all the rest of the men had reached the opposite bank. We were up to our waists in mud by now and the more we struggled, the deeper we sank. It became impossible to move forward at all, and the soldiers up on the bank began to laugh openly at us, offering no assistance. It was terrifying, first of all, to feel like you were going to drown in this stuff which was up to our armpits by now, and even more terrifying to be openly humiliated like this after eleven and a half months of delusion. Then, one by one, the laughing soldiers turned their backs and walked away. I was trying hard to keep from panicking completely. Soon the tide would come breathing in again, and the only thing I could think of was to call a helicopter on the radio and get pulled out. But that could take an hour. It would be a real race with the tide. I could see the tongue of brackish water approaching already, coming around a bend toward us.

This sergeant who was with me was a great guy, but like a lot of other Americans he had no great love for this war or those people, while for me it was the people who made the war bearable at all. He, too, had sworn frequently that he was getting out of the army as soon as he could, foregoing his retirement benefits, but now it looked like we weren't going to get out of the mud, and he lost his temper as much out of fear for his life as frustration with the Vietnamese and he unlimbered his M-16. He was yelling that he was going to shoot the bastards, and I kept trying to calm him down, knowing that it wouldn't do us any good if he did, that they would then be obliged to finish us off and report a terrible ambush. He had the thing locked and loaded and had flipped the safety to full auto, and there wasn't a thing I could do about it because he was too far away for me to grab the gun. In the end, it was our yelling at each other that brought a few of the soldiers back. They looped a bunch of rifle slings together and pulled us out. We came back to the village caked with black mud, and in the stony silence of anger and humiliation. My friendship with the sergeant remained as strong as ever, but for both of us the war would never be the same. We had seen how the soldiers really felt about us, and it was definitely time to go home.

The area we were in was a sort of thoroughfare between the sanctuaries of Cambodia and the Rung Sat, so along with the local Viet Cong there were also North Vietnamese occasionally passing through, and one night while we were all watching television, Tu and his men captured a young North Vietnamese lieutenant. They found him wandering about in a rice paddy after a short but sharp firefight, and brought him into our room. He was soaking wet and shaking with fear, but too good a prize to torture and kill. In my naïveté, with whatever last vestiges of innocence I had left, I saw this as a great opportunity to meet the enemy, especially one of equal rank, so I sat this young man down at our kitchen table and offered him a cigarette, which he refused, sensing that he only had a few more minutes to live. I offered him a beer, which he also refused. Tu was with me, barely tolerating my indulgence as I tried to loosen our captive up and get some camaraderie going, but it soon became clear that he took this war a lot more seriously than I did. He would glance at the glowing television, which held the rest of our team in rapture. He would stiffen, as though expecting blows from behind, when ever anyone moved about the room. Finally, after about two hours, he did drink half a can of beer and confided that he had worked in a bicycle factory outside Hanoi before joining the National Liberation Front. By the end of the evening, I was ready to sign a confession myself, having been completely worn down by him. His resolve was so much stronger than anything we could muster, I wished he would stay with us, instead of being hauled off to prison camp the next morning.

It was, as Tu had said after our dinner in Cholon, a case where we were making a bad situation progressively worse. Worse yet, as the days dragged on, was the realization that I was going home soon. The war would be over for me. I had no vested interest here, no family, no commitment beyond a year's tour of duty. Of course the Vietnamese had known this all along, and that was why they took such advantage of us. It is fortunate that I could not see farther into the future, that I could see only my own plans, and not what still lay ahead in Vietnam. After all, peace talks had been in progress since May. Who could imagine that the peace talks would drag on for years and years, just as it would take so long for my father to die, or that we could turn our backs on the mess we had created so completely, and go back to mowing our lawns while the North Vietnamese tanks finally swept down Highway Thirteen.

I had come to love this village I lived in, loved the people as well as the food and the sky and the cycles of rice planting and harvest. The promise I had first seen in An Loc, in the village of the Montagnard charcoal makers had been fulfilled. I had won many friendships, especially among the children, who would follow me everywhere when I took my evening strolls. They would stroke my hairy arms and beg to be picked up. I would sing "Old Man River" to them and there would be gales of laughter among them, voices like bells, with the great river flowing back and forth with love, as the clouds drifted in from the South China Sea, as the palm fronds swayed in a gentle cooling breeze.

It was my love for the place, and especially the children, that brought me the most pain in the end. Truths that had been hinted at, sensed as an infantryman, suggested by the four skeletons huddled together on the floor of a burned hut north of Di An, suddenly became vividly clear. Just as the buildings were pockmarked, riven by shells, so were the people, day after day, year after year. Sure, we were doing good work in the village, too. I'm certain that even the gestapo did good work at times, giving toys to the orphans they had created, that sort of thing. We distributed food and medicine and other goods among the villagers, especially when ABC News came to film us. We even had two army nurses with us on that day, helping out in front of the cameras. But perhaps the greatest service we provided was the air ambulance, by means of our radio and helipad. It took a long time to be fully realized, but as trust grew, people in the village and later in the surrounding countryside learned that they could bring their most critically injured to us, and in this way I began to see what the war was really doing, doing in a day to day way to the people.

This was an entirely different horror from that of the firefights, and one that changed me in more profound ways. It is a sight that soldiers are usually spared, although Saipan, where the civilian casualties outnumbered the military tenfold, was an exception. My river, flowing through the village, gradually became an ever widening river of blood. This was mostly the blood from old people and young children, carried to us by their desperate, often hysterical families. Some came from the western part of the village, such as when the Viet Cong mortared us, which they frequently did. I remember an eight-year-old boy I knew with shrapnel in his beautiful neck. He could have been my own son. More came from the eastern part of the village, like when an American shell landed short and removed the lower jaw from an eighty-year-old woman. She could have been my own grandmother. But with most of the casualties, it was best not to ask where they came from. These were almost all children; two and six and ten years old, often at the edge of death or slightly over the edge with the huge, ragged holes made by artillery and rockets. This was what Co Dep had warned us about, when Mike Division attacked rubber trees. This was the real war, the one soldiers never saw, where the bullets and shells that seemed to be just going off into nowhere finally came to rest.

I inadvertently contributed to this river of blood myself, sending a young boy I knew to the civilian Saigon hospital where, rumor had it, stray dogs roamed the hallways looking for amputated limbs. (I know this rumor to be false, that it was the other way around. Any stray dogs were immediately eaten by humans.) This boy got into the cans of napalm that I had placed around our helipad for night landings, thinking the jelly might be good to eat. It wasn't. Then he smeared some on his arms and chest. It began to sting his skin so he ran back to his mother and stood beside her cooking fire and burst into flames. Another time I shot a guy in the foot with the fifty-caliber machine gun. There was a firefight going on right at the eastern edge of the village at the time, and Tu pointed at a certain grass hut and said the VC were in it, but he was wrong. ARVN soldiers were in it. At least that time it was fellow soldiers and not more civilians.

There was unexploded ordnance everywhere. There were forgotten land mines, grenades with rusting pins. Being a VC was often a family affair, especially so in the VC-controlled areas. VC families would collect unexploded bombs and shells, remove the fuses, and melt out the TNT while sitting in a circle by the cooking fire. Aircraft in trouble would have to jettison their ordnance. Artillerymen would inadvertently leave out a powder bag, or leave an extra one in. Until I lived in the village, I had no idea this was going on, and as my time in Vietnam drew to a close, it seemed more and more true that everything we did, whether out of guilt or innocence, anger or love, turned to shit. Even our municipal improvements, such as the bulldozing away of airplane wreckage in the market place. For five months afterward, the villagers would wait for low tide, and then resume retrieving the building stones from the river. Other well-intended aid — weapons, medicine, building materials — became mediums of exchange, sources of power, and likely as not ended up in enemy hands.

It was definitely time for me to go home. The same thing that had happened to me after half a year with Mike Division, was happening after nearly six months in the village. I was becoming paralyzed by love, no longer able to move against the enemy, repelled by my own country, repelled even by myself and what I had done out of misguided loyalty and guilt. My relationship with Tu began to deteriorate. We realized we had betrayed each other. I was not so powerful as he had hoped. His aggressive tactics would not win him much after all. I was sickened by what he did. And he, in turn, became greedy, more closely resembling his fellow officers. He wanted to get what he could from me before I deserted him and went home, leaving him with my war. We exchanged addresses and promised to write, but he said he didn't expect me to write, and he was right. This was the place of broken promises.

Our team was falling apart. After our captain left, we got a new captain for a while who seemed insane. Our team divided along racial lines, foaming with animosity. I got the captain relieved of duty, and he vowed to get me, no matter how long it took, no matter where I went. I became the team leader, but the animosity remained. I went through the wallet of a North Vietnamese soldier Tu's men had killed. There was some North Vietnamese money in it, with a portrait of Ho Chi Minh. I stared at the portrait long and hard. Then it began to haunt me. I began to be repelled by the fact that, for the moment, things seemed to be going so well for us, that in our brutal way we were getting ahead, at least for a while. But it was like the way we kill chickens. Americans kill chickens by cutting their heads off. A Vietnamese would begin to kill a chicken by picking it up and cradling it in one arm. He would calm the chicken down by gently stroking it with one hand. Then with the free hand, he would slowly slit the chicken's throat with a very sharp knife. The chicken would remain calm. It would not know that it was bleeding to death. Nor, it seemed, did we.

For me, the distinction between who was enemy and who was not became completely blurred, a thing of the moment rather than dogma. I couldn't fight anymore. Tu couldn't stand this. Yet still, the war went on. Yet still, the river rose and fell. My country had become like my father, hanging on tenaciously, even grotesquely, in an angry daze of morphine psychosis. I walked around the village unarmed, feeling it was my only sanctuary, and once, during those dwindling days, I think I even went canoeing with the Viet Cong. I was hailed by three elderly men in a dugout while on my evening stroll. They seemed to be having some sort of a party, with a bottle of *bac si de* among them, and they motioned for me to join them. As soon as I got in a drink was pressed on me, and then another while the man in the stern poled us along the fringe of the river and the man in the bow silently stroked his small, Confucian goatee and cocked his head, staring at me.

It was an exceptionally fine evening, the kind the village was well known for, the kind that had once drawn wealthy Saigon businessmen. Furthermore, the perspective offered by a boat is so different from that of land, as my father knew well. We were cruising past the backyards now, where people cooked and did laundry, and I hardly noticed that we were going into the eastern part of the village, the people were so friendly. They would see us in the canoe and wave and shout greetings. This was a part of the village I had never seen from the water, never seen at all except during quick raids. This was where the fishermen lived. Nets hung in great sweeps from poles, drying in the breeze, and each home had a rickety little dock where the family boat was tied, brightly painted eyes leering from the bow. In these narrow threads of the river the trees enclosed us overhead so that it was already twilight. Children shouted and chased each other about on the hard dirt beneath the shade trees, and the bell at the Cao Dai temple was ringing its evening song.

We were going farther east than I had expected. Palmetto swamp was closing in on the left. People on the shore were fewer, more silent, staring expectantly. Still, the man in the bow stroked his goatee, and there was the constant swish of the pole in the water. A wave of terror swept through me as I realized I was probably being canoed about by Viet Cong, without a weapon, with nothing but my silly grin. I said that I had to get back and of course they understood, but the only reaction was to nod agreeably and keep poling toward where *punji* pits surrounded every house. Palm fronds trailed in the dark, slowly moving water. Viscous black mudbanks glistened, ready to suck me in. It was, I suppose, another test like the kind that Tu administered all the time, or perhaps a joke at my expense, shared by those in the canoe with those who watched silently from the shore. At any rate, they waited until my discomfort was such that I was thinking about jumping. Then the canoe slowly turned, and they brought me back to the village just as darkness was finally settling in. When I told Tu about this later he was furious, not so much because of my own danger, but because I had crossed some sort of boundry.

When I had only about a week left I heard that my old unit was back in Di An again, so I decided to take the jeep and drive up there for the day. I found the barracks where they were staying, but most of the company was out on operations. I did run into Roy Wakefield, though, which was great. He was going home in a few days, too, having spent the rest of his tour as Bravo Six's romeo. He told me that Mike Division had virtually ceased to exist after I left; most of the guys had transferred to Recon, as they had said they would. The North Vietnamese never did storm us at Loc Ninh, and the quiet times continued until toward Christmas. Then the fighting got intense again. Redfeather's best friend in Recon got killed, and this time Redfeather went completely crazy and had to be evacuated. Nobody knew what became of him. And Millhouse got killed while walking point. He was carrying the CAR-15 I had given him, not the crossbow. For one fatal moment, he must have been distracted by something, or perhaps he was overly tired. This time they saw him first, and killed him with a single shot in the forehead.

There was a big party in the village the night before I left, with Tu and his men and our team pigging out on food and drink. At about one in the morning, long after we had all retired, somebody fired a couple of rocket grenades toward our hooch from the swamp to the west, but his aim was off. The rounds passed high over the roof and exploded harmlessly in the rice paddies far beyond our outhouse. Perhaps he had been to the party, too, and had too much to drink. Or perhaps it was another joke. Then I went home. It was like a film of being flushed down a toilet run backward. It left me feeling dizzy as I emerged from the vortex.

It was fun at first to be one of the tall thin people obsessed with sex chasing each other around in short fat automobiles. It was fun to be alive, but I secretly mourned for Mike Division and the village of Long Thanh. I longed for children of my own. I could not accept the vision of the world, of my future, offered to me by corporate America any more than I could accept the visions offered to me by my father, like the toy tugboat he had made for me so long ago. We had grown closer together in some ways, each of us doing recon instead of joining the crowd, and I accepted many truths he had hit upon, all the while growing farther apart. I had wounds that wouldn't heal, wounds that got infected with the city soot. What I had hoped would be the end never really ended at all. Tu, Redfeather, Millhouse, Baby-San, Defiant Six and the Viet Cong all followed me to Vermont. We watched the war together on a small black-and-white television. The reception was poor. Ghost images floated past. It was taking too long, so much longer than anyone could have imagined possible, like my own father clinging to his own life beyond what was proper or even logical, his chest refusing to give up its heaving rhythm, his mind and soul lost in a morphine rage.

Once, toward the very end, I went in to awaken him for treatment. He looked as though he was dead already, the way the almost-dead do when they are sleeping; cadaverous, mouth open, but he stirred when I touched his shoulder and his eyes met mine for an instant and during that unguarded moment his eyes were filled with love. It was the only time I had seen that look, the only time all his defenses had been breached and it only lasted a second, but I took that home with me like an ember, a gem. Far below, as I flew, the hills were covered by a late spring snow. They turned pink, then purple as the sun set.

Then it was back to the war, back to machine guns and the great chest heaving, choking on the mucus of corpses. North Vietnamese tanks ran back and forth freely in the slime. Vast populations fled in a panic, like an immune system running amuck. Systems failed in a cascade; whole battalions, even divisions began to fibrillate on the shores of the South China Sea while America mowed her lawns. Tu, Redfeather, Baby-San, Defiant Six and the Viet Cong watched with me as Saigon fell. We watched people desperately chasing after fleeing airplanes, watched helicopters being pushed off the decks of aircraft carriers. Our flags came down. Theirs went up. Surely this was the end, and it was, and it wasn't. My father became impossible to keep around, grotesque and haunted by the poison he had been forced to drink, shattered by the grenade he had fallen upon and cradled to his chest. He became dangerous, tried to strangle his wife when she came close to him, and had to be put in a ward for the dying and finally, finally expired propped up in front of a television. I wondered what stupid show was on at the time as his final companion, such a sad ending it was.

I was peeling cedar logs myself when the call came. I went back to the woods and resumed the job. This is what my ancestors in Vermont did. The bark comes off clean in long strips in the spring, revealing moist and creamy white wood beneath, which seems to have its own musculature, clean and sweet as fresh snow. I split the logs, driving steel wedges with a sledge. The blows ring through the woods like the bells of the Cao Dai temple, and when the log splits the sweet cedar incense pours forth.

This then is the end, and it is, but it isn't. On my oldest son's twenty-first birthday, I gave him a high-powered sharpshooter's rifle. He seems healthier now than ever; this is but one of the blessings bestowed upon us. We went into the woods together looking for deer. He carried the gun as my machine gunners sometimes did, upon the shoulder, held by the bipod, and we shared the mystery of men and guns and woods. I gave my middle son flying lessons for his sixteenth birthday. I go up with him now and then. He takes to it naturally, concentrated yet at ease, feeling the glory of man and machine in the sky as I did. I gave my eight-year-old "Leggos." He assembles Leggo armies and maneuvers them on the living room rug, already a leader.

I have friends in Vietnam today, American friends I correspond with who were there once as soldiers and now have gone back because they came to love the place and the people as I did. They tell me that there the war is over. They send me photos and videotapes of a nation at peace, while we remain belligerantly at war, both at home and abroad. They tell me that in several instances, during the final days, when South Vietnamese military units found themselves surrounded by those of the North and knew that they all would soon die, their last act was to strip off all their clothes. They preferred to die naked, as a final renunciation of the government that had led them to such an end.

Meanwhile, one after another, my own three sons have discovered my old fatigues and put them on, rolling up the sleeves, shirttails dragging on the ground. I might have burned the clothing or buried it long ago, but I couldn't do so any more than I could bury the ghosts of Vietnam. This was my father, my family, this is me, and so they get these hand-me-downs like a faulty gene, like cystic fibrosis, a mutation borne on the wings of love. Sometimes, in the evening, that same light returns. The hills are cast half in shadow, half golden light. We are at peace, we are at war. There is movement in the bushes by the barbecue. Shadows lengthen. The voices of my sons ring like bells as they attack phantom enemies.

A NOTE ON THE AUTHOR

Nat Tripp lives with his wife and five children in northern Vermont, where he works as a television producer,
writer, and part-time farmer. *Father, Soldier, Son* is his
first book.

❖

A NOTE ON THE BOOK

The text for this book was composed by Steerforth Press
using a digital version of Sabon, a type face designed by
Jan Tschichold and first cut and cast at the Stempel
Foundry in 1964. The book was printed on acid free
papers and bound by Quebecor Printing ~ Book Press
Inc. of Brattleboro, Vermont.